EVEN THE BIRDS STOPPED SINGING

Dearest Jeanne,
with warmest best wishes, memories & love from

Charlie xx

Published by Parafotos

PO Box 269, Pewsey, Wiltshire SN9 6PD

First published in 2019

ISBN 978-0-9554257-2-1

Copyright © Charlie Shea-Simonds 2019

The right of Charlie Shea-Simonds to be identified as the author of this work has been asserted by him in accordance with the Copyright, Designs and Patents Act 1988.

Designed by Hawk Editorial Ltd, Hull

Printed by Book Printing UK Ltd, Peterborough

EVEN THE BIRDS STOPPED SINGING
Fifty years of fun in the clouds

by

Charlie Shea-Simonds

'Perfect speed is being there'

Jonathan Livingston Seagull by Richard Bach

Dedicated with all my love to Julie, my beloved partner and best friend, and to my offspring, Patrick, Lucy and Philip, and to my grandchildren, Alexander, Emily, Ieuan, Eleanor and Peter.

And to remember Jim Crocker, a charismatic, larger-than-life sporting aviation enthusiast.

CONTENTS

Foreword: Air Chief Marshal Sir John Allison KCB CBE vii

Introduction 1

Chapter 1: Fire! 3

Chapter 2: Ancestors and Influences 7

Chapter 3: Learn to Test – Test to Learn 14

Chapter 4: Return to Peace 21

Chapter 5: Down With Skool 26

Chapter 6: Serve to Lead 32

Chapter 7: Utrinque Paratus 44

Chapter 8: Falling Free 52

Chapter 9: Aldershot, Hythe, Warminster and Bahrain........................ 60

Chapter 10: Aldershot Again! 71

Chapter 11: 1 PARA and Aden 82

Chapter 12: 4 PARA (V) and the Ravens 87

Chapter 13: Grindale Field 110

Chapter 14: Those Who Can, Do – Those Who Can't, Teach 119

Chapter 15: BPA National Coach and Safety Officer 142

Chapter 16: Chief Judge 1977, 1981 and 1983 157

Chapter 17: The Tiger Club and the Dawn to Dusk 173

Chapter 18: DH82A Tiger Moth G-AGZZ 189

Chapter 19: The Diamond Nine Team 200

Chapter 20: Turbine Time – Thank You Dr Pearson! 223

Afterword 237

FOREWORD

by Air Chief Marshal Sir John Allison KCB CBE

The author of this exciting personal story and I have much in common. We share the same birthday, albeit one year apart. We both chose a military career. We both have a lifelong passion for flying. But – apart from the small matter of preference for Army versus RAF – there is one big difference between us. Charlie's love of aviation was not sated merely by piloting aircraft; he went further by jumping out of them, initially for professional reasons and later for sport and fun.

I have always striven to stay firmly strapped into my nice safe pilot's seat, but from that vantage point I will admit to unbridled admiration and respect for those who have the cold-blooded courage to leap into the void. Charlie is such a person and his book is about his life in both flying and parachuting.

It is often said that everyone has one book in them, i.e. their life story. Charlie has certainly vindicated that theory, but he has the enormous advantage of having lived a life of variety, excitement and achievement, borne along by his fun-loving, adventurous spirit and spiced by doing things that have an element of danger. In this context, I was pleased to discover, on reading his introduction, another bond between us. Charlie and I share a common disdain for the effects on society of health and safety legislation. Charlie's life, exemplified by a disciplined and sensible approach to aviation, without sacrificing the fun, is living proof that the formal bureaucracy of risk assessments and so forth is redundant where there is intelligent application of professional knowledge and common sense to achieve safe outcomes.

The reader also finds that Charlie has been an unwitting trailblazer in another aspect of contemporary society. I refer to the current vogue for target setting. But unlike targets set by political leaders and officials for others to attain that (because it is so easy to do) might reasonably be called soft target setting, Charlie does it the hard way. He sets difficult goals for his own life, then goes out and attains them. For example, he had a goal to own a Tiger Moth. He could not afford one, so he bought a wreck and rebuilt it himself. Another example is the remarkable achievement of winning the prestigious Duke of Edinburgh Trophy in the Dawn to Dusk competition, not once but three times, and, incidentally, raising a lot of money for various charities along the way.

Also in the book, we learn about Charlie's forbears, his early life, his exciting and action packed career in the Parachute Regiment, his distinguished service to national and international sport parachuting in major leadership roles, his wide and varied flying career, his love affair with Tiger Moth G-AGZZ and, inevitably in so adventurous a life, his brushes with disaster.

Charlie's story is vividly told. It is populated with a rich cast of notable characters that seem to abound in the gutsy world of parachuting and is choc a bloc with entertaining stories. The book is full of Charlie's friends and it is clear that he has a gift for friendship. The story is factually but modestly told. For example, Charlie was the moving spirit behind the founding of the famous Diamond Nine Tiger Moth formation team, which he then led "because nobody else wanted the job".

As Charlie's life in parachuting and flying unfolds before the reader's eyes, he/she can see the energy and gusto, the adventurous and brave spirit, the willing acceptance of responsibility, the multiple achievements, but above all, it is the sheer sense of enjoyment with which he has lived that leaves the most lasting impression. Ultimately Charlie's story is about more than aviation. It is about the art of living; the human values that shine through the pages mean that there is something for everyone in this splendid and unusual book.

INTRODUCTION

'You should live gloriously, generously, dangerously – safety last!'
Sagittarius Rising, Cecil Lewis

Reflecting on the late, great Cecil Lewis's wonderfully inspirational words written in the 1920s, I'm sure they'd receive little support in the 'nanny' state in which we now live. On the other hand, I certainly didn't want this book to be an endless catalogue of 'there I was inverted at 12,000ft and nothing on the clock but the maker's name' type stories. I have to admit, however, that there are always one or two adrenalin pumping moments when 'living dangerously – safety last!' What follows, however, is an attempt to capture some memories of early influences and something of the amazing atmosphere of a hugely enjoyable and fulfilling fifty-plus years of aviation before the fun police of health and safety moved in to persuade the regulators that excitement is unacceptable. Whilst my log books record hours flown (nearly 6,000) and parachute descents made (just over 2,000), they have also stimulated the ageing brain cells to remembering some extraordinary aviation characters, both pilots and parachutists, encountered along the way who, in eulogy-speak, have enriched my life – indeed Cecil Lewis, with whom I flew on two occasions, was one of them. I've often thought that the satisfaction of a particularly enjoyable flight or memorable skydive or the adrenalin rush experienced when things have not gone according to plan, are somewhat selfish, being as they are personal and of the moment; whereas friends with whom we have shared the skies are very much more important and should never be taken for granted. My one big regret in putting this volume together is that I don't have the same gift of words as that great aviation writer Ernest K. Gann whose evocative *Fate is the Hunter* is, in my view, the all-time aviation classic. Therefore, Gentle Reader, I crave your indulgence!

As for the title of this book, I am indebted to Will, son of the late Rod McLoughlin, for kindly giving me permission to use his father's words. Rod was a talented English teacher and skydiver who in 1969 wrote a delightfully funny piece in *Sport Parachutist*, the British Parachute Association's magazine, entitled 'Even the Birds Stopped Singing'. Part of Rod's colourful description of the apprehension experienced by a group of student parachutists waiting to emplane for their first parachute jump is worth quoting:

> *They are milling anxiously about in front of the aircraft uttering little whimpering cries of despair and peering nervously towards the windsock which is hanging vertically in the still air. A group of visiting instructors stand nearby watching in stunned disbelief. They are all stripped to the waist and are wearing very brief shorts and para-boots. They are very relaxed so as not to make their muscles ripple too much and all of them are smoking each others' cigarettes because none of them has any of his own. The students on the tarmac sense a crisis and huddle more closely together,*

tugging pathetically at each others' equipment and bleating with fear. So far only one of them has managed to pop his reserve and he is now attempting furtively to stuff the canopy down the front of his overall. The jumpmaster appears around the hangar and a sudden hush descends. Even the birds stop singing.

Both during and after his glittering RAF career Air Chief Marshal Sir John Allison KCB CBE has enjoyed flying aerobatic and vintage aircraft and gliders – he is an accomplished pilot. He has also enthusiastically and diligently worked with the Historic Aircraft Association, the Light Aircraft Association, the Royal Aero Club and Europe Air Sports for the promotion of safe sporting aviation within sensible regulatory parameters. I feel privileged, therefore, that he found time to write such a generous foreword for which I'm hugely grateful – thank you, John.

Finally I am reminded of the words of Polish-born travel author, Rom Landau, who wrote: 'Most of us cherish imaginary romantic notions about ourselves and only rarely succeed in breaking through the crust of self-deception. In books of an autobiographical background an occasional word of self-criticism is usually out weighed by pages of self-praise, however cunningly disguised.' I do hope that my splendid grandchildren, for whom this book was originally written, don't think Landau's words apply to this one – I simply hope that they find it interesting and enjoyable!

Charlie Shea-Simonds
Upavon 2019

CHAPTER 1
FIRE!

Sunday, February 5, 1989, dawned a crisp clear winter's day with a light breeze. It had been eagerly anticipated as it held the promise of a memorable day's flying in one of my favourite aeroplanes – the de Havilland DH 89A Rapide, a classic, elegant twin-engined taper-winged bi-plane of nineteen thirties design. G-AJHO was a lovely example which had been the Army Parachute Association's first aeroplane and from which I'd parachuted on numerous occasions in the sixties before finally getting to fly her in 1988 after she'd been lovingly restored. She looked immaculate in the red and black livery of Brooklands Aviation and the aroma of the newly covered grey leather passenger seats wafted around her interior.

Fellow Diamond Nine Team member, Colin Dodds, flew her for the first flight of the day from Netheravon to Oxford, Kidlington, whilst I sat behind him in the navigator's jump seat trying not to be impatient at the thought of soon flying her myself – in the Rapide the pilot sits up at the pointed end in solitary regal splendour. The thirty-minute flight was uneventful. Having parked on the apron in front of the control tower, Colin and I changed seats and he left me to it, while he wandered off to check that the Cessna 172 RG, the aeroplane he was to fly next, was ready to go. With the two Gipsy Queen III six-cylinder engines ticking over contentedly, I carried out the pre-flight checks and, having received a thumbs up from Colin and taxi clearance from air traffic control, I released the brakes and guided this graceful, historic aeroplane around the taxiway to the holding point for runway 20.

Taxiing for take-off at Kidlington, Sunday, February 5, 1989

I had to wait for a couple of minutes for two Piper PA 28 training aircraft to land before I could line up for take-off, so I repeated the checks – all OK – and, strangely, I remember pulling up the straps of the shoulder harness to hold me more firmly in the seat. ATC gave me departure clearance, so I lined the old girl up on the centre line of the runway, eased open the throttle levers to full power and accelerated along the tarmac. With a 2,050 rpm indication and normal oil pressure for both engines, the speed built up quickly. Gentle forward movement of the control column raised the tail off the ground at about 55 knots and she lifted off the runway as the speed continued to increase through 75 knots. ATC recorded our take-off in their subsequent report:

1104: Dragon Rapide G-AJHO departs Oxford for Shoreham (VFR) one POB, R/W 20 240/10.

I eased her in the climb on to a south-easterly heading for Shoreham, some seventy nautical miles away.

G-AJHO airborne for the last time

The excellent visibility ensured easy map reading – 'HO's only aid to navigation was a single P11 compass as, of course, this was pre-GPS days. At 1,500ft I gently lowered the nose and eased the power back to 2,000 rpm a side. I was just in the process of juggling the levers to synchronise the propellers to a steady beat, when I noticed the starboard rev counter unwinding, indicating the engine failing on that side. The Rapide responded to the loss of power by yawing to the right – I instinctively counteracted with left rudder to prevent it worsening. I turned the aircraft to the left, which was the shortest way back towards Kidlington, before glancing to the right towards the failed engine. *Shit* – the bloody wing was on fire! I called ATC, which recorded:

1107: G-AJHO reports emergency, returning to field with starboard engine failure. Subsequently reports having a fire – requesting emergency landing. Airport Fire/Safety Services called out. Full emergency initiated with 999 call.

By now the fire was more than alarming, and was rapidly gaining hold of the Rapide's wood and fabric construction. I was unable to turn off the fuel cock as the lever had been wire-locked into the 'on' position. Suddenly there was an audible crack, the aircraft lurched abruptly as the lower wing appeared to jump and simultaneously the upper wing bowed upwards. The rear spar of the lower wing must have burnt through. It was frighteningly obvious that I had to get her on the ground in a hurry. I spotted a large field off to my left and turned towards it. ATC were trying to be helpful:

1108: 'HO' offered R/W 02 230/10. 'HO' response was negative, have major fire, going into a field. A/C 'PW' reports O/H Rapide and watching him. Subsequently reports that 'HO' has turned over in a field and on fire.

Their final sentence, while accurate, missed some of the more interesting detail that I was experiencing. The tubing to the pitot head, located on one of the starboard inter-plane struts, had obviously burnt through as the airspeed indicator was now reading zero. It only remained to fly the Rapide by feel, aided and abetted by a generous measure of good luck. I set her up for an approach into my chosen field. Only a couple of landing checks were necessary – brakes off, leave the flaps alone as the right-hand one would almost certainly be damaged by fire, and the shoulder straps were already tight. Then I saw them – a line of 11 KV high-tension cables stretched across the field and right in my flight path – bloody hell, not my day! I eased the control column gently back. Even then it looked like I might still hit them, but mercifully we skimmed safely over.

Now it was concentration for the landing – control column back carefully – I sensed we were going too fast… too bad, I had to get her down. The wheels touched – we skipped into the air again. Control column hard back and she landed firmly. What I'd thought was a smooth grass field proved to be three or four inches of wet, winter wheat. The surface was sodden. The wheels started to sink in. I held the column back as far as it would go. No need for brakes – the wheels simply dug into the ground. Momentarily I thought we'd got away with it, but no such luck. Like a slow-motion piece of film she tipped over on to her back. The shoulder straps held me firmly – but upside-down. I released them and struggled to get myself right side up. I wasted a few seconds trying to bash my way out through the perspex windscreen. It held firm so, being acutely aware of the heat of the flames, and crouching I made my way down the fuselage to the door on the left-hand side. But it wasn't there – of course not, you bloody idiot, thinks I – the aircraft was upside-down so the door was on the other side. One firm bash and it flew open. Years before on a demolitions course in the Army I'd learnt that you measured the required length of safety fuse based on how long it took to walk away to safety – never run, you could easily trip up. So I remember walking deliberately away from the flaming wreck of that beautiful Rapide. After about 75 yards I turned around just at the moment the fuel tanks exploded into a mini-mushroom cloud of smoke and flame. ATC recorded the arrival of the local police helicopter:

1109: Helicopter 'Police 05' responds to emergency. 'PW' gives position of accident as 2 miles to the A/F side of Beckley Mast, with pilot safely out of A/C.

Then:

1112: 'Police 05' reports landing at site with A/C on fire and pilot safely out and walking.

Never had the grass looked so green, nor had the sky looked so blue.

Even the birds stopped singing!

About a month later, an investigator from Air Accidents Investigation Branch came to talk to me about its findings. He entered my office with the words:

"May I touch you?" I must have flinched perceptibly, but, with a cheerful grin, he continued, "I just hope that some of your extraordinary good fortune might rub off on to me."

He then went on to explain that only the shells of the engines hadn't been consumed by the fire, and the following is an extract from the published AAIB report:

'Examination of the right side engine and the remains of pipework found in the ashes showed that the initial failure was the number four cylinder head gasket. This allowed the release of hot cylinder gases in an area close to the carburettors and fuel interconnection pipe. The type of fuel pipe fitted to the aircraft was made of rubber with an internal steel braid. Deterioration of the rubber due to the escaping cylinder gases allowed fuel to escape and cause an intense fire which was sufficiently hot to locally melt the steel cylinder fins and the steel braid on the hose. A hole 3/8in diameter was eventually made in the steel braid and this allowed large quantities of burning fuel to escape and run back from the engine cowling on the lower wing, causing the fire to spread very rapidly.'

Exactly!

CHAPTER 2
ANCESTORS AND INFLUENCES

My great-great uncle, George Blackall Simonds (1843-1929), was an accomplished sculptor who had studied under Professor Johannes Schilling in Dresden. He later had a studio in Rome where, between 1870 and 1874, he created what as generally regarded as his masterpiece, a colossus of *The Falconer*, which now stands proudly in Central Park, New York. It's hardly surprising, therefore, that later he became founder president of the British Falconers' Club in 1927. He was also a founder member of the Art Workers' Guild and became its first chairman in 1884. Two years later he created the massive cast-bronze Maiwand Lion, which now stands impressively in Forbury Gardens in Reading as a memorial to the 328 all ranks of the Berkshire Regiment, the 66th of Foot, who died at the battle of Maiwand in Afghanistan in 1880. Whilst in Rome he had met an American lady, Gertrude Prescott, whom he later married in 1877 and their only son, George Prescott, was born in 1881. Having been appointed a director of H&G Simonds, the prosperous family brewery in Reading, George Blackall retired as a sculptor in 1904 after he had completed more than two hundred works. He devoted the remainder of his working life to the brewery and became the company's chairman in 1910, a position he held until his death in 1929. Their son, George Prescott, having survived Army service in the Boer War, was called up as a 33-year-old reserve officer in the 1st South Wales Borderers in 1914 – he arrived with the battalion on September 19 and was killed a week later on the 26th near Vendresse in north-eastern France.

In 1862, George Blackall's sister, Mary Simonds, married Dr John Shea, a surgeon at the Royal Berkshire Hospital and Reading's Medical Officer of Health. Of their

George Blackall Simonds as Master of the Art Workers' Guild in 1909

The Falconer in Central Park, New York

GBS as president of the British Falconers' Club

The Maiwand Lion in Forbury Gardens, Reading

four sons, Steven Victor (born June 11, 1874) was my grandfather and the youngest, Geoffrey Norman (born December 28, 1880), who won the Sword of Honour at the Royal Military Academy at Sandhurst in 1900. He was commissioned into the Royal Munster Fusiliers before finding himself on active service during the latter days of the Boer War in South Africa. His South Africa medal has the following five clasps: South Africa 1901, South Africa 1902, Transvaal, Cape Colony and Orange Free State. The Regimental History starkly records that in 1902 in the Orange Free State: 'Second-Lieutenant Shea was killed at Schotland West District, Kroonstad, on April 20, whilst doing duty with the Mounted Infantry Company.' The Armistice was signed six weeks later on May 31. He was laid to rest in the Kroonstad Garden of Remembrance and, eighty-one years later, Julie and I placed a bouquet of flowers on his grave. In this place of tranquillity it was easy to recall Rupert Brooke's poignant words:

If I should die, think only this of me;
That there's some corner of a foreign field
That is forever England.

Meanwhile, Steven had joined the Queen Victoria Rifles, a London Territorial Army regiment. He went to war with the battalion as a 40-year-old captain and company commander, in November 1914, thus qualifying him for the Mons Star medal. The regimental history records that on his first visit to the trenches he was accompanied by one of his young officers, 2Lt Harold Woolley, who, early the following year, won the first TA Victoria

Geoffrey Norman Shea's South Africa medal and his resting place in the Kroonstad Garden of Remembrance

Cross of the Great War and who later also won a Military Cross. After the war Woolley was ordained and in the Second World War he served yet again, but this time as an Army chaplain. Steven was badly wounded in January 1915 and, having been Mentioned in Dispatches by Field Marshal Sir John French, he spent the remainder of the war serving in a training capacity.

Soon after he returned back to England he was appointed a director of H&G Simonds and, as the company had never had a director who wasn't a Simonds, he added his mother's maiden name, Simonds, to his own, thus Shea-Simonds. Steven had, before the war,

Steven Shea's First World War medals

The Prince of Wales visits the H&G Simonds Brewery in Reading in 1926, with Steven Shea-Simonds arrowed left and George Blackall Simonds arrowed right

married Victoria La Trobe, a granddaughter of Charles La Trobe, who had been the first Lieutenant-Governor of the state of Victoria in Australia. My father, Geoffrey Patrick La Trobe Shea-Simonds – their only child – was born on July 26, 1917. My maternal grandfather, Ernest Cross, was at theological college in 1914 and, after the outbreak of war, he decided to place his religious studies on hold before he was commissioned into the 17th Battalion of the West Yorkshire Regiment. The 17th Battalion was also known as the 2nd Leeds Pals or the Leeds Bantams. Bantam battalions were made up of enlisted men who had originally been less than the Army's minimum height requirement of 5ft 3in – this was reduced to 5ft for the first time in Birkenhead where a number of coal miners had originally been rejected for Army service for not being tall enough. Ernest survived the war to resume his theological studies – having taken holy orders he was vicar of East Knoyle near Shaftesbury for eighteen years and later became a Canon of Salisbury Cathedral. He'd married my grandmother, Lydia Hughes, in 1915 and they had three daughters, the second, born on January 18, 1919, was my mother, Archisadella Anne Cross. My grandmother's brother, William Barton Hughes, born on September 21, 1899, was the first aviator in the family – he was commissioned into the Royal Naval Air Service and started his flying training at Chingford on October 6, 1917, finally gaining his flying wings on March 31 the following year. The next day on April 1, 1918, the RNAS and the Royal Flying Corps were amalgamated to form the Royal Air Force and on May 17, 1918, William, now a probationary Flight Officer RAF, took off from Dover in a Clerget-engined Sopwith Camel for a practice flight before flying to France. The aircraft suffered a dramatic engine failure and tragically William was killed in the subsequent forced landing. He was 18 years old.

My father, as the only son of a prosperous brewing family, had something of a privileged upbringing based around the Village House in Bradfield. He was educated at Uppingham where his Uncle Percy was a house master. Apart from my grandfather insisting that my father drank a pint of Simonds beer after lunch every day and two years

William Barton Hughes in the RNAS (left) and in the RAF (right)

My father, Geoffrey Patrick La Trobe Shea-Simonds (top right), at the
Reading Aero Club with a Miles Hawk in 1934

The Speed Six Bentley outside the Village House, Bradfield, in 1936

as a member of the school shooting VIII, his school days would appear not to have been very distinguished and ended in 1934. Thereafter he enjoyed a playboy lifestyle based, it would seem, around a succession of exotic sports cars, including a 1931 4.5-litre TT Invicta, a 6.5-litre Speed Six Bentley (which he raced at Brooklands) and, bizarrely, one of Count Zborowski's Chitty-Bang-Bangs which was powered by a 23-litre Maybach Zeppelin engine, the thirst of which was an impressive three gallons to the mile! And it was in September 1934, aged seventeen, that he started to learn to fly in a Miles Hawk at the Reading Aero Club at Woodley Aerodrome, which was also the home of Miles Aircraft Ltd. He went solo (iconic, memorable moments recorded with pride in every pilot's log book) a month later after seven-and-a-half hours of dual instruction. By March of the following year he had recorded a total of thirty-four hours in his logbook after which he apparently didn't take to the skies again until he started his military flying course in the Royal Navy during the war.

My mother had a more modest start to life, being educated at St Brandon's Clergy Daughters' School in Bristol where she developed a love of the theatre. On leaving school in 1936 she gained a place at London's famous Central School of Speech and Drama and she started the two-year course there that autumn. One of her tutors was John Laurie, a prolific Shakespearian actor who had also trained at the Central, but earlier in 1921 – he later found unexpected fame playing the gaunt-faced undertaker, Private James Frazer, throughout the ten-year run of the TV sitcom series *Dad's Army*. Indeed, John Laurie had himself served in the Home Guard during the Second World War, having seen traumatic service in the Honourable Artillery Company during the First. His coaching of my mother could well have been instrumental in her being awarded the Central's Gold Medal for 1938.

Meanwhile, my father had survived a year at Queen's College, Oxford, before an extremely short interview without coffee with the Master, who is recorded as saying: 'Frankly, Mr Shea-Simonds, you don't need us, and we don't need you!' He then decided on a stage career following that of his mother who, in her youth, had been an aspiring actress and, maybe, his father was getting bored with funding his playboy lifestyle. He arrived at the Central a year after my mother in 1937 for the less comprehensive one-year course. In those days the Central was based at the Royal Albert Hall in what is now the Elgar Room and it was almost certainly here that they met. My mother later confessed that she was literally swept off her feet by this obviously wealthy and handsome 6ft 4in 20-year-old, who was soon courting her around London in his Speed Six Bentley. What my grandfather, the Reverend Ernest Cross, Vicar of East Knoyle in Wiltshire, made of this blossoming relationship is anyone's guess. But by now Herr Hitler was making his belligerent influence dramatically felt all over Europe and the day after war was declared on September 3, 1939, Pat Shea-Simonds and Della Cross were married by the Reverend Ernest Cross in St Mary's Church, East Knoyle, on September 4. They started their near-fifty years of married life together living in my grandfather's Cross Cottage in the delightful little Wiltshire village of Brixton Deverill. It was here that their first born child was born on March 24, 1942. Unfortunately for my parents, it was me!

CHAPTER 3
LEARN TO TEST – TEST TO LEARN
(The motto of the Empire Test Pilots' School)

My father, having been commissioned into the Air Branch of the RNVR – the Royal Naval Volunteer Reserve – gained his naval pilot's wings at Lee-on-Solent early in 1941. The highlight of his naval flying was his selection as a candidate on the very first course of the Empire Test Pilots' School at Boscombe Down in June 1943. For the fifteen months prior to his posting to Boscombe Down he had commanded the Communications Flight at the Royal Naval Air Station at Hatston in the Orkneys, where part of his responsibilities involved being the workshops test pilot. The latter gave him the opportunity to fly more than three hundred hours as pilot-in-command of fourteen different aircraft types, which included Tiger Moth, Gladiator, Spitfire, Hurricane, Walrus, Martlet, Roc, Skua, Swordfish, Albacore and Douglas A-20 Havoc. The latter, a large twin-engine attack aircraft, played host to a couple of amusing incidents which both involved one of father's good chums, an Engineer Officer, one Duncan Hamilton, who, post-war, achieved considerable success driving Jaguar sports cars at Le Mans and winning the race in 1953.

On the first occasion in late May 1943, the two of them were on a local flight when Duncan discovered an aluminium dust sea-marker canister to be used if a submarine was spotted from the air. His curiosity got the better of him and he managed to set it off in the fuselage. Both of them were covered in a thick coat of aluminium dust and they subsequently emerged from the aircraft resembling silver aliens. Only four days later, and again with Duncan as his co-pilot, they took off for what is described in father's log book as 'flight round islands' with a passenger simply designated 'Commander, US Navy'. During the flight Duncan was taken short but mistook the voice communications tube for the 'pee' tube – the Commander, US Navy, was not amused to experience a warm, wet feeling around his ears. The latter story is also recounted in Duncan Hamilton's highly entertaining 1960 book, *Touch Wood*. Luckily reports of these two incidents failed to reach higher authority otherwise his posting to ETPS might well have been in jeopardy. But all his flying experience, combined with his having qualified as an Engineer Officer during his time at Hatston, were useful experience before he started on No. 1 Course, ETPS, the following month.

Wing Commander Sam Wroath, the first commandant of ETPS, was something of a legend in the RAF test flying world, having been a sergeant test pilot at Martlesham Heath in the early 1930s and whose enlightened approach was evident from day one. The candidates on this first course were flying all manner of different aircraft from the moment they arrived. During the first three days my father flew six different aircraft types: Hurricane, Curtiss Seamew, Halifax, Lancaster, Anson & Firefly, and by the end of the course in February 1944 he'd added another twenty-two different types to the list. This totalled sixteen hours on four different four-engine types, sixty-three hours on twelve different twin-engine types and forty-four hours on twelve different single-engine types. Even today this policy remains in being. John Killerby, an ex-RAF chum who, nearly seventy years later, recently flew twenty different types during his ETPS course

No. 1 Course ETPS 1943 – Patrick Shea-Simonds, front left

which he completed successfully, and this in an age of austerity. So it can readily be seen that the ETPS course, even today, remains the ultimate military flying experience in terms of the extraordinary variety of aircraft flown. On March 8, 1944, the red-ink entry in his logbook records: 'Completed successfully No. 1 Test Pilots Course, Test Pilots School, A&AEE, Boscombe Down. Technical Ability: "Exceptional".' The following day, the newly qualified test pilots were split up to be seconded to the various aircraft manufacturers to gain further experience, and my father, as a naval pilot, was attached to the Fairey Aviation Company – one long associated with the design and production of naval aircraft.

Two days later on March 11, having taken off from Eastleigh and during his fourth flight for the company and his third that day in an Albacore – a naval torpedo bomber – an unexpected problem suddenly manifested itself. His logbook entry is brief and to the point: 'Acceptance Test from Eastleigh. During the test flight the engine disintegrated and the greater part of it, together with all cowlings and the propeller, broke away from the aircraft. The aircraft was therefore forced landed in a field South of Chilbolton aerodrome.' In his full report of the incident he noted: 'I realised at once that all or most of the engine must have broken away, and, as the nose of the aircraft rose to a steep climbing angle, I pushed the control column fully forward to the limit of its travel – rather more instinctively, I imagine, than from any real hope of being able to control the aircraft. While holding the control column fully forward with my right hand, I opened the upper port side cockpit window and the sliding roof with my left hand and prepared to abandon the aircraft. To my surprise, however, the nose of the aircraft began to fall again very slowly in response to the forward movement of the control column and this caused me to reconsider my decision to abandon the aircraft.' As my father was 6ft 4in he would probably have had some difficulty getting out in time, but he pulled off a successful forced landing anyway. Fairey's initial reaction of was to have the Albacore dismantled and returned to Eastleigh, but my father suggested it might be simpler to fit a new engine

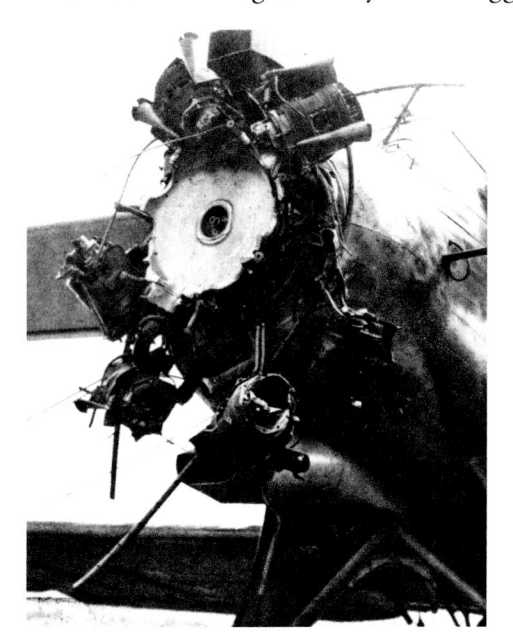

The Albacore and part of its engine and propeller after the forced landing near Chilbolton

to the aircraft in situ and then fly it out from the same field. Thus, a week later on March 18, he was able to record in his log book: 'Flew aircraft out of field into which it had previously been forced landed, after new engine had been fitted. Completed Acceptance Test during the flight to Hamble.' I believe he was later somewhat embarrassed to have been awarded a military MBE for having had little option other than to have forced landed the Albacore in the way that he did. On the other hand he was thrilled to have subsequently received a silver cigarette box engraved 'from the Directors of the Fairey Aviation Company Ltd' with his name and 'Albacore N 4188 March 11th 1944'. On the inside of the lid are positioned two photographs – one of the Albacore standing in the field minus most of its engine and the second is of the remains of the engine, together with the cowling and the three bladed propeller lying in an adjacent pasture – a fitting memento indeed.

After his spell with the Fairey Aviation Company and a short secondment to Blackburn Aircraft at Brough, where the Blackburn Firebrand II was produced – and, as will be recounted later, this was not an aeroplane for which he had any lasting affection. He then spent July 1944 at the Royal Navy Aircraft Repair Yard at Fleetlands near Gosport testing naval aircraft which had been repaired or overhauled, specifically 23 different Barracudas, Spitfires and Swordfish. On the 27th he took off from Fleetlands in Seafire MB356 for a flight that he recorded in his logbook as: 'Test following Major Inspection. The engine cut completely at 8,000ft – the skew gear on the magneto vertical drive shaft having stripped – and the aircraft was therefore forced landed on Worthy Down Aerodrome with chassis lowered and no damage to airframe'. Then he was posted to 'C Flight, Performance Testing Squadron, A&AEE at Boscombe Down where he was involved in the testing of naval aircraft – these included most of the famous names of the era: Barracuda, Hellcat, Avenger, Wildcat, Helldiver, Corsair and the recalcitrant Firebrand II. Of the latter DK 377 he wrote in his logbook on September 16: 'Handling: stick force per "g" and CO contamination Tests. At the conclusion of the tests the throttle jammed in the closed position, and the aircraft was therefore forced landed on Boscombe Down Aerodrome – slight damage being sustained as a result of collision with an obstruction marker post.' He recalled later that he was pleased to have played a small part in preventing the Firebrand II entering naval squadron service.

At this point it is worth recording that statistically test flying was proving to be a dangerous business. During the first five years of its existence, ETPS had 123 candidates attend its first five courses, and, of these, twenty-nine (or 23%) were killed in flying accidents – on No. 2 Course two candidates were killed in flying accidents during the course itself. But towards the end of the war in September 1944, the test flying of military aircraft, however dangerous it was proving to be, was essential to the war effort, and I believe my father was actually delighted to have been posted to Vickers Supermarines at High Post to work under their legendary Chief Test Pilot, Jeff Quill, on the development of the later marks of Spitfire and the innovative Spiteful with its newly designed 'laminar flow' wing. The latter was introduced to reduce drag at air speeds approaching Mach 1. Sadly my father's predecessor at High Post was killed test flying the prototype Spiteful. He was Frank Furlong, another RNVR pilot, who had achieved horse racing fame when he won the Grand National in 1935 on his father's horse Reynoldstown. Jeff Quill was convinced that Frank Furlong's crash was caused by the aileron push/pull rods

Patrick Shea-Simonds in a Spitfire XXII...   **...and in a Sea Otter**

jamming during a high 'G' turn, but this was unknown when my father started further development flying on the Spiteful when he first flew the prototype NN 664 on April 8, 1945. In the meantime he was mainly occupied carrying out development test flying of the later marks of Spitfire, particularly the Mk XXI and Mk XXII. The latter was his favourite and is evidenced by the look on his face in the cockpit of the prototype PK312 in a classic aerial photograph taken by Charles E. Brown on April 18 and which, even now, hangs on my office wall. During the year he was at High Post he flew more than 350 hours in ten different types – not including numerous marks of Spitfire – but which did include a Meteor and this was the first time he flew a jet-engined aircraft. He also flew more than ten hours in Supermarine's last amphibian, the Sea Otter, a beefed-up version of the legendary air sea rescue aircraft, the Walrus. He is clearly recognisable flying Sea Otter JM831 for another splendid Charles E. Brown photograph taken on July 27.

Two months later on September 27 he once again tempted the fates while flying the first production Spiteful, RB515, from High Post. His logbook entry is brief and to the point: 'Handling C.G. 9in aft of datum: at 30,000ft, the first stage rotor disintegrated practically destroying the engine. The aircraft was successfully landed (wheels up) at Farnborough.' His subsequent report of the incident records an uneventful climb to altitude before continuing:

> *Shortly after the engine rpm and boost had been reduced to give maximum cruising power and the indicated airspeed had increased to 240 mph just below 30,000ft, there was a loud explosion and I saw something fly past the cockpit on the starboard side. At the same time the engine began to vibrate very violently, oil began to stream back over the windscreen and cockpit hood and the engine rpm rose rapidly to a reading of 4,000. I took what action I could to deal with the situation: I closed the throttle, brought the constant speed control lever back to positive course pitch, pulled the engine cut-out, turned off the fuel and switched off the ignition. At the same time I pulled the nose of the aircraft up to reduce the airspeed to 140 mph. I then opened the cockpit hood, released my safety harness and prepared to abandon the aircraft as I fully expected the engine either to disintegrate completely or to be torn from its mountings. The vibration and high rpm persisted for some ten to fifteen seconds while oil and glycol streamed back around and into the cockpit and I saw a crack develop in the starboard side of the cockpit immediately aft of the windscreen side panel. Then the rpm fell rapidly, the airscrew came to a stop and the vibration ceased. I called Boscombe Down on the R/T and informed them that my engine had blown up and that I was preparing for a forced landing. I felt that as long as the aircraft did not catch fire it was essential to try to land it in the hope of discovering the cause of the engine failure. Boscombe Down then asked me to give them an approximate position and I replied that I was going to attempt a landing at Farnborough which was within gliding distance to the South East. By the time I had descended to 5,000ft it seemed that there was no longer any risk of the aircraft catching fire. Accordingly I re-fastened my safety harness and proceeded to approach the long runway at Farnborough from the South West. This would*

bring me in to a downwind landing, but the surface wind was very light and I preferred to come in over open country rather than over the town. I also decided not to attempt to lower the undercarriage either by means of the hydraulic hand pump or the CO^2 emergency system as I could not be certain of the extent of the damage caused by the blowing up of the engine, and I did not want to run the risk of getting the undercarriage jammed only partially down. I selected flaps down and operated the hydraulic hand pump until resistance ceased. The trailing edge indicators fitted to the flaps of this particular aircraft then showed that they were about ¼ down, and continued use of the hand pump brought about no increase. I therefore made my final approach with the aircraft in this condition and landed wheels up on the grass alongside the long runway.

The first production Spiteful RB515 after the forced landing at Farnborough on September 27, 1945

The total disintegration of the supercharger caused considerable residual damage to glycol and oil pipes together with substantial crankcase damage. It was fortunate that there was no fire and this allowed my father to keep flying the aircraft rather than abandoning it with parachute and leaving it for an uncontrolled crash. In January 1946 he received a letter which reads:

Sir,

I am directed by the Minister of Supply and of Aircraft Production to inform you that His Majesty the King has been graciously pleased to award to you, at the New Year 1946, the Commendation for Valuable Service in the Air. The Minister wishes me to convey to you an expression of his warm congratulation on this well-merited distinction.

I am, Sir,

Your obedient Servant,

O.S. Franks, Permanent Secretary.

Towards the end of the previous September Jeff Quill had offered my father a permanent peacetime position as a company test pilot. I am sure that my mother played her part in persuading my father not to accept the job as they now had two sons who were soon to be joined by my youngest brother, George. A postscript to this chapter is that Mike Lithgow, another Royal Navy pilot and graduate of No. 2 Course ETPS, subsequently took the job and, in 1947, became Supermarine's Chief Test Pilot and flew with distinction for the company for the next sixteen years, during which time, in 1953, he established the world air speed record in the Supermarine Swift of 735 mph. Tragically he was killed on October 22, 1963, during development test flying of the BAC 111.

CHAPTER 4
RETURN TO PEACE

Like countless others, my parents had to adjust their lives to cope with peace, and for both of them a return to the theatre seemed the obvious thing to do. Seasonal repertory is hard work but generally accepted as valuable experience for budding actors and actresses, and, in 1947, my parents were fortunate enough to be taken on, for two summers by a seasonal repertory company in Ventnor on the Isle of Wight operated by legendary actor Tod Slaughter and his wife, Jenny Lynn. Tod Slaughter had established a reputation in the 1930s as an actor/producer specialising in gory Victorian melodramas, which culminated in two classic 1936 films of the genre. Tod's maniacal and deliriously hammy performances in *Sweeney Todd – The Demon Barber of Fleet Street* and *Maria Marten* (or *Murder in the Red Barn*) received popular acclaim and Jenny subsequently told of how she'd lost count of the number of times Tod had 'murdered' her on stage as he performed numerous different roles with such wonderfully scripted lines as: 'May my dying shriek ring in your ears as a never-ending curse!' It's hardly surprising therefore, that, as an impressionable five-year-old, having watched Tod 'strangle' my mother during a matinée of *Maria Marten*, I refused to talk to Tod, having been introduced to him in his dressing room after the performance. In 1948 my father, in his stage persona of Patrick Addison, landed his only screen role as Captain Hugh Alston with Tod as William Hart in the film *The Greed of William Hart*, based loosely on the story of the early nineteenth-century body-snatchers in Edinburgh, William Burke and William Hare. A recently acquired DVD copy of the film revealed conclusively that Tod was the star, whereas my father definitely wasn't!

Patrick Addison (my father) with Henry Oscar, Dennis Wyndham and Tod Slaughter in *The Greed of William Hart*

In 1950 my parents established a seasonal repertory company of their own, Addison Productions, which operated for the next five summer seasons at the Princes Theatre in Clacton-on-Sea. One memory is of the company staging a Bulldog Drummond story every summer for the week on either side of my father's birthday. The fictional hero, Captain Hugh 'Bulldog' Drummond, an officer of the equally fictional Royal Loamshire Regiment, had won a DSO and MC in the First World War and, bored with civilian life thereafter, becomes a gentleman adventurer. The author of the original stories, Cyril McNeile, had himself won an MC serving with the Royal Engineers during the Great War – hence his pseudonym, 'Sapper' – and he later commanded the 18th Battalion of the Middlesex Regiment on the Western Front. His son, Michael McNeile, was a member of the company, so it was inevitable that he would be cast as Bulldog Drummond, with my father playing Algy Longworth MC, one of Drummond's henchmen, while my mother played the part of Irma, the femme-fatale wife of Drummond's evil nemesis, Carl Petersen. For a ten-year-old prep school boy this was all good 'Boy's Own' stuff reminiscent of the works of G.A. Henty and John Buchan!

Meanwhile in 1947 my father had taken to the skies again and, having flown an Auster from Thruxton on a couple of occasions, he bought one for himself in the autumn of that year – a pretty little Lycoming-engined Auster V, G-AJTM, which he flew for the first time on October 19. It was a significant date for me as it states in the 'remarks' column of his log book: CHARLES SHEA-SIMONDS – PASSENGER – HIS FIRST FLIGHT. According to his post-war logbook, I flew more than eight hours with him in the Auster during the five years he owned it, though only one flight stands out in my memory. Father had also acquired a J2X Allard which he occasionally raced in club events, usually at Thruxton or Silverstone.

Patrick Shea-Simonds racing the J2X Allard at Silverstone in 1952

On April 19, 1952, while one of his chums drove the Allard to Silverstone, my father took his three sons, aged ten, eight and six, in the Auster. It was a warm spring day with mild turbulence which was enough to provoke my youngest brother to throw up first, echoed by my middle brother following his example, and then, inevitably, I couldn't restrain myself either. Father was not amused as his colourful language proved during our cleaning up of the Auster with grass after we landed at Silverstone. One of the characters who I remember from those days at Thruxton was a legendary pilot by the name of Stewart Keith-Jopp who had lost an arm and one eye and was equipped with a steel skull-cap, all as the result of aerial combat while flying with 1 Squadron, Royal Flying Corps, on the Western Front. He flew again during the Second World War as a ferry pilot with the wartime Air Transport Auxiliary and during this time he delivered more than 1,300 aircraft. After the war he became interested in photographing archaeological sites from the air for which he and my father often flew together. In June 1952 my father had been to the Isle of Man for the TT races after which he had flown from Ronaldsway in a Rapide to Speke, Liverpool, where he hoped Stewart Keith-Jopp would be waiting for him with the Auster. The weather was horrid – low cloud and rain – and the pilot of the Rapide only just managed to scrape into Speke at his second attempt. Father didn't think Stewart would have had any chance of flying in from Thruxton in the Auster in such vile weather conditions, but as he got out of the Rapide, he spotted his stalwart chum sitting in the rain on an old oil drum alongside the Auster, whereupon he remarked, 'What kept you so long, dear boy?' Father subsequently recounted that he didn't enjoy flying the Auster back to Thruxton as the weather hadn't improved and he didn't want to appear to be too apprehensive about it – even if he was – but he remained a huge admirer of this colourful, courageous character.

When he was issued with his civilian private pilot's licence in 1946, my father was authorised to fly 'all types of landplanes and seaplanes' – an authorisation now unavailable in the bureaucratic age in which we live. This enabled him to apply for an interesting job. The Israeli Air Force had in the late 1940s acquired a number of Spitfire Mk IXs from the Czech Air Force. In 1954, thirty of these aircraft were sold by the Israelis to the Burmese Air Force. The problem was that the Iraqis might discover that the aircraft were all ex-Israeli Air Force so they were flown to Cyprus where their military markings were changed to Burmese before being flown across Lebanon and Iraq to Burma. The word got around that a company called Air Services Ltd was on the lookout for service or ex-service pilots with Spitfire experience to ferry these aircraft to their new owner. So in early December the chosen pilots were split into groups of three and flown to Cyprus where the Spitfires were waiting at Nicosia airport. One of the other pilots in my father's group was Lt Cdr Jack Overbury RN, a Fleet Air Arm graduate of No. 12 Course ETPS, who was on leave from the Royal Navy – whether the latter knew that he would be flying an ex-Israeli Air Force Spitfire across Arab countries is unlikely! My father was allocated Spitfire IX UB 447 powered by a Rolls Royce Merlin 66 engine and, bearing in mind that he hadn't flown a Spitfire for more than nine years, he carried out two air tests of the aircraft, the first of an hour-and-a-half on December 1, followed by another of an hour's duration the next day. He recounted later that, while these Spitfires were technically airworthy, they weren't in their first flush of youth as the pilot trio discovered later. Early the following morning they took off from Nicosia to land two hours and forty five minutes later at Baghdad. The flight of the first two groups of three had gone to plan, but, by the time my father's group had arrived, the Iraqi authorities had smelt a very whiffy rat resulting in the intrepid trio being apprehended. A short piece in the *The Iraq Times* of Wednesday, December 8 recorded: 'The Three Burmese Air Force planes detained here since Friday are due to leave Baghdad back to Cyprus today escorted by Royal Iraqi Air Force Planes to Iraq's western frontier. Due to bad weather and engine trouble in one of the three Burmese Spitfire fighters, their departure was delayed till today. They landed in Baghdad on Friday on their way to Burma without permission from Iraqi military authorities.' In fact they didn't get away to return to Nicosia until the following day. Unfortunately one of the three Spitfires developed a glycol leak over Lebanon, so a swift landing was necessary before the engine overheated and ultimately seized solid. The three had agreed before they originally left Cyprus that in the event of any problem they would stick together, so they diverted as a trio into Beirut where they were immediately arrested, pending an investigation into the Spitfires' origins. From my father's scrapbook, another newspaper cutting from Beirut's *Daily Star* published on December 19 accounts what happened under the headline: 'Burma Planes Fined (sic) For Illegal Landing In Beirut.' It went on:

> *Three British pilots who landed three Burmese military planes December 9th in Beirut International Airport without prior permit were fined £500.00 each by a Beirut court yesterday. The pilots were forced to land in Beirut for refuelling while en-route from Baghdad to Cyprus. They were detained six days in Baghdad after reports said they were of Israeli origin (sic). After the court's verdict was issued an official spokesman said the planes will continue to be detained until investigation into their origin is completed. The Ministry of Public Works has contacted Iraqi and Cyprus authorities for information about the origin of the planes. The pilots confessed that they flew over Lebanese territory without permit but said their 'intention was good'. The verdict ordered the pilots to pay the fine or else they would be imprisoned, one day for every five pounds they fail to pay.*

Meanwhile, back in England my mother came to pick me up from my prep school at the end of the Christmas term – this was usually father's chore. So 'Where's Dad?' I asked. 'He's in jail in Beirut!' My mother replied before explaining as much as she then knew. In Beirut the British Consul proved to be a formidable negotiator who not only paid the fine, but also managed to arrange for the three to be repatriated back to the UK where they arrived on Christmas Eve – but with the three Spitfires being left behind at the airport, their ultimate fate unknown.

Then there was the saga of the Thruxton Jackaroo – the brainchild of Sqn Ldr Jimmy Doran-Webb, the managing director of the Wiltshire School of Flying, and so named after the Australian 'jack-of-all-trades'. The idea was a conversion of the ubiquitous Gipsy Major-engined DH 82a Tiger Moth tandem two-seat trainer into a four-seat utility aeroplane by widening the mid-section of the fuselage from 24 to 37 inches. An alternative was a single seat crop spraying version with the same widened fuselage. My father disclosed later that there had been discussions about replacing the four-cylinder 130 hp Gipsy Major with the larger 205 hp six-cylinder Gipsy Queen engine, but this sensible idea was rejected as being too expensive – when the original concept was taking shape in late 1956 the conversion of an existing airframe was to cost about £600 and about £995 if purchased outright with a reconditioned engine. Another option was a conversion pack for export to sell at about £530. The design work and stress calculations were undertaken by Ronald Prizeman and my father agreed to take on the task of the development test flying. The latter started with the first flight of the prototype G-AOEX on March 2, 1957.

He flew nearly four hours in two weeks in the four-seat prototype before flying the crop sprayer prototype, G-AOEY, for the first time on March 14. During the next three months my father carried out further test flights with the two prototypes and these are meticulously recorded in his logbook with the comment in the 'remarks' column for March 22; 'Solo: handling at increased AUW (all up weight)'. This aspect of the aeroplane's performance was already causing my father some concern. It had been marginally improved by the fitting of a metal propeller and on April 4 he recorded: 'Solo: handling and performance at AUW 2,100lb' – the maximum AUW of a Tiger Moth is 1,825lb. In reminiscing about this flight he subsequently came out with the old gag so often used by pilots to describe poor aircraft performance: 'The only thing that got me airborne was the curvature of the earth!' After thirty-one hours during forty-five test flights of the Jackaroo, my father remained concerned about its performance, which led to his falling out with Jimmy Doran-Webb and their parting company after he had flown G-AOEX for the last time on June 7, 1957, and this proved to be his last ever flight as pilot in command, to which the last entry in his logbook bears testament – and this nearly twenty three years since his first solo in 1934. Subsequently the test flying programme was completed by Commander 'Doc' Stewart and twenty-six Tigers were later converted to become Jackaroos. Many of this number were used by the Wiltshire School of Flying in a training role well into the 1960s, but the Jackaroo cannot really be considered a success story – evidence the fact that over the years the majority were converted back to being Tiger Moths again. Nevertheless, the Jackaroo will be mentioned again within these pages!

CHAPTER 5
DOWN WITH SKOOL!

In 1944 my parents bought the 17th-century thatched Melrose House in Figheldean, a lovely village nestling alongside the River Avon on Salisbury Plain. It was to become our family home for fifty years. In the immediate post-war years Figheldean was a thriving community that boasted a butcher's shop, a bakery, a haberdashery, a general store, the Working Men's Club and, most importantly, the Wheatsheaf Inn. When I was twelve my father took me to the Wheatsheaf for my first pint of Strong's best bitter, and which then cost one shilling and five pence of old money (or 7p today and now worth £1.10). The village also had a separate post office which was the small front room of an old cottage where the imposing, flaming red-haired postmistress rested her ample bosom on the counter. Believe it or not, her name was Mrs Titt! Sadly over the years the village lost all these amenities with the one exception which remains today – the Working Men's Club.

Just before my eighth birthday my parents sent me off to a boarding prep school, Hawtreys, in Savernake Forest and established in 1946 at Tottenham House. This gently decaying stately home was built for the 1st Marquess of Ailesbury in 1820. I can't say I enjoyed my time there – the headmaster was an enthusiastic believer in the benefits of corporal punishment and I was a frequent recipient of his energetic application of this form of correction – and I wasn't the only one. After the end-of-term exams had been marked, a queue of under-achievers were lined up outside the headmaster's study for what had been endearingly christened 'The Grand Execution' with the first in line being thrashed for his sins, the next receiving a 'good talking to', the next being thrashed and so on alternately. Those of us standing at the back of the queue nervously counted the number of those standing in front of us in an attempt to work out which form of punishment we were likely to receive. Inevitably I drew an odd number in the line-up of miscreants.

It was in 1953 while I was doing time at this ghastly institution, that the classic Geoffrey Willans book, *Down with Skool!*, so brilliantly illustrated by Ronald Searle, was published. I well remember thinking at the time that St Custards, the 'skool' in question, must have been inspired by Hawtreys. It was the result of squinting at blackboards in an attempt to read what had been written thereon that it was discovered that I was short-sighted, so corrective spectacles were prescribed. I now looked even more like Nigel Molesworth, the self-proclaimed curse of St Custards and the unlikely hero of *Down with Skool!*, and at a stroke I realised that my early dream of becoming a Fleet Air Arm pilot like my father was unlikely to be fulfilled. Meanwhile my parents had themselves become so disenchanted with Hawtreys that my two younger brothers were sent to a much more enlightened school near Guildford. It was here that my parents became friends with the parents of a boy called Kim Ross, who was destined to go on to Uppingham at the same time as I was. We both found ourselves going to Lorne House and, as sharing a study was mandatory for the first two years, we managed to fix it that we shared together. There was never any doubt about Kim's future – he had already decided he was going to be a Guardsman, which is exactly what he became – he later commanded the 1st Battalion the Scots Guards before finishing a rewarding Army career as a Brigadier; he remains a good friend and I was thrilled when he and his splendid wife, Cathy, asked me to be godfather to Alice, their number-two daughter, who is an absolute delight.

Uppingham in Rutland, founded in 1584 and rich in tradition, was a different establishment from Hawtreys altogether with discipline usually enforced by the school or house prefects (known as praepostors or 'pollies') – straw boaters were badges of office for the former. Corporal punishment canings, known as 'bimmings', having necessarily been sanctioned in each case by the housemaster, were dished out by the pollies after house prayers in the evening. We all knew when some unfortunate was about to receive six of the best as we were obliged to sing the bimming hymn, *Thy Kingdom Come O God*, fortissimo because it contained the unforgettable line: 'Break with thine iron rod the tyrannies of sin!' For really outrageous behaviour the headmaster could expel the culprit. I only remember this happening on one occasion and even then the unfortunate young gentleman was within two weeks of the end of his final term anyway. His crime was literally applauded as it occurred during the school variety show. He came on to the stage from between the curtains and, with a deadpan expression, he recited the following:

Mary had a little lamb,
She put it in a bucket,
And every time the lamb climbed out,
A bulldog tried to…
…pick it up and put it back in again!

The headmaster was not impressed. But it was felt that the punishment system was fairly administered with the result that standards of behaviour generally were considered acceptable. Apart from academic study, sport was considered almost as important, as was the school's Combined Cadet Force (CCF). The latter was mandatory and, apart from a dominant Army section, it also had small RAF section. As Hawtreys had been a soccer school I initially struggled with rugby at Uppingham, but I thoroughly enjoyed the game even though I was a lacklustre player. I positively hated cricket, however, because the attitude at my prep school was that, unless you were in the 1st XI, none of the staff were interested or qualified in coaching those of us who were less talented in the game. In the summer term the alternatives to cricket were full-bore rifle shooting and athletics, which suited me perfectly. Apart from wanting to follow my father's example by qualifying for a place in the school's shooting VIII, participation permitted the use of a bicycle to get to the school's five-hundred-yard open range which was located a couple of miles out of the town in open countryside. Two events enhanced my enthusiasm for shooting. The first was at Bisley where in 1957 Uppingham won the public school's prestigious Ashburton Shield with a record score of 529 out of a possible 560. Suddenly shooting became fashionable in the school. Secondly my Lorne House housemaster, who was related by marriage and with whom I'd had an uneasy relationship for my first two years – probably because he loved cricket and I didn't – finally stood down after 29 years in the job. For me his replacement was a breath of fresh air. His name was Ian Bridges and, unlike his predecessor, he hadn't led a sheltered academic life – far from it. His grandfather, the Reverend Thomas Bridges, was found as an abandoned baby under Bristol Bridge (thus the name 'Bridges') in 1842 and he became the first missionary to settle in Tierra del Fuego with his wife and baby daughter in 1871. Ian's father, Stephen Lucas Bridges, was born there three years later in 1874. He subsequently wrote the classic book, *Uttermost Part of the Earth*, about the family's work among the Yaghan Indians during late 18th and early 19th centuries. Stephen Lucas survived serving in the Royal Artillery during the First World War during which time he had married.

Ian, my housemaster, was born in 1921, and was himself educated at Uppingham. He was about to take up a place at university but when he saw that war was imminent he put the plan on hold, and, like his father, he was commissioned into the Royal Artillery and served throughout the war, after which he finally went up to Cambridge. There is no question that that he was a major influence during my last three years at Uppingham. This wasn't altogether surprising as he commanded the CCF, and was the master in charge of both shooting and cross-country running. At the end of my first term as a member of the school shooting VIII, I became by default the Captain of Shooting (which included small-bore during the winter and spring terms) simply because the three members of the team senior to me completed their time at the school. At the same time because shooting was linked to the cadet force, I was promoted to the dizzy rank of lance corporal, presumably to give me some degree of authority while wearing uniform when we competed at the various schools' rifle meetings. At the end of the four summer terms 1957, 1958, 1959 and 1960, I attended two weeks' annual cadet camp at Windmill Hill (near Tidworth), Towyn, Catterick and Cultybraggan respectively, while during the Easter holidays of 1959 and 1960 I attended two cadet leadership courses in the Welsh mountains. During the latter, which were basically seven-day cross-country treks, I kept a diary that recorded that it had rained for most of the time but, in spite of this, the report about our section's efforts during the 1960 course recorded: 'The first four named attended in 1959 and this was certainly the outstanding section. Hampton unfortunately suffered from sinus trouble on the first day and dropped out. All four remaining did splendidly; if anyone was the leader it was probably Wilkinson with Shea-Simonds as chief morale maintainer. This section were bang on course throughout, gradually gained on their schedule and finished in great heart.' All this, coupled with the fact that I had been promoted steadily through cadet ranks to that of 'under-officer', convinced me that the regular Army offered me an interesting future.

During my last two terms at Uppingham I thoroughly enjoyed myself to the detriment of much academic achievement. In the spring term I gained a place in the school cross-country running VIII, while, during my last term, the shooting VIII were placed first in three important schools' rifle competitions – Beckingham with a score of

I receive the Bell Trophy from the 'Auk' at Six Hills, July 1960, with Ian Bridges in the background

503/560, Cambridge with 523/560 and Six Hills with 517/560. The latter remains a significant memory, enhanced by a much-treasured photograph of my being presented with the trophy by the magnificently impressive Field Marshal Sir Claude Auchinleck GCB, GCIE, CSI, DSO, OBE. For my money the 'Auk', a formidable man of total integrity, was arguably the greatest general of the Second World War. He first came to prominence in 1940 when he was given command of the Anglo/French land forces in the ill-conceived and doomed Norwegian campaign. By early 1941 he had risen to become Commander-in-Chief of the Indian Army. In July 1941 he then succeeded Wavell as Commander-in-Chief, Middle East Command where, in July 1942 and in spite of continued interference from Churchill, he stemmed the tide of Rommel's eastward advance across the desert towards Alexandria at the first battle of El Alamein. This provided Montgomery with a firm base from which to defeat Rommel at the second battle of El Alamein in October 1942. The Auk then returned to India having been appointed Commander-in-Chief for the second time in June 1943 and in this capacity he was able to provide General (later Field Marshal) Bill Slim with the resources he required for the latter's 'forgotten' Fourteenth Army to defeat the Japanese in Burma. His illustrious career came to a sad end when he had debilitating job of winding up the magnificent old Indian Army at the time of Partition in 1947, but he remained in command of all British forces in India and Pakistan until late the following year. He was a very great man.

In 1942 a young officer serving in the Royal Tank Regiment was wounded during the war in the Western Desert, captured and incarcerated in the Campo 21, a notorious

POW camp in northern Italy. Because he was already a classical musician of some distinction when war broke out, he approached the Italian authorities and persuaded them to provide him with enough instruments to form a symphony orchestra. The result was a number of orchestral concerts that did much to relieve the boredom of both the inmates and their Italian guards. After the Italian surrender in September 1943 he escaped twice, the first time from a moving train, and, after the second he was on the run for six months before he was finally recaptured. After the war he became the wonderfully enthusiastic head of the wind instrument department at Uppingham and he taught me to play the clarinet. His name was Tony Baines and it now seems amazing that, at our time at Uppingham, none of us knew of his extraordinary wartime career, as now, every time I pick up my clarinet I simply remember him as a mildly eccentric character who was an extraordinarily talented musician and an inspirational teacher.

Needless to say I failed my A-levels and was thus forced to seek an alternative means of qualifying for entry to the Royal Military Academy at Sandhurst. I needed a job where, during any spare time, I could study for the alternative – the necessity of passing the Civil Service Exam. Ian Bridges discovered that the headmaster of Hazelwood, a boy's prep school near Oxted in Surrey, was on the lookout for a temporary schoolmaster for the autumn term, so this seemed to be a good solution. During the summer holiday I managed to pass my driving test and persuaded my mother to lend me her car to drive myself to Hazelwood for the job interview – it proved to be the shortest imaginable. The headmaster was standing solidly on the steps to the front door as I pulled up. He was smoking a huge pipe and had a rugby ball secured under one arm. He wasted no time in small talk and, having introduced himself, he demanded: 'What can you teach?' Surely he must have guessed that, at eighteen, I'd never taught anything.

'Er, I'll have a go at teaching anything,' I replied, with as much confidence as I could muster.

'Jolly good – you play rugby of course?'

'Yes, Sir, I do.'

'Excellent,' he replied, releasing a billowing cloud of tobacco smoke, 'See you on September the 21st!'

I drove away from the place in a daze without having discovered any of the essentials, such as how much I was to be paid (£90 for the term), or whether I could have time off to travel to London to sit the Civil Service exam (it wasn't a problem). I started my short, undistinguished three-month teaching career on September 21 as instructed and found myself on the staff of an institution which, like Hawtreys, appeared to have much in common with St Custards. Sport was obviously more important than academic achievement and, whilst it was easy to encourage the boys on the rugby field, the headmaster never once appeared in my classroom to see what knowledge a totally unqualified teenage member of his teaching staff was imparting to his pupils. Character building was high on the agenda and exemplified on November 5 when the headmaster instructed the boys to ask their parents to supply each of them with a box of fireworks. We, the staff, built and lit a huge bonfire before retiring to our common room to witness through the large bay window the headmaster dishing out boxes of matches to the boys who were basically told to get on with it. Throughout the ensuing flame-ridden chaos the female members of the staff, led by the headmaster's wife, manned the equivalent of a minor field hospital to treat the boys' numerous wounds and burns.

One of the least eccentric members of the teaching staff was an impressive-looking man called Vernon Scannell. Vernon had persuaded the headmaster to allow him to teach boxing which of course fitted into the character-building ethos of the place. All I knew about Vernon at the time was that after he came out of the Army at the end of the war he had earned money as a fairground boxer before becoming Captain of the Leeds University boxing team. What I didn't know was that he had served initially in the Argylls and then in the Gordons, first seeing active service in the North African campaign where he deserted after enduring three days of devastating artillery fire and the dying screams of wounded men. His behaviour would today be diagnosed as post-traumatic stress disorder, but he was subsequently court-martialled and sentenced to three years in prison. He was then prematurely released on a suspended sentence to take part in the Normandy landings where he was badly wounded before going on the run a second time. He later wrote about all this in *Argument of Kings* (1987) and, in another autobiographical book, *The Tiger and the Rose* (1971), he wrote of Hazelwood: 'There was something dreamlike about much of school life, moments of Alice-in-Wonderland craziness, an unnerving sense of lunacy in command together with a vague sense of déjà-vu which I think must have come from residual memories of my reading the *Magnet* and the *Gem* when I was about the same age as the boys I was teaching.' I found Vernon to be stimulating and interesting company and now, reflecting on those days in late 1960, I find it extraordinary that, although he knew of my intention to join the Army, he never tried to discourage me. He later became a much-respected poet and writer, and, after he had written *The Tiger and the Rose*, I re-established contact with him when I asked him to sign my copy – in it he wrote: 'To Charles Shea-Simonds with best wishes and memories of Hazelwood school where we both did time, Vernon Scannell.' Later he wrote in my copy of *Argument of Kings*: 'For Charles Shea-Simonds who, as an ex-soldier, will understand what this book is about. With warm regards from Vernon Scannell.' Indeed I do understand. He died aged eighty-five in 2007 and I still have fond memories of him at Hazelwood. In retrospect the place can't have done me much harm as I managed to pass both the Civil Service exam and the Regular Commissioning Board to gain a place at the Royal Military Academy at Sandhurst.

CHAPTER 6
SERVE TO LEAD
(The motto of the Royal Military Academy, Sandhurst)

In the 1960s the Royal Military Academy, Sandhurst, was co-located with the Army Staff College on the northern edge of Camberley. It consisted of three colleges – the original Old Building (thus Old College) housed cadets in companies named after 18th and 19th-century battles, Blenheim, Dettingen, Inkerman and Waterloo, with New and Victory colleges housed in the New building which was built just before the First World War. Victory college companies were named after Second World War conflicts; Alamein, Normandy, Burma and Rhine with New College companies named after First World War battles; Marne, Somme, Gaza and Ypres. In early January 1961 I became a member of Intake 30 and was assigned to Ypres Company along with sixteen others, all of us initially designated as 'Juniors'. We were a disparate group. We had two overseas cadets, Simon Uwakwe from Nigeria, and Dick Lockley, a tall, good-looking cadet from Rhodesia (now Zimbabwe). My immediate neighbour in the corridor was one R.A. (always known as 'Ra') Wilson who was an enthusiastically dedicated participant in the London social scene. A couple of doors away was Robin Sjoberg, for whom sailing has always been a passion – as he was such an accomplished sailor perhaps he should have joined the Royal Navy and gone to Dartmouth instead. Mike Robjohn was another memorable character who was always the butt of the Guards Sergeant Majors' and Sergeants' barbed comments – but, and with great resilience, he took it all on the chin – even when on one occasion he was forced to have three haircuts in one day! Martin Tinniswood was a naturally talented athlete in spite of being a chain smoker, whilst Warwick King-Martin turned out to be a gifted pop singer whose spirited rendering of *Wimoweh* with his group the Figleaf Five remains memorable more than fifty years later. Almost from day one Norman Arnell and Bob Clarke stood out as being the keenest members of the platoon and it came as no surprise that the latter ultimately became the platoon's Senior Under Officer. The company was commanded by Pat Dawson, a delightful major in the Lancashire Fusiliers and the Company Sergeant Major was Idris James, a splendidly impressive Welsh Guardsman who, on our very first parade, announced: 'I call you Sir, and you call me Sir – the only difference is you mean it!' (Every officer cadet at Sandhurst has heard this from one Sergeant Major or another!)

To us at the time the Foot Guards were the memorable backbone of the Academy staff, led at that time by the legendary Academy Sergeant Major, J.C. (Jesus Christ perchance?) Lord, late of the wartime Grenadier Guards and the Parachute Regiment, of whom more later. The personalities of the guardsmen we encountered first hand remain permanently etched in our collective memories, none more so than our Platoon Sergeant, Joe Ford, of the Grenadier Guards for whom we developed the greatest respect. From the start and for the first couple of months, Joe Ford chased us relentlessly, but it was never bullying and it was seldom administered without a twinkle in his eye. He was always immaculately turned out with his magnificent ginger handlebar moustache impeccably groomed – he led by example and never swore, though he did have an extensive repertoire of brilliant gags: 'Mr Robjohn, Sir, you're handling your rifle like the Countess stroking a navvy's tool!' For the first two or three weeks we were kept busy from six in the morning until at least ten at night, either attending a variety of parades for the many aspects of Army training or pressing our uniforms, and cleaning our equipment and rooms so that they were immaculate and satisfied whoever it was who conducted the infinite number of inspections which took place.

Joe Ford impressed upon us three vitally important lessons that have remained an indelibly imprinted part of my life ever since. Firstly the knots in our ties were not permitted to have flutes in them – in this context a flute is a vertical crease below the knot and was a definite no-no! Secondly we learnt how to hang our trousers properly with the trouser legs being placed in opposing directions over the horizontal bar of the coathanger – this way the trousers maintain their carefully ironed creases and are discouraged from falling off the hanger. Thirdly our boot laces when tied could not be diagonally criss-crossed – they had to be passed horizontally between the lace holes. Kit inspections followed each other in quick succession with our ability to 'bull' our boots – by the traditional method of 'spit and polish' practised by generations of British soldiers – to the highest standards set by the Guards. Later we wised up and purchased extra illicit pairs of boots that were designated 'show' boots – they were never actually worn but were secreted away to be produced solely for inspections. Similarly, we were subjected to the practice of folding our sheets, blankets and pillows into 'bed blocks' of specified dimensions and which took so long to make up that a number of us slept under our beds rolled up in our heavy Army greatcoats. Fortunately the requirement for bed block fabrication didn't last more than a couple of weeks and, mercifully, neither did 'changing' parades. The purpose of the latter was to speed up our changing from one form of dress to another in double-quick time. We'd be formed up on the square – that hallowed expanse tarmac to be found in all Army barracks – in, say, battle dress and, on the word of command, 'GO', we'd have two minutes to sprint off the square and back up to our rooms to change, for example, into PT kit and then dash back down the stairs to renew our places on the square, where we were inspected to ensure that we were properly dressed. Two or three minutes later the exercise was repeated with another change of dress being designated. Robin, Ra and I had the fortuitous advantage of our rooms being located close to the stairs, so we had a head start over those members of the platoon whose rooms were at the far end of the corridor. After about forty-five minutes of a number of frenzied changes we were all dropping on our feet.

Much of our time in our first few weeks was spent on New College square undergoing various forms of drill. I was reminded recently by my stalwart Parachute Regiment friend, John Ball, of when he was sent on a drill instructor's course at the Guards Depot at Pirbright and learnt the Guard's definition of drill: 'The object of drill is to develop in the individual soldier that instinctive sense of obedience that will enable him to carry out his orders at all times under all conditions.' Apart from that, drill was the means of instilling into us a variety of basic military skills – and all taught by numbers, of course. They included how to march in slow and quick time, how to halt, how to turn at the halt and on the march and, most importantly how to salute – longest way up, shortest way down. 'Saluting is not a servile act, but dates back to olden days when knights used to raise their visors to their opponents as a mark of respect.' So it went on with Bicycle Drill proving to be an hilarious highlight. Behind the Academy grounds was the adjoining 'Barossa' training area and the use of bicycles to access it was a sensible option – but to start with we had to learn how to ride them as a military drill. Bicycles had first been used by the British Army in the Boer War and the machines we had to sign out from the bicycle sheds were probably those left over from campaigning in South Africa sixty years previously, and it looked like the two ancient retainers who maintained them were of a similar vintage. Having signed for our respective bikes we were met on the square by Sergeant Major James who revealed to us the mysteries of bicycle drill. We formed up with our bicycles to our right in a single rank with Dick Lockley on the right of the line with Simon Uwakwe next to him. The first word of command was: 'Bicycles, Right dress.' Eyes smartly right and we bounced our steeds into line. Then: 'Eyes front,' followed by: 'Prepare to mount.' We reached down to adjust the left pedal so it was closest to the ground. Then: 'Bicycles, right incline.' We instantaneously turned the handlebars 45° to the right – our intended direction of travel. So far, so good. Sergeant Major James's executive word of command boomed across the square: 'MOUNT!' Unfortunately, and until that January day, Simon Uwakwe had never seen a bicycle – never mind ridden one. His bike slid noisily from under him causing the remaining sixteen of us to topple over in rapid succession like a stack of dominoes. We lay on the square interlocked with our bikes, unable to contain our laughter, while our revered Sergeant Major desperately tried to keep a straight face. We subsequently learned that, because it needed both hands on the handlebars to control an Army bike, the right arm couldn't be used to salute when appropriate, thus a smart 'eyes right' was the solution which we reckoned was equally as hazardous. Mercifully our pathetic bicycle drill efforts failed to be an influence when we took to the square on a later occasion to take part in the inter-company Juniors' Drill Competition which we managed to win and, at the end of our first term, we followed this up by also winning the New College Inter-Company Juniors' Cup. Thanks to Joe Ford we had developed into a tightly knit team, which was of course the object of the exercise.

The first and last terms of our two years at Sandhurst were devoted exclusively to Army training and this was mixed with academic studies during the intermediate terms. Military history was an important subject which was enthusiastically taught by a brilliant team led by the charismatic Brigadier Peter Young – a distinguished wartime Army Commando whose gallantry had earned him a DSO and three MCs. He was supported by two other equally erudite historians, David Chandler and John Keegan. We were fortunate indeed to have been inspired by these outstanding, knowledgeable teachers. We were also able to choose an additional academic subject and initially I selected mathematics as I'd failed the subject at A-level and was grateful of another opportunity. It seemed

Our platoon winning the Juniors' Drill Competition, Sgt Joe Ford at the rear, C S-S in the rear rank, third from left

to me, however, that, apart from the military historians, those members of the academic staff who taught us were not so gifted and lacked essential teaching skills – indeed one of them wrote in one of my reports: 'He is far keener on the Army than on mathematics.' Too true! Luckily I was permitted to change to studying additional military history instead – perfect. The variety of military training was extensive and included everything from weapons – rifle, light machine gun, mortar and 3.5in rocket launcher – to map reading and military law. The latter included the dubious advice that, if you can't get the accused for any specific offence, try the 'catch all' of Conduct to the Prejudice of Good Order and Military Discipline contrary to Section 69 of the Army Act 1955. We also had a memorable visit to the Army School of Health and Hygiene where we received a wonderfully funny presentation on how to dig various types of latrines in the field from a poker-faced Royal Army Medical Corps warrant officer. His performance had been carefully perfected over the years, with the result that his timing was impeccable. Finally he could tolerate our laughter no longer: 'Gentlemen,' he announced solemnly, 'it may be shit to you, but it's my bread and butter!' He received a well-earned round of applause for that one.

The Green Howards (Alexandra, Princess of Wales's Own Yorkshire Regiment) were, as their title suggests, a proud Yorkshire Regiment until 2006 when the ghastly ogre of amalgamation took away their historic cap badge and they became part of the 4th Battalion, the Yorkshire Regiment. My father had a Green Howard friend, one John Bade, who, before I went to Sandhurst, persuaded me to opt for his regiment as my first choice. I spent three enjoyable days at the Richmond home of the Green Howards and learned much about their distinguished regimental history. This included eighteen of their number being awarded VCs, one of whom in the First World War, Private Henry Tandey, was also awarded a DCM and MM, making him the most highly decorated private soldier in the British Army. During my last term at Uppingham I was fortunate enough to have been one of a CCF group to visit No. 1 Parachute Training School at

RAF Abingdon where we witnessed a number of Parachute Regiment soldiers undergoing military parachute training. This must have been a strong influence because, when at Sandhurst we were ordered to nominate a second regiment of choice, I opted for the Parachute Regiment believing that I had little chance of being accepted because of my short-sightedness.

The end of our first year was marked by Ypres winning the competition to become the Sovereign's Company and Pat Dawson finishing his stint as Company Commander – his place was taken in January 1962 by Major Mike Walsh of the Parachute Regiment. Mike Walsh had been commissioned into the Kings Royal Rifle Corps in 1945 and transferred to the Parachute Regiment in 1955. During the Suez Operation 'Musketeer' in November 1956 he had parachuted on to El Gamil Airfield as a Company Commander with the 3rd Battalion – he was to change my life completely. Within days of his arrival he sent for me, having spotted in my file that I had nominated the Parachute Regiment as my second choice – this obviously offended his Regimental pride! He went straight for the jugular: 'What's all this about the Parachute Regiment being your second choice?' I explained that I thought my short-sightedness would be a decisive stumbling block.

'Nonsense,' he replied firmly, 'If we want you, we'll have you – do you want to join the Parachute Regiment or not?'

'Well, yes Sir, I do – but what about the Green Howards?'

'Don't worry, I'll fix them, and you'll be on Regimental interview next week'

And a few days later, having attended the interview, I received a letter dated February 2, 1962, from the Regimental Colonel:

Dear Shea-Simonds,
With reference to your interview on February 1, I am writing to tell you that the Colonel Commandant will be pleased to accept you for a commission in the Parachute Regiment.
Yours sincerely,
Graham Mills.

Interestingly the Colonel Commandant at the time was a hugely distinguished parachute soldier, General Sir Gerald Lathbury GCB DSO MBE, who had commanded the 1st Parachute Brigade in the 1st Airborne Division at the famous Battle of Arnhem in September 1944 where the following month, and in spite of his wounds, he had managed to escape back across the Rhine. What an example! I've no idea how Mike Walsh 'fixed' the Green Howards, but now the Parachute Regiment was the goal, and this was made more challenging by the thought that my red-bereted company commander would be watching my every move. During our Easter leave Mike had arranged a three-week visit for the four of us now accepted for the Regiment to the 3rd Battalion then stationed in Bahrain. Roly Gibbs, the Commanding Officer, was a delightful but resolute soldier who, like Mike Walsh, had been commissioned into the KRRC. He had served throughout the war during which time he'd won a DSO and an MC. He later became one of the British Army's last Field Marshals before the rank was abolished in 1995. He made us most welcome and we were delighted to be simply treated as 'toms' – the Regiment's enduring nick name for its private soldiers ('tom' – a derivative of Kipling's 'Tommy Atkins') – when we took part in a seaborne assault exercise with the Royal Navy. It proved to have been a thoroughly worthwhile visit.

Back at Sandhurst I had my first face-to-face encounter with Academy Sergeant Major John Lord, who before the war had been a Grenadier guardsman. In 1941 this magnificently impressive man was appointed the first Regimental Sergeant Major of the 3rd Battalion, the Parachute Regiment with whom he subsequently parachuted into Arnhem in September 1944. Here he was badly wounded before being captured and being sent to Stalag XIB. This proved to be an 'other rank' prisoner of war camp where the conditions were very unpleasant. As on arrival he found himself in the position of being the senior warrant officer, he immediately set about instilling some discipline by initiating kit inspections and drill parades to promote some self-respect and raise morale among the inmates. Initially the wound in his right arm was serious enough to prevent him saluting German officers as required by the Geneva Convention, but eventually he gathered his senior NCOs together and informed them that, as his wound had now recovered, he intended to seek out the German camp commandant and give him the smartest salute possible – he let his intention sink in with his horrified audience before, and with great timing, he announced: 'But I'll be thinking "bollocks"!' Within 24 hours all the POWs were enthusiastically saluting every German officer they encountered. Morale went through the roof and therefore it was not surprising that, when the camp was relieved by the Recce Troop of the 8th Hussars, they were met by an immaculately turned-out guard of airborne soldiers led by the inspiring figure of RSM Lord. The MBE he received was well deserved. Our platoon was formed up on Old Building square as we watched him come to attention in front of us with his pace stick locked firmly under his left arm.

'Gentlemen, when I come to each one of you in turn, come to attention and give me your number, rank and name and regiment of first choice.' He paused in front of me. I came to attention and, with as much confidence as I could muster, shouted out: '23855166 Officer Cadet Shea-Simonds, Sir, the Parachute Regiment!'

He took a pace away from me before executing a perfect double-take as he stepped back. 'Which battalion, Sir?'

'The 3rd Battalion, Sir!' I replied.

'Not if I can help it, Sir!' he said as he strode away!

On the military history front our platoon were instructed to produce a presentation on D-Day Normandy 1944 for the rest of the New Collage intake. Warwick King-Martin and I decided it would be a good idea to ask Field Marshal Montgomery if we could tape an interview with him about this historic military operation. We drove to his house at Isington Mill near Alton and rang the bell. An imposing member of the staff came to the door and we explained our mission. It was solemnly pointed out to us that this was not the way to approach the Field Marshal, and it was suggested that we write to him detailing our request. Having been put firmly in our places, we returned to Sandhurst where I wrote the letter. A couple of days later Warwick and I were somewhat surprised when my letter came back with, in Montgomery's unique, distinct handwriting, the following words written in red ink at the bottom: 'The field-marshal cannot do as you ask. Secretary 26.6.62.' Very odd! The envelope had the same handwriting.

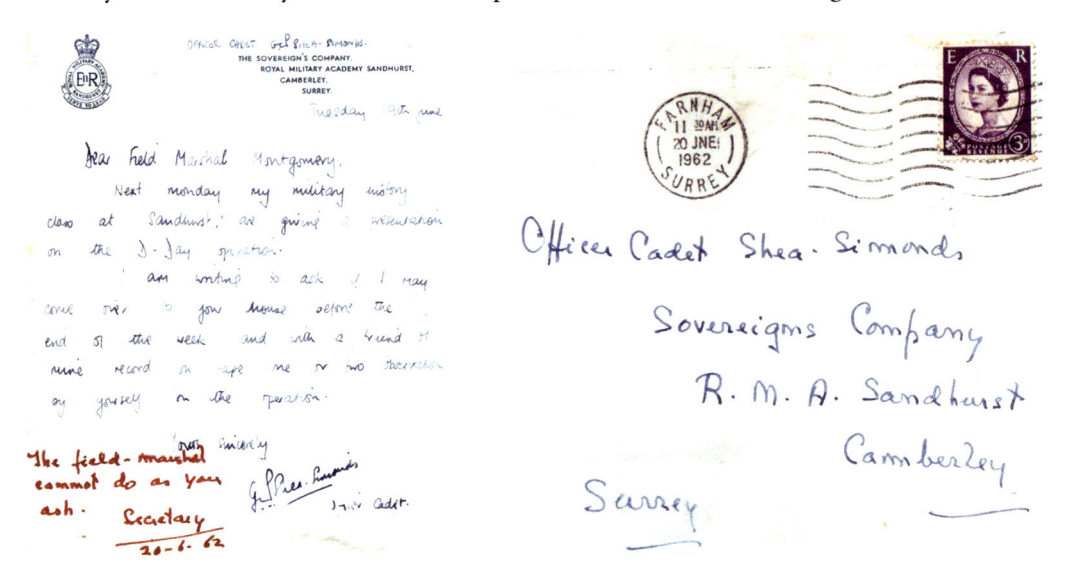

The letter and envelope and, below, a sample of Montgomery's handwriting from his memoirs

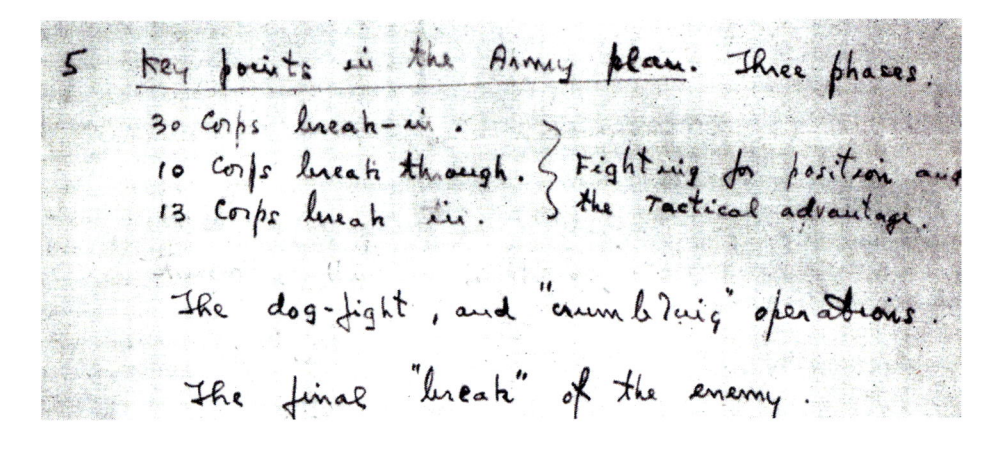

In July we became the senior platoon in Ypres Company and, as we had predicted, Bob Clarke became our Senior Under Officer with Dick Lockley, Martin Tinniswood and me as the three Junior Under Officers – I was fortunate to be given command of the intermediate platoon as they were a good crowd. Among their number was David Skinner who in recent years has become a good friend and staunch supporter of our

Army Parachute Association flying operations at Netheravon. Another was Mike Jackson who had an illustrious career in the Parachute Regiment before finally becoming Chief of the General Staff – he had obviously taken on board everything I told him! In 1950 Officer Cadet Edward Bear (a 14in Teddy) became the mascot of the voluntary military parachute courses organised for Sandhurst cadets by No. 1 Parachute Training School of the Royal Air Force, and during the twenty-five years the courses were run he made more than four hundred parachute jumps. He now resides in dignified, well-earned retirement in the RMA Sandhurst museum.

In September 1962 No.1 PTS was based at RAF Abingdon and, for those of us soon to be commissioned into the Parachute Regiment, the course was compulsory, which was just as well as places were limited and keenly sought-after. The seven-jump course was the same as the full military parachute course, but without the requirement for a night jump. During the course introduction we were proudly told by the staff that the PTS motto was – and still is – Knowledge Dispels Fear. This has always struck me as being bloody silly as it implies that we were almost expected to be fearful of parachuting until the RAF parachute jumping instructors (PJIs) had worked their magic on us – perhaps Training Reduces Apprehension would be nearer the mark! Our course officer, Flight Lieutenant Bill Paul, had been a wartime PJI and later, in the 1970s, Bill and I worked together for the British Parachute Association. All PJIs came from the physical training branch of the RAF and our section's PJI, Sgt Pullin, was no exception with an India rubber physique and a rich catalogue of hilarious gags. He had just given us the first lesson on the use of the reserve parachute when the inevitable question was asked:

'Staff, what happens if the reserve doesn't open?'

'The Royal Air Force has a drill for that,' which he proceeded to demonstrate. 'You must quickly cross your legs and extend your arms out sideways, level with your shoulders, and prepare to land!'

He held the position until the next obvious question: 'Why do you do that, Staff?'

The deadpan response: 'So that when they get to you they can unscrew you!'

The French military parachute instructors have a different answer to experiencing a similar emergency: 'Make sure you keep your left hand held high!' And following the innocent response of 'Why?' comes the answer: 'It ensures that your wristwatch isn't damaged so it can then be useful to the guys on the ground!'

After hours of practising exits, controlling our parachutes (which were basically uncontrollable), and forwards, sideways and backward landings, we were assessed as being ready for our first parachute jumps, which were to be the first of two balloon jumps on the course and to be made over Abingdon airfield itself. At the end of the war there were any number of barrage balloons stored away and these hydrogen-filled monstrosities with a 'cage' suspended beneath them to lift five paratroopers and a dispatcher were considered an ideal and economic vehicle from which training jumps could be made.

Balloon jumping

I was to be number four out of the five in our stick and, with Sgt Pullin leading us, we boarded the cage for our first totally unforgettable parachute jumps. There was a degree of apprehension amongst us evidenced by the nervous laughter as the order was shouted out: 'Up 800ft, five men jumping!' The balloon cage lurched into the air and immediately the floor tilted at an uneasy angle towards where the door would have been had the cage had one – a horizontal metal bar was the only thing stopping us from making a premature exit. Sgt Pullin hooked up our static lines to the strong point before occasionally looking down to see if the signal flag showed we were at jump altitude. We grinned sheepishly at each other in the swaying silence of the cage – we realised that none of us could possibly refuse to go in front of our chums – let's just get on with it. Sgt Pullin lowered the metal bar and ordered: 'Number one – stand in the door!' Number one had no sooner positioned himself than: 'GO!' from our grinning PJI, who watched the deploying canopy before the procedure was repeated for number two.

In no time at all it was my turn and I edged gingerly downhill on the sloping floor towards the exit – I was concerned about falling out before the order had been given. Then: 'GO!' and, adrenalin-charged, I launched myself forwards, aware of a heart-thumping surge of excitement as instantaneously gravity took control. I was conscious of a firm tugging at my shoulders as first the suspension lines and then the canopy itself were pulled rapidly in sequence from the bag. The positive deceleration as the canopy quickly deployed was reassuring and a glance upwards to check the 28ft diameter circle of khaki nylon revealed no cause for alarm – phew! A look around permitted me a swift appreciation of a magnificent view of Oxford some four miles off to the north-east before remembering that I only had another 40 seconds or so to enjoy the ride before arriving back on terra firma. Feet and knees tight together slightly bent, back rounded, chin on chest and elbows tucked in – I'm ready for the landing… oh no, I'm bloody not – in the last couple of seconds the grass rushed up sharply up at me – I hit the ground like the proverbial sack of potatoes with a firm, audible thump. I sat on the grass, grinning stupidly – I'd survived! We carried out the second balloon jump the same day and the five aircraft jumps during the following three days. In the early 1960s the RAF's two parachute dropping aircraft were the Handley Page Hastings and the Blackburn Beverley.

The Blackburn Beverley and the Handley Page Hastings

We were allocated the latter during our course and this ungainly, bulbous-looking aeroplane was a great workhorse as it could be used both for dropping personnel and for the heavy parachute dropping of guns and vehicles. After the peace and quiet of balloon parachuting, aircraft jumping was a much more dramatic affair with the noise of the four engines competing with the noise of shouted orders for hooking up the static lines, checking our equipment and, when the red light above the door came on, shuffling in step towards the exits on either side of the fuselage. All eyes were now on the green light above the doors – when they were illuminated they constituted the order to 'GO!' It seemed like pandemonium as we reacted to the 'Go – go – go' of the PJIs. We struggled to keep closed up to the man in front as we lurched in turn towards the door. Suddenly it was there: 'GO!' and I hurled myself out into the blast of the propellers' slipstream. A couple of confused seconds of adrenalin-enhanced disorientation followed before the reassuring deployment of the parachute pulled me towards the vertical. I was relieved to see that my canopy was OK and that there was nobody else in my bit of the sky before, on our last two aircraft jumps, releasing my weapons container so that it fell away to dangle on nylon cord 15ft below me. Then, all too quickly as before, I was thumped on to Weston-on-the-Green's welcoming grass for the qualifying seventh landing of the course – made it! We couldn't stitch the light bulb-like parachute badges on to our uniforms quickly enough! And in October, after a refresher jump at last light on to the Everleigh drop zone on Salisbury Plain, we parachuted into Brittany in France for a two-day exercise, 'Tipperary', against cadets from L'Ecole Spéciale Militaire de Saint-Cyr, the French Military Academy. I can't remember who won, but it didn't really matter – we had all carried out our first military parachute jump overseas.

Made it! My parachutes and weapons container on Weston's grass and having landed in Brittany, October 1962

For our final exercise we were flown out to Cyprus in December. By now we were a real 'band of brothers' ready to tackle anything as a team, so it was a memorable few days and our last together before our 'passing out' parade later in the month. Late in the afternoon before we flew back to the UK I made a huge faux pas. As a JUO I was 'volunteered' with Warwick to travel in two three-ton trucks with two Royal Corps of Transport drivers to deliver all our heavy packs safely to the RAF at the Nicosia airport. On arrival, and, having unloaded the packs, we were informed that we had to complete a substantial amount of paperwork – a necessary chore to which our two RCT drivers could obviously contribute nothing. Being a considerate sort of chap I suggested that, in the meantime, they could relax in the cabs of the trucks. The form filling took longer than anticipated and when it had finally been completed we returned to the trucks – the drivers were nowhere in sight. Warwick and I eventually found them very much the worse for wear in a nearby bar. We persuaded them to down considerable quantities of black coffee, but even then it was obvious that they were in no condition to drive for the hour or so back to the barracks. Warwick and I quickly came to the conclusion that, despite the fact that neither of us had driven a three-tonner before, we would have to drive them ourselves. So, with our RCT drivers snoring loudly in the passenger seats beside us, we drove the two trucks very carefully back to the vehicle park in the barracks. Having woken our two drivers and pointed them in the right direction, we reported mission accomplished with the bonus of having learned a useful lesson in man-management!

Back at Sandhurst we prepared for the big day of our Commissioning Parade. As related earlier, my great-uncle, Geoffrey Norman Shea, had won the Sword of Honour at Sandhurst in 1900 before being tragically killed in South Africa in 1902 while serving with the Munster Fusiliers. I was fortunate enough to have inherited the sword and, as an under-officer, was keen to carry it on my own passing-out parade. I sought permission from our Company Sergeant Major who informed me that only the Academy Sergeant Major could grant such permission – gulp! At the end of a parade a few days later I plucked up courage and marched across to the great man. I came to a halt in front of him and, looking at him straight in the eye: 'Sir!' I said, with as much confidence as I could muster.

'Yes, Sir,' he replied, 'what is it?'

'Sir, I request your permission to carry this sword on my passing-out parade.'

'What is its significance, Sir?'

I told him.

'Allow me to have a look at it, Sir.'

I passed him the sword and he read the inscription on the blade before handing it back to me.

'Carry it with pride, Sir!' And at the Sovereign's Parade on December 20, 1962, I did just that. Admiral of the Fleet Sir Caspar John, First Sea Lord, took the salute and, out of the hundred and eighty-two of us commissioned that day, Norman Arnell was third, Bob Clarke was fourth while I was seventeenth in the final order of merit – better than anticipated! Our two years at Sandhurst had been utterly memorable in every way.

My RMAS Comrades in Arms – Ypres Company, Intake 30 – our final photocall. Left to right: Simon Uwakwe, Robin Sjoberg, Dick Lockley (with kepi), Chris Brown, C S-S (with shotgun), Charles Innes, Herbie Howard-Harwood (in heavy disguise), David Daniell, Mike Daunt, Bill Snell (with dumb-bell), Mike Robjohn, Bob Clarke (in part no. 1 dress), Ra Wilson (in bowler), Ollie Hackett (on shooting stick), Martin Tinniswood (with racquets), David Cross, Norman Arnell (with kepi) and Warwick King-Martin

CHAPTER 7

UTRINQUE PARATUS
(READY FOR ANYTHING)
(The motto of the Parachute Regiment)

By the time I joined the 3rd Battalion of the Parachute Regiment (3 PARA) in early 1963, Lt Col Anthony Farrar-Hockley had succeeded Roly Gibbs as the Commanding Officer. TFH, as we referred to him, was one of the most extraordinary soldiers of his generation. On the outbreak of the Second World War in 1939, aged 15, he had enlisted in the Gloucestershire Regiment. His being under-age was soon discovered and he was discharged. In 1941 he tried again and the following year, having gained his parachute wings, he was granted an emergency commission in the Parachute Regiment. Aged 20 he was in command of a company in the 6th Battalion in Greece where he won an MC. After the war and having served in Palestine, he returned to the Glosters as Adjutant and went with them to Korea in 1950. At the battle of Imjin his conspicuous gallantry and leadership won him his first DSO after which he was captured and, in the two years he was a POW, he escaped six times and became an authority on the Chinese indoctrination to which he had been subjected – his book, *The Edge of the Sword*, which records these experiences, has become a classic of military writing.

To have TFH as my first Commanding Officer was to prove interesting. The Parachute Regiment is the youngest infantry regiment in the British Army and was formed in 1941 as the result of a memorandum sent the previous year to the War Office by the then Prime Minister, Winston Churchill. Its unique short history continues to provoke huge pride in its achievements for all ranks both past and present. Many writers more qualified than I have expressed the view that battalion life is akin to being a member of a large family with the wives of all ranks also taking pride in its unique esprit de corps – definitely 'all for one and one for all'! 3 PARA had its own special character which is exemplified by the fact that so many of my brother officers from those memorable days remain lifelong friends. A legendary 3 PARA character from that time was one Cpl Joe Grout who was the last serving member of the battalion who had jumped and fought at Arnhem in September 1944. For this Joe was respected throughout the battalion, but also because he had the misfortune to suffer from a cleft palate. One day on the ranges the targets were not going up and down as swiftly as they should have been. On the firing point one 3 PARA subaltern asked another to phone the butts to speed things up, not knowing that Joe Grout was commanding the Butt Party.

'Buths here, Cpl Grout thpeakin'.'

The subaltern on the phone turned to his chum.

'There's a fucking idiot on the end of this phone!'

'Yeth, and ith not thith fuckin' end either!' was Joe's classic response!

But before I could join the battalion it was necessary for me to undergo some refresher parachute training – which would include a night drop – at No.1 PTS at Abingdon. Unfortunately it was a particularly hard winter with heavy falls of snow bringing the country, and the Royal Air Force, to a virtual standstill for the whole of February. As the battalion was due to fly to Malaya for jungle training and a major exercise, TFH was determined to go with a full compliment of officers and, as I learnt later, he became impatient with the RAF, informing them that my refresher training would be done at a later date with the RAF parachute detachment in Aldershot. So I drove to Aldershot and Blenheim Barracks, where I was welcomed by Major David Callaghan, the Second in Command.

'Welcome to 3 PARA,' he said, 'I'm afraid the CO's away on a recce in Malaya at the moment, but he'll see you when he returns next week. You'll be commanding 7 Platoon in C Company, so go and report to Rufus Lazell, your Company Commander, and when you can find a moment I suggest you introduce yourself to the Quartermaster and the Regimental Sergeant Major – they're the two most important people in any battalion.' How right he was and it proved to be useful advice. I found C Company and the OC's office – Rufus was a dynamic American on an exchange posting from the 82nd US Airborne Division who turned out to be a delightful and encouraging company boss for a very 'green' 2nd Lt. I took over 7 Platoon from Ian McLeod who I had met in Bahrain during our visit from Sandhurst. Ian, who later was to become the battalion's Intelligence Officer, had left the platoon in good shape, although my Platoon Sergeant, Banks Middleton, was new to the job having only just been promoted from having been a corporal in the Signals Platoon. My brother officers were a fantastic bunch of individuals who were warmly welcoming, especially Martin Stratton, whom I had first met when we were both about eight or nine during his father's ministry as vicar of Figheldean.

When TFH returned from his 'recce' I was summoned into his presence. One of the first questions he asked was whether I had yet selected one of my soldiers to be my batman – I had to admit that so far I hadn't – I felt I was capable of looking after myself. But TFH told me that having a batman was important in the field, for example, to prepare meals from the contents of the 24-hour ration packs while, as platoon commander, I had other responsibilities to occupy my time. I was certainly in no hurry to appoint one of my 'toms' to the job especially as I was expected to pay him for his efforts from my own pocket. It's worth recording that my first year's pay as a Second Lieutenant was £950 with an extra 7/6d a day (£135 a year) parachute pay – totalling about £22,000 a year in today's money, with today's total being about £27,000. A few days later I was interviewing my toms when one of them, Private John Stokes, came into my office. Stokes was a twenty-year-old Cockney 'likely lad' with an irrepressible sense of humour. He didn't waste any time.

'Are you looking for a batman, Sir?' He asked cheerily.

'What's the catch?' I replied, smelling a rat.

'No catch, Sir, I'll do the job for nothing if, when we're in barracks, you give me the first couple of hours a day off parade!'

I agreed to his suggestion on a month's trial basis. I soon discovered his batman skills were rarely practised because, if I popped into my room in the Officers' Mess during a morning coffee break, I would invariably find Stokes on my bed sleeping off a hangover from the night before. In the field his culinary skill with 24-hour ration packs was also unimpressive – he'd open all the tins and mix all the contents together with a liberal dose of hot curry powder in a heated mess tin. Curried pork and beef mixed with vegetable mayonnaise and treacle pudding was hardly cordon bleu. His other regular bit of mischief was to ask if I was using my suit on a particular evening. 'Why, Stokes?' I replied innocently, but already suspecting I knew the answer: 'Well Sir, I've got a date and I was wondering if I could borrow it?' I granted his request on three or four occasions until one evening my suit was rendered hors de combat during one of the regular Saturday night skirmishes with a bunch of 'crap hats' at the Aldershot NAAFI Club – a 'crap hat' was our rather unfair and derisory term for any soldier not serving in Airborne Forces. But he often excelled himself. TFH had ordered me to take my platoon down to Salisbury Plain to take part in a week's filming for an advertisement for the Army. Every morning Stokes drove with me in my somewhat temperamental 1936 Austin 7 Nippy from the barracks in Tidworth to the filming location close to Figheldean.

7 Platoon do battle on Salisbury Plain – C S-S with pistol and with John Stokes on the left of the photo

One morning while passing Carter Barracks near Bulford, the Nippy died of fuel starvation. On opening the bonnet I saw that the union on one end of the fuel line to the carburettor had come undone. I'd left my tools back in Aldershot so I asked Stokes if he'd pay a visit to the MT section of the barracks' resident Royal Welch Fusiliers to ask if he could borrow a 3/8in spanner so I could tighten the union properly. About twenty minutes later he returned aboard a massive Scammel recovery vehicle which was covered with impressive cranes and winches and manned by the Fusilier MT Sergeant and REME fitter. The latter were clearly unimpressed to discover they'd come to administer aid to an ancient Austin 7. The union having been successfully tightened in about fifteen seconds, the Scammel and its humourless crew withdrew. I sought enlightenment from Stokes: 'What the bloody hell was all that about?'

'Well, Sir, I told the MT Sergeant that Colonel Shea-Simonds was stuck down the road in his staff car and could they come and fix it!'

'Why, Stokes, for chrissake?'

His response was priceless: 'I reckoned that if I'd simply asked the MT Sergeant if I could borrow a 3/8in spanner, he'd have told me to fuck off!'

Yes, Stokes, he probably would have!

After 7 Platoon's filmed battle scenes on Salisbury Plain it was time for the Battalion to fly to Malaya for a concentrated spell of jungle training. It took twenty-two hours' flying time to Singapore staging via Akrotiri, Bahrain and Gan in Britannias of RAF Transport Command, before we finally reached Kluang where we were soon learning the skills required for jungle warfare. However hard we tried it was almost impossible to keep the various creepy-crawlies at bay – mosquitoes obviously appreciated my O-positive blood, thus becoming my constant enemies, whereas Rufus's blood group attracted leeches by the dozen. I well remember one occasion when I had been summoned to receive up-to-date orders. Company headquarters was located by a stream in a jungle clearing where our revered company commander was standing stark-naked in the water with at least a dozen revolting-looking leeches hanging from his legs, while Charlie Altass, our seasoned Company Sergeant Major, was administering the tip of a lit cigarette to each in turn in an attempt to discourage further blood letting – I think I preferred the mosquitoes.

It was during our time in Malaya that I really got to know my 7 Platoon toms. I couldn't have been supported by a better bunch and, in common with all Parachute Regiment soldiers, they came from all regions of the United Kingdom. To differentiate between the more common surnames in the Army such as Smith or White, they had the last two digits of their Army number added so they were known as, for instance, Smith 36 (three six) or White 27 (two seven) – though I never did meet the apocryphal Jones 00 who was inevitably known colloquially as 'Jones fuck-all!' The training went well but with navigation in dense jungle proving something of a challenge. Luckily 7 Platoon didn't suffer the indignity of getting lost and then having to fly the colourful hydrogen balloons with which we had been issued above the jungle canopy to attract the attention of any aircraft sent to look for us. During a break back in barracks in Kluang, TFH sent for me.

'I understand you know the King-Martins?' He inquired.

'Not exactly, Sir,' I replied, as I'd yet to meet Warwick's mum and dad – the latter then a gunner Brigadier serving as CRA of 17 Gurkha Division in Kuala Lumpur. 'But their son, Warwick, was a good chum at Sandhurst and he spent a couple of leaves with me and my family.'

'Well, they obviously wish to repay the hospitality as you've been invited to stay with them for the weekend, as have the Brigadier and I – we're going to fly up in an Auster and you'll follow on in a Land Rover with the bags.'

TFH didn't believe in officers driving themselves in military vehicles but, as it was a weekend and he didn't wish to have one of the toms detailed for what was essentially a social occasion, he made an exception in my case – the Army Air Corps Auster pilot obviously wasn't his responsibility. I viewed the whole exercise with a degree of apprehension. Here was I as a totally insignificant second lieutenant soon to be socialising with my CO, TFH (DSO & MC), Brigadier Johnny King-Martin (DSO & MC) and Brigadier Michael Forrester, the Commander of 16 Parachute Brigade, thus my brigadier whom I had yet to meet. The latter was a highly decorated fighting soldier. He had been awarded the MC as a second lieutenant in Palestine in 1939, and a second MC leading a group of Cretan partisans in a bayonet charge against German paratroopers in the battle for Crete in May 1941. A New Zealand officer who witnessed the charge said later that it was the most thrilling moment of his life. He then went on to win two DSOs while commanding his battalion of the Queen's Royal Regiment – the first in Italy and the second in Normandy after D-Day. In the event I need not have worried as it was a very relaxed visit. It ended with my driving TFH and Michael Forrester back to Kluang as the Auster

C Company 3 PARA march past HM the Queen in 1963

was unavailable on the Sunday. During a break in the journey to have a swim in the sea at Port Dickson, my Brigade Commander asked me how I was enjoying soldiering with the Regiment. Inevitably I couldn't stop myself bubbling over with enthusiasm for what I was experiencing in 3 PARA, and from then on he kindly reciprocated by keeping a fatherly eye on my progress. I feel privileged to have known him. Back in Aldershot we learned that Her Majesty, the Queen, was due to visit the town and that 3 PARA had been selected to provide part of the military contingent for the march past from the Royal Garrison Church of All Saints. It proved to be a memorable occasion with Rufus, as probably the only Yank present, being, I'm sure, the proudest officer on parade when he led C Company with Alec Larkman and I positioned immediately behind him.

The next exercise after returning from Malaya was a C Company night drop into Denmark to support a troop of 22 SAS against the Danish Home Guard (HJV), the volunteer but highly motivated fourth service of the Danish military. This was to be my first night drop and it was certainly memorable. The RAF managed to drop us more than half a mile to one side of the planned run-in heading. This shouldn't have been a problem, but, as it was a clandestine drop, we had to clear the drop zone carrying our main and reserve parachutes together with our normal kit. This meant crossing two massive water-filled dykes to get to the rendezvous (RV). With the parachute jump-induced adrenalin still coursing through our veins we made light of tackling the dykes and C Company soon gathered together successfully at the RV where we met up with our SAS guides. All I remember of the next forty-eight hours was the long night march finishing close to the objective, lying up undiscovered in a wood during the next day, and a noisy night attack followed by our successfully ex-filtrating unseen to the coast from where we embarked on a Danish Navy destroyer for a short voyage to Copenhagen. The exercise culminated in our experiencing generous Danish hospitality during a memorable visit to the Carlsberg lager factory – the result was fat heads all round during the flight back home the following day. But sometimes things didn't go so well.

Following our return to Aldershot we were all soon heavily involved in competing in the battalion's inter-platoon competition – a wicked contest that encompassed a variety of military skills and which had all of us young platoon commanders panicking seriously throughout the near six weeks of its duration. Rufus left his platoon commanders in no doubt as to his views on the subject:

'Gentlemen,' he said, during his briefing and without a glimmer of humour, 'I want you to understand – I can't stand to lose!' Oh dear!

This came to mind as I marched on to the square in front my platoon towards David Callaghan who, as Second in Command, was judging the Drill Competition. The immaculate and impressive figure of Arthur Channon, the Regimental Sergeant Major, ex-Coldstream Guards and Guards Parachute Company, stood rigidly to one side. I was immediately aware of his microscopic scrutiny of my indifferent performance even before I came to a halt. Looking the Second in Command straight in the eye, I raised then lowered my sword in salute.

'7 Platoon, C Company, 3 PARA formed up and ready for your inspection, Sir!' I reported with all the confidence I could muster.

'Thank you, Mr Shea-Simonds,' replied the 2i/c, 'how many men have you got on parade?' The bottom fell out of my world – I simply hadn't a clue – I just knew that all who should have been on parade were on parade. I also knew I couldn't bluff my way out of this one, but my response was pathetic:

'I'm sorry, Sir, I've no idea.'

'Then I suggest you count them,' he replied icily, and I knew instantly that the situation was slipping from my grasp. I turned about and, without thinking, started to count them using the blade of my sword as a pointer. My platoon sergeant raised his eyes heavenwards, while the RSM's groan of disbelief could be heard on the other side of the square, and my toms, bless 'em, fought valiantly to smother their laughter. Our drill competition score, or lack of it, ensured that 7 Platoon had no chance in the overall placings and my subsequent interview with Major Rufus demonstrated perfectly why he 'couldn't stand to lose'.

My chance at redemption followed quickly when, at short notice, the Battalion entered a number of teams into Aldershot District's Evelyn Wood Ten Mile March and Shoot Competition. Each company made up a platoon of its fittest toms and I was given command with one, Sgt Bill Scarratt, as my platoon sergeant. I couldn't have been more fortunate as Bill was as fit as a butcher's dog and, as I had only recently been 'volunteered' to take over as officer i/c cross-country running and was already a member of the 3 PARA team, I was reasonably fit myself. Luckily Bill and I hit it off immediately and he was to become a stalwart chum. He was later to have an impressive military career culminating in his winning a well-deserved Distinguished Flying Cross while serving as an Army Air Corps helicopter pilot in Northern Ireland in 1975 – he was also an accomplished sport parachutist.

During the three weeks leading up to the competition itself we took the toms on three ten-mile marches a week against the clock. We were expected to complete the ten miles in two hours in full battle kit which is why we set ourselves a training target of finishing the ten miles in well under the two hours. And after the march finished on Ash ranges we were to be inspected to make sure all our equipment was intact before we carried out a rifle and machine gun shoot. Our short training regime prepared us for the big day as well as could be expected, so much so that we hoped that we could prevent the Guards Parachute Company, who had won the competition in 1961 and 1962, from scoring a hat-trick. The 7 Platoon toms did magnificently with none of them dropping out and we finished third as the highest placed 3 PARA team behind the Guards Parachute Company and 9 Parachute Squadron, Royal Engineers, who were winners and runners-up respectively. It was a satisfactory result that pleased Rufus no end. Indeed, from my point of view, it was a fitting end to his exchange posting from the 82nd US Airborne Division and we were sorry to see him leave us to return to the United States. I certainly couldn't have had a better first company commander and I remember him with considerable affection. His successor was posted into 3 PARA from outside airborne forces to be OC C Company and, in contrast to Rufus, I found him somewhat uninspiring – he certainly took his time adjusting to the way the battalion operated. His first challenge was the battalion's test exercise held in the autumn. We were due to drop on to the Otterburn Training Area but, while we were drawing and fitting parachutes at RAF Colerne, it was announced that, because of torrential rain and high winds in Northumberland, the drop was cancelled. Whereas an adrenalin-charged arrival by parachute always provides impetus to the start of any operation or exercise, the converse is equally true. So it was on this occasion – we were flown in the Hastings allocated for the drop to RAF Middleton St George – now Durham Tees Valley Airport – from where we were transported for a miserable three-hour drive in three-ton trucks for the 70-mile drive to Otterburn where the weather was every bit as dire as forecast. In spite of the energy sapping conditions and lack of sleep throughout the three days of the exercise, my 7 Platoon toms remained as resiliently energetic and cheerful as ever. TFH's command of the battalion obviously impressed the Brigadier who was forced to notionally 'kill off' the CO, whereupon David Callaghan, as second-in-command, assumed command. Sadly, nearly twenty years later, this situation occurred for real during the Falklands campaign when Chris Keeble, second-in-command of 2 PARA, so ably took over command of the battalion in the middle of the Goose Green battle after the tragic death of CO 'H' Jones, to whom the posthumous award of the VC continues to inspire.

In November, 16 Parachute Brigade flew to Cyprus for Solinus II, an airborne exercise that remains memorable for two reasons. We were being briefed for the battalion drop when a member of the brigade staff interrupted the proceedings to announce the shocking news of the assassination of President John F Kennedy in Dallas on November 22. That night 3 PARA dropped on to the Morphou DZ located near the north-west coast of the island. I was number one of the port stick of the Hastings and, as it was to be my first battalion night drop, I was determined to have a forceful exit. 'Green on, GO!' I hurled myself into the pitch-black night. As the deploying canopy tugged reassuringly at my shoulders I was aware of the Hastings continuing on its jump run and of a few lights twinkling on the DZ below. It seemed that I'd barely had time to lower my weapons container for it to swing on its nylon rope 15ft below me before I crashed violently into the rock-strewn DZ. It was immediately obvious from the pain that I'd damaged my right shoulder – it proved to have been dislocated. As the DZ was close to the coast we were all equipped with lifejackets and small clip-on 'esco' lights to be used if we landed in the sea. We were also briefed to switch on our 'esco' lights to attract attention in the event of our becoming DZ casualties. My toms responded enthusiastically – and with typically wicked humour – resulting in my being abandoned on the DZ lit up like a Christmas tree! The Brigade's Parachute Field Ambulance quickly reduced the dislocation and I was 'casevac-ed' back to UK to take no further part in the exercise – altogether it was an inauspicious and mildly embarrassing conclusion to my first year in 3 PARA. But 1963 also remained memorable for some other interesting happenings.

CHAPTER 8
FALLING FREE

Until the early 20th century it was widely believed that anybody falling any distance from an aircraft before deploying a parachute would quickly lose consciousness – after all, it was well known that the terminal velocity of a body falling free, reached after about ten seconds from exiting the aircraft, is about 120mph. How could such a speed be survivable? It was left to Leslie Irvin, an American barnstorming parachutist and occasional member of a military test jumping team at McCook Field, Ohio, to demonstrate that such pessimism was unfounded. On April 29, 1919, he exited a DH 9 biplane flown by his colleague and the parachute's designer, Floyd Smith. From 1,500ft he quickly accelerated to near terminal velocity before successfully deploying his parachute and landing safely albeit sustaining a broken ankle in the process. The result was that manually deployed parachutes were quickly adopted as effective emergency life-savers, especially for military aircrew. For the next twenty-eight years, thousands of lives were saved as aircrew tumbled uncontrollably from stricken aircraft before manually opening their parachutes and landing safely.

In early 1947, Leo Valentin, a young French Air Force parachute instructor, was giving some thought to solving the problem of tumbling uncontrollably before parachute deployment. Valentin reasoned:

> *Let me see: if I jump with my body extended, i.e. with hollow back, extended neck, chest thrust out, arms and legs splayed and slightly backwards, I present to the air a compact surface, so to speak, of a more or less convex form. I already look more like a bird than the common sack of sand I am when I fall in a jack-knife position. I turned this idea over and over in my mind, and imagined myself up aloft cleaving the air with my body like a rounded prow, already gliding… No more loops, spins or wild somersaults. I could hardly refrain from jumping up and down and dancing for joy: I'd found it. The day of my great challenge to the sky had really come.**

On May 23, 1947, he had the opportunity to test his theories. He exited a JU52 at 9,000ft over the military airfield of Pau just north of the Pyrenees in the Aquitaine region of France and, during his 45 seconds of freefall, he did indeed discover that he could fall with a measure of bodily control which he perfected during a series of jumps that he made over the next few days.

Little did either of these two pioneering parachutists appreciate that their discoveries would do much to initiate the acceptance of freefall parachuting, not only as an impor-

---

*Birdman, Leo Valentin, Hutchinson 1955

tant military skill, but also as an officially recognized aviation sport by the International Aviation Federation, before, in 1951, the first World Parachuting Championships were held at Bled, Yugoslavia. By 1962 both the British Parachute Association and the Army Parachute Association had been formed with a small number of civilian and military clubs operating around the country. The military also appreciated that freefall parachuting offered an alternative method of delivering small groups of special forces personnel into battle, and this resulted in the Royal Air Force starting to provide freefall courses based on those already being operated by the L'Armée de l'Air in France. The first two courses were laid on specifically for the SAS with the third course for the Parachute Regiment being held in 1961. Lieutenant Edward Gardener was one of the two officers on that course (Rod Liddon was the other) and, as will be recounted, he subsequently made a unique contribution to the development of freefall parachuting within the Regiment. During my snowbound attendance at No. 1 PTS at Abingdon in early 1963 I had shared a room in the mess with Mike Little, a sapper officer from 9 Parachute Squadron, Royal Engineers. Mike was a participant in the RAF freefall course running concurrently with the static line course I was on, and, such was his enthusiasm for the exhilaration of falling free, that I was immediately infected likewise – I simply had to attend a freefall course as soon as I possibly could. After the battalion had returned from Malaya I decided that the time was right for me to apply. Jeremy Hickman, the adjutant, was such a genial officer that I felt confident he would approve my application without delay. I was dead wrong. He wasted no time in reminding me that, as an insignificant second lieutenant of only a couple of months' standing, I should get my priorities right and concentrate on learning the job of regimental soldiering. That put me firmly back in the box!

John Ball was, and still is, a genuinely irrepressible, larger-than-life character who was then a corporal in the 3 PARA mortar platoon. We encountered each other for the first time on the ranges a few days after my failure to gain a place on a RAF freefall course. John suggested that if I was still keen to freefall I might consider joining the British Skydiving Centre, the civilian club at Thruxton Aerodrome near Andover, where he and a few of his chums in the battalion were enthusiastic members. So in early May I drove to Thruxton where John introduced me to Bernie Green, who had not only founded the club, but he was also the first secretary of the British Parachute Association. Bernie was a delightfully cheerful, laid-back individual whose enthusiasm was infectious – as one of the club's instructors he started my training right away. At that time the majority of parachute equipment used in the sport was US military surplus, principally aircrew B4 pack and harness – the latter which was modified to enable a 24ft reserve parachute to be clipped to its front. The pack usually contained the ubiquitous C9 28ft flat circular parachute canopy, though originally designed for one emergency jump only, it was in turn modified with two of the 28 gores and a number of panels removed to give it more stability and controllability (each gore had four diagonally cut panels). The canopy was carefully folded into a sleeve designed to slow the canopy's deployment as it was pulled away from the pack by a spring-loaded 'pilot chute'. Inevitably there was some paperwork to be completed, the first of which was the requirement to join the British Parachute Association – interestingly membership numbers started at 101, with mine being 475 and, since its inception over 50 years ago, BPA has had more than 1.38 million members! The other bureaucratic requirement was a strange one. Article 36 of the then current Air Navigation Order prohibited pilots dropping objects from aeroplanes. Thus every sport parachutist required an individual exemption from Article 36 to be issued by the Department of Trade and Industry (the forerunner of today's CAA) to 'legalise' the sport of parachuting. Initially a 'restricted' exemption was issued which only allowed student parachutists to jump under the supervision of a BPA instructor.

After a couple of poor weather weekends, Sunday, June 9, was perfect for my first sport jump. It proved to be something of an inauspicious start to fifty-two amazing years of fulfilling participation in the most dynamic of aviation sports practised by an equally amazing bunch of people. A final briefing by Bernie preceded our emplaning in the DH89A Rapide G-AGJG often used by the club as a parachuting platform or 'jump ship'. Little could I appreciate at the time that, ten years later, I would be flying this self-same elegant old biplane for parachuting myself. Some fifteen minutes after take-off the pilot, John Heaton, had established 'JG on the run-in at 2,500ft above the airfield. Bernie hooked up my static line and motioned me towards the opening on the port side from where the door had been removed. A shout to John up front resulted in the power being reduced to allow me an easy climb out on to the wing facing forwards to grip the diagonal strut with both hands. Then: 'GOOOO!' and I launched myself backwards, tumbling inelegantly into space shouting: 'One thousand… two thousand… three thousand,' as I felt the pilot 'chute tugging the rigging lines from the sleeve which in turn slid off the canopy to allow its staged deployment. The Rapide's engines' noise faded away as I checked the canopy and orientated myself to the drop zone on the north side of the airfield where I'd pre-positioned my old Land Rover. During the couple of minutes under the canopy I had time to appreciate that control of this parachute was considerably more than that I had experienced in the military parachuting world – but it was something I had yet to master as evidenced by the succinct comment I wrote in the 'remarks' column of my virgin sport parachuting logbook: 'Arrived spot on my Land Rover!!' Luckily I was completely unscathed and, being totally exhilarated by the experience, I immediately asked Bernie if he could put my name down for the next available lift. Within a couple of hours I'd repeated the experience with the result that I was now well and truly hooked. Bernie sensed my enthusiasm and, demonstrating keen entrepreneurial acumen, he offered me the opportunity to buy a second-hand 'rig' – a B4 pack and harness complete with a 28ft camouflaged US T7A canopy and a T7A 24ft reserve. As these two canopy types were designed for use by paratroopers they were inherently stronger than the C9 option. The whole combination cost me £22.10 and served me well until I acquired a brand new custom-made US Pioneer sport canopy fourteen months later.

By the end of July, regular visits to Thruxton with John, Sgts Dick Wallace, Joe Reddick and SSI Don McCarthy, had enabled me to clock up a total of twenty sport jumps – five static-line, three three-second delays, three at five seconds, three at ten seconds, three at twenty seconds, two at forty-five seconds and the first of many from 12,000ft with a sixty-second delay – this was considered something a bit special in those days as I wrote in my log book in red-ink capital letters, 'THE MAGIC MINUTE!' And it certainly seemed magic as it also qualified me for the grant of a General Permit and this permitted me to jump without an instructor overseeing my progress. As one of the Thruxton instructors was Mick Turner, a tough, colourful Irish Staff Sergeant in 9 Parachute Squadron RE, who delighted in writing caustically derogatory, and probably well-deserved remarks about my mediocre (2nd Lieutenant perchance!) performance in my logbook, I was happy to be free of his strict supervision. But, as he proved convincingly, Mick was a dedicated and outstandingly competitive sport parachutist who later that summer became National Champion.

A Parachute Regiment team – 1963, C S-S, Charlie Gowens, John Weeks and Ed Gardener

By the end of the year I had logged fifty-eight descents, gained my BPA Instructor's Rating, and, apart from Rapides, jumped from Jackaroos, Austers, Tiger Moths, Army Air Corps Beavers and Royal Navy Whirlwind helicopters. I had also been fortunate enough to have been invited by Major John Weeks, an experienced Parachute Regiment sport parachutist who was also first secretary of the recently formed Army Parachute Association, to be a member of an ad-hoc Regimental Display Team over two separate weekends. The first was with John and Don from a Beaver at a show on Rochester Airfield and was uneventful, while the second, with John, Ed Gardener and an experienced 'tom' skydiver, Charlie Gowens, didn't go entirely according to plan. We were to parachute at one event on the Saturday followed by a second drop at another on the Sunday. For both displays John and Charlie were to jump from one Auster, while Ed and I had the use of a second. Unfortunately somebody had failed to tighten up the oil filler cap on our's which, as a result, popped off about ten minutes after we got airborne. As Ed was sitting by the open door frame he copped a shower of hot oil which dramatically blackened his pristine white, tailored painter's overalls. Luckily the pilot managed to fly us safely back to Rearsby airfield before all the oil drained away and the engine seized solid – meanwhile

John and Charlie carried out the display successfully on their own. Later Ed's fiancée, Janet, and now his lovely wife of more than fifty years, spent an entire detergent-soaked evening attempting to restore her beloved's overalls to their former glory. The following afternoon we took off again in the two Austers from Rearsby to jump into a posh, fundraising Garden Party at Prestwold Hall. Armed with two smoke grenades each to mark our freefall trail, the four of us exited the two Austers at 6,000ft. I recorded the jump for volume 1, issue 1 of the BPA magazine, *Sport Parachutist*. This is an extract:

> *I watched the crowd surge towards where John and Ed are going to land. I'm still 1,000ft up. Only one of John's smoke canisters has gone off and his shock of hitting the ground sets off the other one. Dense clouds of red smoke envelop him. I'm going to land behind the crowd about eighty yards away. Seconds later, feet and knees tight together, bump, and I'm safely on terra firma. I'm red hot and dying for a pint but I find it difficult to stifle my disappointment when we're handed petite glasses of sherry. An elegant lady of quality, who had probably overdone the self-same sherry, tapped John on the shoulder. 'Young man,' she said, 'were you the one that was on fire?'*

John Weeks and C S-S walk off the drop zone at Prestwold Hall

Another memory from my first fifty-eight sport jumps occurred during my summer leave from the Regiment while staying with the family in Figheldean. With a favourable forecast for the morrow, I phoned Bill Leary, a Thruxton flying instructor who was a good friend, and asked him if he could fly me for a couple of jumps early before the aerodrome officially opened the next day. With my younger brother, George, I drove straight to the aircraft hangar and we had pushed the Jackaroo out on to the grass by the time Bill arrived at seven o'clock. Bill and I were airborne fifteen minutes later and climbing for a twenty-five-second freefall from 6,000ft. The jump went well and George drove across the grass with a second rig to where I'd landed. I swapped rigs while Bill landed the Jackaroo and taxied across to join us – I climbed aboard and we repeated the exercise; up and down to 6,000ft twice in forty minutes and back to Figheldean in time for breakfast!

The thirty-ninth day after I had dislocated my shoulder in Cyprus was New Year's Day 1964. This was a good enough reason to take to the skies again. For the two jumps from a Jackaroo I was joined by Helen Flambert, a delightful young lady from a local farming family who lived about a mile from the airfield at Thruxton. Helen was one of only a handful of ladies regularly sport parachuting at the time, as was Penny Seeger who had served in the WRNS and was married to Ram, a tough Royal Marine and himself a press-on sport parachutist – we never did discover Ram's Christian names, thus he was always known by his initials. Both Helen and Penny became very competitive parachutists and were soon selected to be members of the British Ladies' Parachute Team. Another Thruxton regular at that time was John Meacock, a single-mindedly determined competitive parachutist who later became National Champion and founder of the Peterborough Parachute Centre, one of the country's first full-time sport parachuting facilities. Funding for the establishment of the latter was partly provided by the payment that John received for jumping out of a 'burning' Heinkel III during the shooting of the epic film, *The Battle of Britain*! Later John became a much-respected chairman of the British Parachute Association. Another character from those Thruxton days was Ken Vos, a dynamic personality who owned a printing company in London. Ken had learnt to fly during his national service with the RAF and now freefall parachuting presented another challenge to which he applied himself tenaciously. Everything for Ken had to be bright red – his Jensen Interceptor, all his parachute equipment and, later when he also got back into flying, his beautiful little aeroplane – a French Super Emeraude. All the Thruxton regulars became good friends – probably because we shared a real pioneering camaraderie as 'skydiving', as it's now called, was still very much in its infancy.

Early in 1964, Regimental Headquarters of the Parachute Regiment came up with the inspired idea of establishing a full-time Parachute Regiment Free Fall Display Team, subsequently re-named the Red Devils (after an appropriate nickname bestowed on the Regiment by its wartime enemies in North Africa) and the regimental elders wisely appointed the one person who was qualified and experienced enough to meet the challenge of becoming the first team leader – and that was Ed Gardener. He was allocated a minute office in the garret of the Victorian building that housed RHQ in Maida Barracks in Aldershot and was told to get on with it. Much credit is due to Ed for the enthusiasm and energy with which he tackled the daunting task of finding manpower, equipment and aircraft support – and so successful was he that in late 2014 we were able to enjoy a splendid dinner to celebrate the fiftieth anniversary of what quickly became and remains arguably the most respected and accomplished military parachute display team in Europe. I'm sure that in those days Ed must have considered me a 'pushy' young officer and this was probably confirmed when, after I'd heard that he was organising a three-week training session and team selection to be hosted by the Army Air Corps at Middle Wallop, I asked him if I could join in as the dates coincided with 3 PARA being on Easter leave. Regimental duties precluded my selection as a team member, but Ed very kindly allowed me to participate with the result that my logbook records that I made eight jumps from Austers and six jumps from Beavers for which, as a pleasant change, I didn't have to pay as I was deemed to be 'on duty'! Ed selected a splendid bunch of soldiers in the Regiment to join him as the fourteen original members of the team and they went on to set standards of professionalism, expertise and enthusiasm which have continued to the present day. So many of them became good friends and I certainly miss Sherdy Vatnsdal and Brian David, both talented parachutists and charismatic characters who became the team's two first Chief Instructors and who are sadly no longer with us. Apart from team selection Ed also managed to persuade RHQ that the team needed its own aircraft and, with the support of Rothmans, the 1944 DH89A Rapide G-AGTM was purchased and named Valkyrie after Richard Wagner's stirring piece of music, *The Ride of the Valkyries*, which is the Regiment's Quick March.

I was never a full time member of the team, but in the early days it was often short of experienced jumpers during each summer's busy display season, so there were a number of us who were lucky enough to have often been invited along as guest jumpers to make up the numbers. 'Spotting' was the skill in deciding the point on the ground over which the jumpers should exit the aircraft to enable them to arrive safely on the drop zone and, as the parachutes we were using fifty years ago were relatively unsophisticated compared with those in use today, the correct 'spot' was all-important. Usually the guest jumpers were first to exit the aircraft and it quickly became obvious that we were there to check the spot. The Northampton Show was a classic example. Sherdy was spotting and directing the pilot as necessary and on his 'thumbs up' signal John Ball and I exited the Rapide on its first pass over the drop zone. After fifteen seconds of freefall trailing smoke, we deployed our parachutes before looking around us to locate the drop zone – and it took some locating! It was very obvious that we weren't going to make it as it was so far away, while we were hanging over Northampton suburbia faced with rows of houses and tiny gardens in which to find a safe place to land. More by luck than judgment I manoeuvred myself to land on a tiny square of grass while the parachute canopy simultaneously draped itself over an apple tree. Almost instantaneously the lady of the house kindly produced a mug of tea, and, while I carefully disentangled my precious parachute from the apple tree, a small crowd soon gathered, one of whom related to me how he'd been at Arnhem – the town in Holland famously commemorated as a Parachute Regiment Battle Honour. Meanwhile the rest of the team, having benefited from our misfortune, had landed safely on target. Having been reunited with them I told Brian David about the onlooker who claimed to have been at the battle of Arnhem. Brian's response was a classic: 'Charlie, there were ten thousand paratroopers at Arnhem – I've met the fucking lot!'

Public enjoyment of parachute displays is always enhanced by the jumpers trailing coloured smoke to mark their fall earthwards. In the early days we used military 'grenades – smoke – 83' which provided about forty-five seconds of smoke and were available in different colours. Eventually the military 'powers that be' announced that the use of smoke grenades for parachute display was unacceptable and thus civilian commercial smoke canisters are now the only option. Either way they could present problems as Sherdy found out during a display for the Southampton Show and which I witnessed first hand. I followed him out of the Rapide for a ten-second delay, having activated our smoke grenades on exit. After a few seconds Sherdy's grenade literally exploded, clouding him in orange smoke and setting fire to his jumpsuit. I watched, helpless, as he tried to beat out the flames with one hand and control the canopy with the other. Luckily he managed both and landed safely in the arena before we lined up as a team to acknowledge the applause of the crowd, who were blissfully unaware of the drama in the air. The following is a quote from the Southampton Echo: 'It was almost uncanny the way the team manoeuvred in the air to come in right on target.' Uncanny it was not – but it certainly was a piece of skilful canopy handling given the fact that Sherdy was on fire for most of his descent!

The six-man team receive the applause of the crowd after their daring display.

Every parachutist has wondered how he or she would react if the time should come when the reserve parachute would prove more than just a convenient place to mount an altimeter and/or stopwatch. I found out while jumping with the team at an agricultural show at Kingston on Soar. After a twenty-second delay I pulled the ripcord to initiate the main parachute deployment, whereupon the pilot chute sprang from the container and wrapped itself neatly around the bracket on the back of my ankle and which held the smoke grenade. The horseshoe shape of the partly deployed main canopy pulled me into a back-to-earth position, providing the instant adrenalin-charged realisation that the mess flapping around my legs was unlikely to slow my fall enough to permit a safe landing. But I was in a perfect position to deploy the chest-mounted reserve parachute. I pulled the reserve ripcord handle and the canopy opened with a reassuring 'crack' – so much so that on checking the canopy I saw that the hard opening had blown four saucer-sized holes close to its high pressure apex. These unofficial holes probably made the reserve canopy a little more stable and the landing in a soft field of plough some distance away from the showground was perfectly acceptable. I picked myself up and immediately became aware that not only was I still clutching the two ripcord handles but that the grass looked especially green and the sky looked especially blue. Even the birds stopped singing!

CHAPTER 9
ALDERSHOT, HYTHE, WARMINSTER AND BAHRAIN

Back in Aldershot, TFH tasked me as Officer in Charge of 3 PARA cross-country running to organise a cross-country race for units located in Aldershot District. A date early in 1964 was selected for the race and invitations were distributed, meanwhile I encouraged the 3 PARA team to intensify their training as, of course, TFH expected them to win. By the due date we had eight teams entered and I had my company commander's support in allowing me to use most of the C Company toms as markers for the six-mile course around the local training area. Race day arrived with fog reducing visibility to a couple of hundred yards – retrospectively I realised that I should have recommended either postponement or even cancellation of the event to TFH, but, given his press-on reputation, I simply wasn't brave enough! Foregoing lunch to allow myself plenty of time, I ran the course positioning the markers as I went, ensuring that each was close enough to see his neighbour in the fog, which showed no sign of dispersing. By the time I arrived back at the Blenheim Barracks end of Queen's Parade the opposition teams had arrived, followed by TFH suitably armed with a starting pistol. The latter's sudden loud report prompted the competitors' fleet of foot departure down Queen's Parade and, yes, you've guessed it, half of them got lost in the fog – and, inevitably, they were the ones that we officers i/c cross-country were expecting to appear first at the finishing line! TFH was definitely not amused and he quickly disappeared back towards Battalion HQ without saying a word. Meanwhile, everyone else enjoyed post-race tea and sticky cakes in the 3 PARA cookhouse and I resolved to avoid TFH for a few days.

In May 1957 the Parachute Regiment had been granted the freedom of the town of Aldershot. So in early April 1964, with the Battalion's imminent departure for a nine-month tour to Bahrain, we exercised the privilege of our freedom by proudly marching through the streets of Aldershot 'with bayonets fixed and colours flying'. But I was to remain in the UK to go on my Infantry Platoon Commanders' Course at Hythe and Warminster. This was intensely frustrating as soon after 3 PARA arrived in Bahrain it was committed to a short but intense little campaign against Yemeni insurgents in the Radfan, a mountainous region some 100km north of Aden. The battalion quickly achieved its objectives with TFH deservedly winning his second DSO, and chum Ian McLeod, now the Intelligence Officer, winning a Military Cross. 3 PARA also won another MC, one MM, a BEM and a number of Mentions-in-Dispatches. TFH and Ian had been together in a Scout helicopter flown by Major Jake Jackson of the Army Air Corps and were conducting a recce when enemy fire disabled the aircraft, forcing it to land in unfriendly territory. Luckily they safely rejoined the battalion and escaped serious injury although Ian had received a minor bullet wound to his wrist.

Meanwhile, I was at Hythe attending the Weapons Training and Methods of Instruction parts of the Course. This was run by specialist instructors from the Small Arms School Corps. We had been split into squads of ten, each with an enthusiastic SASC Warrant Officer or Staff Sergeant in charge – except in the case of our squad. We discovered on day one that we were to be taught by the only non-SASC instructor at Hythe at that time – a Royal Marine Staff Sergeant by the name of Brian Bellas. In view of the traditional intense rivalry between the Parachute Regiment and the Royal Marines I was expecting to be given a hard time, but my fears were totally unjustified. Brian was, without doubt, the finest instructor I have ever encountered bar none whatever the discipline, whether it be weapon training, parachuting or flying. He taught me so much about instructing, particularly the importance of body language and personality, that I owe him a massive debt of gratitude.

Apart from Brian's inspirational instruction, my time at Hythe was particularly memorable for the Great Inter-Regimental Boat Race which took place one Saturday morning on the local canal and was organised by a couple of Old Etonian rowers in the Grenadier Guards. The race for teams of two was from the Boat House to a bridge some five hundred yards away along the canal… and back. By the time the Parachute Regiment Team of Joe Vitoria and I had arrived to hire our boat, all the long, slim, built-for-speed craft had been snapped up by the eagerly keen officers of the Foot Guards, leaving the remaining short, podgy tubs of questionable performance for the rest of us. From the 'off' the sleek Guards-propelled craft swept into the lead and away from the indifferent oarsmanship of the Parachute Regiment, the Gurkhas and the Gordon Highlanders. All too soon the Guards had reached the bridge and were speeding back towards the finish at the Boat House, which the rest of us were determined that they shouldn't be allowed to reach. We abandoned our little fat boats and, standing up to our chests in the water, formed them into an impassable barrier across the canal. The Guards' protests at this un-Henley-like behaviour were drowned out – almost literally – as their boats were overturned, leaving their crews splashing noisily about in the water. Understandably the owner of the Boat House was not impressed with our mini-version of the Battle of Jutland, even though we did right the boats and dry them out. Having been summoned, the law soon appeared on the scene and our names were recorded for the Monday morning attention of the Commandant in front of whom the sixteen of us were arraigned en masse for a solemn interview 'without coffee'. He expressed his displeasure by ordering us to undertake orderly officer duties between us until the end of the course and, as this was only a week away, it wasn't much of a sentence!

The second part of the course was held at the School of Infantry at Warminster with the aim of our being taught infantry tactics up to company level. I don't think I was the only one who found the conduct of this part of our young officer training disappointingly uninspiring. We were taught by young infantry captains who tediously relied almost exclusively on the 'directing staff' or DS solutions to the various tactical scenarios and who then prevented constructive discussion about possible alternatives. We were treated like errant Sandhurst officer cadets rather than as enthusiastic young officers who had in many cases been commanding platoons of thirty or so soldiers for about eighteen months – and some on active service. I resolved to accept the situation and rely on weekend parachuting outings either to Thruxton or to the recently established Army Parachute Centre at Netheravon to maintain morale! Occasionally I was able to organise a parachute display and one memorable jump was for the Royal Navy Air Day at Yeovilton where our hosts laid on a Wessex helicopter to lift us to 8,000ft. The fact that five of our eight-man team were civilians bothered the Navy not one bit!

RNAS Yeovilton June 1964: Sgt Dick Wallace 3 PARA, Pat Slattery, Terry Crawley TA SAS, John Meacock, Ken Vos, Des Smythe and Sgt Joe Reddick and Lt C S-S, both 3 PARA

The dreary days at Warminster came to an end early in August and, having received permission from TFH, I remained in the country for the rest of the month to compete in the first Army Parachute Championships to be held at Netheravon. On the third day of practice and my second jump of the day the canopy deployed normally and I steered myself towards the large dayglo target cross. Concentrating with grim determination on the job in hand I failed to notice another competitor who was close by in the sky doing exactly the same thing. At 200-300ft above the ground we collided and our parachutes' suspension lines wrapped around each other. With only about ten or fifteen seconds of flight remaining there was nothing we could do other than hold compact parachute landing positions and hope for the best. We thumped close together into the pea-gravel landing pit for landings that were substantially harder than normal, whereupon I discovered that my 'adversary' was none other than John Weeks. The result was that I was lucky enough to be just somewhat shaken whereas John had sprained his ankle seriously – an injury that effectively put him out of the competition. At the subsequent inquest into what had happened John told me very firmly that I should have been more aware of what was going on around me. I kept quiet as I was only a lowly subaltern and he was a major, but of course it occurred to me that maybe he also should have been aware of what was going on around him! What we didn't know was that a press photographer had recorded the incident on camera and it appeared on the back page of the *Daily Mirror* the following day. What the photograph clearly showed was that I was the low man, so technically it had been my right of way – but there was no way I was going to point that out to John, so once again I kept quiet! The *Mirror* write-up, under the headline 'TERROR FOR TWO', was a classic:

> *It happened yesterday to Army parachute experts, Lt Charles Shea-Simmons [sic] (in the white helmet) [no, actually John was wearing the white helmet, mine was green] and Major John Weeks. Both were practising for the Army parachute championships which began at RAF [sic] Netheravon, Wilts, today… with their 'chutes snagged up, they plunged hundreds of feet together. But they landed safely.*

The *Swindon Evening Advertiser* headline went one better: 'SKYDIVERS IN TANGLE WITH DEATH.' In spite of this little drama my August jump total proved to my best month to date with twenty-nine jumps in the thirty-one days from four different aircraft types – Rapide, Beaver, Auster and Percival EP9. It was now time to rejoin the Battalion in Bahrain.

The remaining six months of 3 PARA's tour provided plenty of variety, which proved both stimulating and enjoyable. We were based at Hamala camp, an isolated complex of air-conditioned huts that had been built over the previous two years by the soldiers of the resident Parachute Battalion Groups. The latter included supporting arms and services from units of 16 Parachute Brigade. 3 PARA's companies were rotated in turn away from Hamala camp to be deployed either at RAF Muharraq or at Jebel Ali in the Trucial States. The airfield at Muharraq was a joint civil/military facility located on a separate island connected to the main island of Bahrain by a causeway and bridge. The RAF hosted the visiting 3 PARA company whose task was the defence of the airfield and this included the security of the RAF's resident 8 & 208 Squadrons' Hawker Hunters and 30 & 84 Squadrons' Blackburn Beverleys when they were deployed there. As far as we were concerned the RAF Muharraq deployment was never very exciting but at least there was the compensation of our being able to enjoy RAF hospitality – the junior service have always known how to look after themselves so it was good to get away to Muharraq – if only for that. In stark contrast the facilities at our tented training camp at Jebel Ali were unbelievably basic with the camp located on a deserted stretch of beach about twenty miles south of Dubai, which in those days was a tiny fishing village with no buildings more than a couple of storeys high, while where our tented camp was located is now a massive sea port. The ingoing company flew down from Bahrain in Beverleys and parachuted on to the salt flats behind the camp.

If then the surface of the flats was firm enough, the Beverleys would land to pick up the outgoing company and fly it back to Bahrain. In spite of the spartan lifestyle at Jebel Ali we kept fit with realistic training, live firing of our company weapons and daily sea swimming. One of my tasks was running the company account which came into its own when we were at Jebel Ali as there were no NAAFI canteen facilities – we simply had a company bar instead. As TFH was keen that all company accounts should be maintained financially in the black, the company bar provided one of the very few opportunities to impress him with entrepreneurial acumen. One of the company commanders hit on a novel approach to the problem. If one of his toms appeared before him on company orders on a disciplinary charge, he would be offered an appealing, but totally unlawful choice – either he be officially fined £10 or he make a donation of £5 to the company account. The result was, of course, that B Company's account was the wealthiest in the battalion – luckily TFH never did discover how this came about! That same company commander became my boss about eighteen months later and, as I will recount in due course, I benefited from his unorthodox leadership style. Every other day while we at Jebel Ali, I collected the cash of the previous evenings' takings from the canteen and then loaned most of it back out again to those toms who were skint – then it was an hour's

A Beverley dropping parachutists over Jebel Ali

drive on sand tracks or across salt flats through Dubai and on to the NAAFI at RAF Sharjah to collect gallons more beer to replenish our canteen's increasingly dwindling stocks. All ranks of C Company 3 PARA enjoyed the festivities of Christmas 1964/New Year 1965 at Jebel Ali and a good time was had by all.

Whilst there was more than enough military static line parachuting during our tour, either on to Jebel Ali or at the start of exercises further afield in the Trucial Oman States, there were no opportunities for any freefall parachuting. The RAF has always had a somewhat parochial outlook on the provision of military parachuting – static line or freefall – in that only military trained personnel using military equipment are permitted to jump from RAF aircraft. But early in the New Year I took the 3 PARA cross-country team down to Aden to compete in the Middle East Cross Country Championships – we finished runners-up to the locally based Royal Marines – shucks! My personal freefall parachute equipment had come with me as I had discovered that 653 Squadron, Army Air Corps, were operating Beavers out of Falaise Airfield, Little Aden, and I hoped that the AAC pilots might be amenable to my leaping from one of their aircraft. They certainly were, and some five months after my last freefall jump at Netheravon, I made four solo Beaver jumps, one from 5,000ft and three from 10,000ft, courtesy 653 Squadron. Meanwhile, back in Bahrain, Ed Gardener, who had been posted to 3 PARA as Adjutant, had worked a miracle by organising a freefall parachute display for the Ruler, Sheikh Isa bin Salman Al Kalifa, by an ad-hoc battalion team.

Colin Blyth, Gus Martin, C S-S, Ed Gardener, John Balls and 'Mac' MacIntyre before the jump

TFH and the Ruler

The certificate

TO WHOM IT MAY CONCERN

This is to certify that Lt. G.C.P. Shea-Simonds has received as a gift, from His Highness Shaikh Isa bin Sulman al Khalifah, K.C.M.G., the Ruler of Bahrain and its Dependencies, one Swiss made Movado watch No. 1868.

This gift was given purely as a token of friendship and in no way constitutes a means of payment.

(F. E. Mitchell)
Consular Officer

Her Britannic Majesty's Political Agency
Bahrain

February 11, 1965.

It turned out to be the first freefall parachute descent on to Bahrain as on February 6, 1965, we exited a Gulf Aviation (C47) Dakota for a forty-five-second delay from 9,000ft to land in blustery over-the-top winds near Jau in the desert on the south of the island. On landing TFH introduced us to the Ruler (and one of his falcons!) – they must have enjoyed the jump because later in the day we each received a gold watch in appreciation together with a pompously worded certificate from the Consular Office. More than half a century later, my gold Movado watch still keeps perfect time.

A letter from Ken Vos reached me soon afterwards. He announced that he was planning to fly his bright red, two-seater French-built Scintex Super Emeraude G-ASMV to Australia, with Bahrain scheduled as one of his night stops. It was obviously going to be quite an undertaking for both man and machine. Ken had removed the passenger seat and fitted an auxiliary tank to provide additional sustenance to the little Continental 0-200 100 hp engine; this was the only modification and, of course, the tiny 27ft wingspan aeroplane had minimal navigation aids – this being pre-GPS days. A couple of weeks later he landed safely at Muharraq and soon after he arrived at the 3 PARA guardroom at Hamala camp to spend the night as our guest in the Officers' Mess. He was, unsurprisingly, exhausted. I told him he was welcome to stay until he felt he had recharged his bodily batteries as my roommate in the mess was away on an exercise in the Trucial States so Ken could take his place. He replied that if he didn't continue his epic flight the next day he'd probably succumb to inertia and abandon the journey altogether. At five o'clock the following morning he continued on his way ultimately to land in Perth in Western Australia as he'd originally planned. It was a magnificent effort carried out without any sponsorship or publicity – he'd just got in the Emeraude and flown to Australia – it was so typical of Ken's extraordinary enthusiasm and energy. Ten years later I was to renew my acquaintance with Emeraude 'Mike Victor' under very different circumstances.

Soon after Ken had departed, TFH summoned me to his presence. He came straight out with it: 'Why didn't you take part in the auditions for *Doctor in the House*?' This was the proposed 3 PARA production about which everyone was talking, and which most

Sir Lancelot Spratt (Marty Stratton) and Tony Grimsdyke (C S-S)

were desperately trying to avoid. I replied that my being in Aden with the cross-country team had prevented my attendance – I didn't tell him that I was delighted not to have taken part; in spite of my parents having been in the theatre, 'am-dram' had never been of any interest. TFH obviously thought otherwise because, as I discovered later, the whole project was his idea. 'I've had a look at the script,' he countered, 'and I've decided that you'll play the part of Tony Grimsdyke.' I thanked him, saluted and marched out, wondering if his decision constituted a 'lawful command'. It probably didn't but, having obtained a copy of the script, the character of Grimsdyke, played in the 1954 film by Kenneth More, seemed a reasonable enough part. On returning to the Officers' Mess I discovered that my chum, Marty Stratton, had also been 'ordered' to play a part – in his case that of Sir Lancelot Spratt played by James Robertson Justice in the film. When we all met for the first reading we discovered that TFH had also cast his wife, Pat, as the Matron. It had all the makings of a disaster but it proved highly entertaining for us the cast – even if it didn't for the audience. During our second performance and in a scene in Act II of the play, Sir Lancelot Spratt (Marty) was conducting a mock operation for the benefit of the three student doctors on hospital porter Bromley (LCpl Pearce). We were all gathered around Bromley who was laid out on the table in our flat. We were waiting for a line from Marty which would prompt the entrance of Matron (Pat F-H) – it never came as Marty had unwittingly skipped half a page of the script. I leaned across the inert body on the table and whispered frantically to Marty: 'The Matron?!' 'I know!' he replied in desperate sotto voce. The rest of us were close to succumbing to an embarrassing fit of the giggles when Marty came up with a familiar line from at least two pages back in the script from whence we restarted the conversation, thus enabling Matron to make her stately entrance. The audience didn't seem to have noticed the near-disaster. Still, it all helped to pass what time there was left before we returned to Aldershot.

Then there was the saga of the 3 PARA dhow. A number of nautically minded members of the battalion figured it would be a jolly wheeze to acquire a dhow – the traditional sailed fishing vessel of the region – and, at the end of the tour, sail it back to the UK. TFH's approval having been obtained together with grants from various Middle East HQ funds, a committee was established with our C of E padre, Fred Preston, appointed treasurer. Fred was a delightfully punchy character who, apart from his ecclesiastical responsibilities, and, with considerable enthusiasm, helped to train the battalion's boxing team. One afternoon, and without informing his fellow dhow committee members, he set off with a very large bag of Bahraini dinar to the harbour to purchase a dhow. He may have been expecting some divine guidance, but this was obviously not forthcoming as some Bahraini 'Del Boy' gave Fred a catalogue of dodgy dhow sales patter and our worthy vicar quickly found himself the proud owner of an ancient vessel endowed with very suspect seaworthiness. The committee members were appalled and Fred was dispatched posthaste back to the harbour to cancel the sale. Needless to say Mohammed 'Del Boy' had 'imshi-ed' off into the sunset never to be seen again. So the committee was left making the best of a bad job with limited skills in a desperate attempt to make the dhow seaworthy and, at the same time, learn how to sail the wretched thing. Platoon commanders were urged to take their toms for an enjoyable afternoon's sailing in the dhow to allow the red-bereted volunteer crew to gain experience in handling the thing. Word rapidly spread that, far from having an enjoyably relaxed afternoon of sunbathing during short cruises out into the Gulf, the toms spent most of these so-called pleasure trips frantically bailing water out of the saturated hull just to keep the dhow afloat. My platoon made it very clear that I might have a mutiny on my hands if I'd detailed them for an afternoon of acting as bilge pumps and I certainly didn't push the idea. Later the regular crew decided on a longer training voyage sailing the dhow down to Jebel Ali… and back. Unfortunately the 'and back' part of the exercise didn't happen because during the outbound leg a storm blew up off the coast of Qatar and the dhow foundered and sank, luckily not before the crew, having transmitted a mayday call on their radio, were rescued by a RAF Air Sea Rescue launch operating from Bahrain. Inevitably it took a few days to organise a salvage team to recover whatever military stores the dhow had been carrying when it sank, by which time the locals had stripped it bare. Only the Quartermaster was happy at this result – it was extraordinary how much military equipment the dhow had been carrying!

The conclusion of the battalion's tour in Bahrain also marked the end of TFH's tenure as our Commanding Officer. He certainly was a remarkable man and I'm sure we all retain personal memories of him from those days. During a signals exercise held in the desert area on the southern end of the island he approached my radio operator and I soon after we'd conducted a successful notional shoot with Bull's Troop, 7 RHA, 3 PARA's supporting gunners. For a change he was complimentary, but then he went on to ask me where I'd sited my notional machine guns. I told him and he asked me to explain why. I replied that I had assumed that the enemy's most likely approach was from a specific direction whereupon he asked me if I'd ever heard the story of the Rat and the Frog. I confessed ignorance, so he told me.

'Mr Frog was swimming in the middle of the river when he saw Mr Rat arrive at the water's edge. Mr Frog swam over to him and asked him he'd like a ride on his back. Mr Rat thanked him and climbed on Mr Frog's back. Mr Frog started swimming strongly for the opposite bank, but halfway across Mr Rat produced a pistol and shot Mr Frog in the back of his head.

'Why did you do that?' asked Mr Frog in his dying breath. 'I assumed you wanted to get to the other side?'

To which Mr Rat replied as he swam away: 'Never assume anything, brother!'

I've tried not to 'assume' anything ever since!

Throughout his time as CO we continued to be amazed at his talents. He was a Le Cordon Bleu qualified chef and regularly gave talks to the Wives' Club on cookery. He held qualifications in brick laying and wood working, and he was an acclaimed military writer. His First World War books, *Death of an Army* (1967) and *The Somme* (1964) are particularly memorable – indeed, I well remember a talk he gave during our time in

Bahrain about the Battle of the Somme. His sole aid was a map of the Somme on the wall at one end of the hut; he spoke without notes for more an hour and had all of us mesmerised by his telling of the story. Just before our return to the UK we dined TFH out of the Officers' Mess. During the coffee and brandy a small group from the Battalion Band played polite music in the background. Mr Bibby, the Bandmaster, tapped his wand to gain our attention: 'Gentlemen, we are now going to play a tune that was composed by the Commanding Officer when he was a prisoner of war in Korea!' Unbelievable!

However, it would be wrong to suggest, as a recent biography of TFH has done, that he was some kind of military messiah. He was a complex character who, like all of us, had human frailties. As an example I witnessed his severe admonishment of one of his company commanders at the end of an airborne exercise in front of the rest of the battalion – 'praise in public, admonish in private' offers an old proverb! On another occasion (on Christmas Day, for chrissake!) he took umbrage at the toms in the first rifle company he visited because they were all in frantic alcohol-influenced party mode – he placed the Company Commander under arrest and, although he relented later in the day, it was very much an over-the-top reaction. Nevertheless he was a gifted and accomplished professional soldier who concluded a distinguished career in 1982 as General Sir Anthony Farrar-Hockley GBE, KCB, DSO and Bar, MC, and Nato's Commander-in-Chief, Allied Forces Northern Europe. I was privileged to have had him as my first Commanding Officer in the regiment.

CHAPTER 10
ALDERSHOT AGAIN!

Commissioned into the Coldstream Guards in 1944, 'Scrubber' Stewart-Richardson was a larger-than-life character. He was more than usually eccentric even for a Guards officer as exemplified by his unusual nickname, the origin of which has been lost in the mists of time. In 1950 while serving in Malaya with the 2nd Battalion of his Regiment during the early phase of the Emergency he sought a little more excitement, and made his way to French Indo-China allegedly to take some leave. He managed to get himself attached to the 5ème Cuirassiers when Viet Minh insurgents ambushed the convoy in which he was travelling. He gallantly fought alongside his French comrades to silence one machine-gun but was wounded in the thigh while attacking another. He was immediately awarded a Croix de Guerre by General Marcel Carpentier, the French Commander in Chief. Whilst he received the congratulations of his regiment, the Foreign Office hierarchy, however, was not amused, with the result that Scrubber was denied the honour of ever wearing this justly deserved medal. Just before we left Bahrain, Scrubber joined us in 3 PARA as a Company Commander and I was appointed his Second in Command. He had earlier served with the Guards Independent Parachute Company so he was familiar with airborne forces, but as a Guardsman everything had to be immaculate and inspections to achieve that end were one of Scrubber's specialities and they were all too depressingly regular.

One morning he was about to conduct one such inspection when he received a phone call in his office so he asked me to take his place. The platoon commander, Sgt Rawdings, showed me around the barrack block which, not surprisingly, was absolutely spotless. I did notice, however, that on the top of the first tom's bedside locker, the issue octagonally shaped glass ashtray was placed right in the corner. 'Bloody silly place for it to be,' thought I, 'it could easily get knocked off and be smashed on the floor.' I simply pushed it into the middle and moved on to the next tom's bed space. The same situation was evident, so once again I pushed the offending ashtray into the centre of the locker top and moved on. I had just spotted the next ashtray in the same position when out of the corner of my eye I caught sight of Sgt Rawdings moving in turn the first two ashtrays back into their respective locker top corners. I sought enlightenment: 'OK, Sgt Rawdings – what's the story?' Grinning broadly, he explained that Scrubber insisted that the edges of each of the tom's ashtrays had to be lined up precisely with the corners of each of their locker tops. Right then, from now on I'd play the game! Later, after a spell back with the Guards Parachute Company, Scrubber took command of the 10th (Volunteer) Battalion, the Parachute Regiment, in London, where he became a well-respected Commanding Officer. After the ashtray incident, nothing about Scrubber surprised me, but, in spite of his eccentricity, I think of him warmly as he was such a splendid character.

Meanwhile, as soon as I arrived back in the UK, sport parachuting quickly moved back to the top of the list of my personal priorities with two new challenges to be met. The first was camera jumping. In the modern world of skydiving, cameras have become so small that most jumpers have them permanently attached to their helmets. In the mid-1960s, before 35mm motor drive cameras came on to the market, the film therein had to be wound on with a lever between each shot; and movie cameras were almost too bulky to be attached to a helmet. I'd bought a 35mm Pentax single-lens reflex camera during one of my visits to Aden and it was a not too difficult a job to make a mount that secured it to my left forearm. I could then grip it with the fingers of my left hand and operate the shutter cable release button with my left thumb while I used my right hand to wind the film on with the lever before being able to take the next shot. I discovered that I could manage to take seven photos within the sixty seconds of freefall from 12,000ft. The main problem with this setup readily became apparent – it was necessary to bring both arms across in front of me to aim and operate the camera, with the result that I was like a bird without wings and had to rely on whomever I was photographing to do most of the manoeuvring in freefall. Additionally I had to set up the focus and aperture before exiting the aircraft as this was pre-auto focus and auto-exposure – thus camera jumping was something of a hit-and-miss affair. Ken became my regular parachuting model and, with his freefall manoeuvring ability, we managed to create some memorable images together, one of which won me five guineas (£5 – five shillings to the uninitiated) in an *Evening Standard* amateur cameraman competition.

The camera mount   **Ken in freefall over Thruxton**

Parachuting competition in the early 1960s was either 'style' or 'accuracy'. The former was the competitor's ability to complete a series of left and right turns and backward somersaults in line with a massive marker arrow laid out on the ground, whereas the latter was judged on how close the competitor could land to a ten-centimetre disc positioned in the centre of a large target cross. Team accuracy was simply the total score in centimetres of each individual in the team from the target – hitting the disc with one's boot was a dead centre (or zero centimetres) and this was the aim of the event. The lack of manoeuvrability of the early flat circular canopies didn't lend themselves to being the ideal parachutes to be used for precision competition accuracy. But that all changed with the introduction in 1962 of a parachute of then revolutionary design – it was called the Para-Commander. From an idea for a para-sail canopy by a Frenchman, Pierre Lemoigne, it was developed by the US Pioneer Parachute Company into what arguably became the most popular sport parachute ever. I bought mine in September 1965 and during the next ten years I made 1,183 parachute jumps with a succession of Para-Commanders without a malfunction of any kind. Attempting to master its potential was my second challenge of the year. With its lift to drag ratio of 1.16 (nearly twice that of any of its predecessors), the PC certainly made accuracy parachuting more accurate, and display parachuting infinitely safer. It was akin to comparing a pre-war Austin 7 with a post-war Austin Healey 3000!

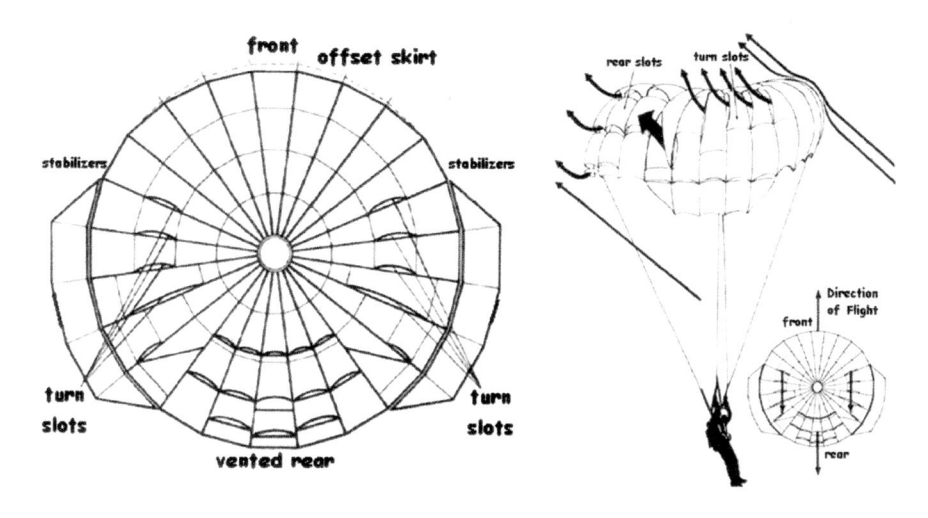

While I competed regularly, without any particular distinction, in the individual events of style and accuracy, they had limited appeal for me because, as I discovered later, I enjoyed sharing aviation experiences with parachuting or flying chums. This is why I enjoyed display parachuting – not because of any showmanship aspect but because, more often than not, we were jumping as a team and sharing the often interesting challenge of flying our canopies into tight arenas, sometimes in marginal weather conditions. Occasionally it also provided the opportunity to jump from a different type of aircraft like when a bunch of us Thruxton jumpers parachuted into the Derby Show from a beautiful DH Dragon G-ADDI (a predecessor to the Rapide and powered by two Gipsy Major engines) flown by the voluptuously glamorous Clare Roberts whose liberally splashed Chanel No 5 wafted around the cabin before accompanying us out of the door at 7,000ft. On another occasion I was a guest jumper with the Red Devils for the Filton Air Day. The Rapide from which we were due to jump became unserviceable at the last minute and Major Mike Heery, who had taken over command of the Red Devils from Ed Gardener and was with us at Filton, immediately set off to find us a replacement aircraft. The Red Arrows, the RAF's justly famous flying display team, were, in those days, supported by an Armstrong Whitworth (later Hawker Siddeley) Argosy, a four-engined transport aircraft which had been introduced into RAF service to replace the ageing Hastings fleet. Mike, who must have known, as we all did, that the RAF only allowed RAF-trained freefall parachutists equipped with RAF parachutes to jump from RAF aircraft, approached the Argosy pilot to see if we could 'borrow' his aircraft for our drop. The Argosy captain was obviously unaware of RAF rules about jumping from RAF aircraft as he couldn't have been more helpful and he readily agreed to Mike's request. Soon we were on board and climbing to altitude. The cloud prevented our jumping from more than 4,500ft but we were able to exit the Argosy from its lowered tailgate – the result was the first Argosy jump and the first tailgate exit recorded in my logbook. We never did discover what happened to the pilot – we simply hoped that his support of the team was never discovered by his superiors as it might have ended a promising career.

On the soldiering front that autumn I was posted to Recruit Company at the depot of the regiment in Maida Barracks, Aldershot, to train young recruits destined for the regiment. It was to prove a thoroughly worthwhile and rewarding two years. Each twenty-two week training cycle included three gruelling weeks of advanced training at the regiment's Battle School at Brecon in South Wales and the basic military parachute course at No. 1 Parachute Training School at RAF Abingdon. All four of my platoons started off with more than seventy strong but, as the result of the high standards we set, none of them finished up with more than thirty on their passing-out parades. The depot's Commanding Officer was Maurice Tugwell, a charming and experienced regimental soldier who, as a nineteen-year-old second lieutenant, had parachuted into the Crossing of the Rhine, the last airborne operation of the war in 1944. My Company Commander was none other than Peter Walter, the wonderfully unconventional officer who had incurred the wrath of TFH on Christmas Day when we were in Bahrain. Peter had won a Military Cross while serving with 22 SAS in Malaya and I found it easy to respond to Peter's unique style of leadership and sharp, dry sense of humour. On day one of their training the newly shaven-headed recruits were paraded in the camp cinema for Peter's opening address. He stood theatrically on the stage with his legs apart and his arms folded firmly across his chest. His opening was unexpected: 'I know why you're all here – you're all here 'cos you want to stick a bayonet up some wog's arse!' My platoon staff struggled to keep straight faces.

Throughout my two years training recruits I was fortunate to have had two exceptional platoon sergeants and a collection of very high-calibre corporal section commanders. My first platoon sergeant at the depot was Jack Henderson, a hard, utterly professional Scot who was always immaculately turned out – it came as no surprise that he later became Regimental Sergeant Major of the 2 PARA before finishing his career as a Major and Quartermaster of the School of Infantry at Warminster. While he was RSM of 2 PARA in Berlin there was a General's inspection of the battalion – inevitably the whole place was spotless with the square swept clear of fallen autumn leaves. During its arrival the General's helicopter flew in low over the trees surrounding the barrack square, blowing the remaining leaves from the branches into an aerial maelstrom. The RSM was not amused. After the General had marched off parade with the Commanding Officer, Jack Henderson had the luckless NCO pilot start up his helicopter to fly it backwards and forwards across the square using the downwash of the rotor blades to clear it of leaves – a novel use of an Army Air Corps asset, although, I suspect, not in the original design specification. My second platoon sergeant was Charlie Buchan, a cheerfully efficient senior NCO who came to the depot having just completed a tour with 22 SAS. He later went on to command the Rhodesian Parachute Training School as a Wing Commander.

Two other characters at the depot were the Paymaster and the RSM. During the war in 1943 the former, Mick Briody, having become an Irish Guards RSM, was posted to the recently formed Glider Pilot Regiment to help install some traditional Guards discipline into what in its early days was an outfit lacking a degree of regimental pride and sense of purpose. Apart from his duties as RSM, Mick Briody also learnt to fly gliders and in September 1944 he flew a Horsa glider with a platoon of the Border Regiment soldiers into the ill-fated battle of Arnhem. Now here he was in 1965 at the depot as a Major in the Royal Army Pay Corps sporting both parachute wings and glider pilot wings, two rows of decorations and a magnificent moustache that bristled with Brigade of Guards pride – and rightly so. The RSM was Jimmy Ferguson, another charismatic Scot who was respected by all of us Recruit Platoon Commanders. Soon after arriving at the depot I took a number of my first platoon which was still forming up to act as a behind-the-scenes general duties squad for a KAPE (Keep the Army in the Public Eye) show to be held near Nottingham and we were to be accommodated in Normanton Barracks, Derby, which, being disused, simply had electricity and running water, and no furniture. As we were only to be in residence for a long weekend I, my staff and our recruits just equipped ourselves with camp beds and sleeping bags. Jimmy Ferguson had for some reason also declared himself in on the weekend and once I had made sure my recruits were settled in I sought him out to discuss details for the following day. I was directed to the last room on the left down a long corridor. Neatly screwed on to the door was an immaculately sign-painted notice which stated in sky-blue letters against an airborne maroon background: 'WOI J. FERGUSON MBE PARA'. A loud very Scottish 'Come in!' greeted my knock. It was difficult to take in the sight that greeted my entry. The RSM was lying back in military splendour on a beautifully made bed complete with tartan eiderdown, reading a newspaper which he lowered reluctantly to identify the unwelcome intruder. There was also a large armchair, bedside locker and reading lamp, a wardrobe and, providing almost stifling warmth, a large electric fire – there was enough kit to fill a three-ton truck, which explained what such a vehicle had been doing in our convoy up from Aldershot that morning. I came straight out with it: 'Bloody hell, Mr Ferguson, this is a bit over the top isn't it?' His response left me speechless: 'Well, Sir, any fucking idiot can be uncomfortable!' Quite!

Three weeks later the depot was subject to the annual Administrative Inspection as it was then called. A general arrived at Maida Barracks to go through the place like a dose of salts upsetting all of us in his determination to find fault. During the two weeks my platoon had been formed up they could just about come to attention when ordered to do so and I knew all their names – and that was about it. I was therefore somewhat concerned to be told that the general would inspect my platoon during a drill parade – I just hoped that he'd been briefed that my recruits had so far only received two weeks' basic training.

At the appointed hour I marched across the square to the dais on which the general was standing. I saluted him with my sword. 'Sir, 298 Recruit Platoon, the Parachute Regiment, formed up and ready for your inspection – there are seventy-two men on parade.' At least this time I didn't have to count them with the point of my sword.

'Thank you, Mr Simonds,' he replied unsmilingly, 'and as I come to each man you will introduce him to me by name and then I may or may not ask you a question or two.'

'Sir!' I acknowledged.

The problem was that most of his questions could, I was sure, easily be answered with reference to the platoon book in which we recorded each of the recruit's weekly progress, but of course I didn't have it with me on parade. That he'd got my name wrong grated and that he wasn't wearing a red beret or parachute wings revealed that he wasn't a member of the 'airborne family'. But I was determined not to be distracted and managed to bluff my way through the questions he asked about the front rank of recruits. We moved to the tall gangling youth who was right of the line in the centre rank. 'Private Clemans, Sir,' I announced.

The general turned towards me. 'And whereabouts does Clemans come from?'

Somehow all I knew about Clemans was that he was a north country man. 'Yorkshire, Sir.' I hoped it didn't sound like another bluff.

In the event, the general called it by turning to Clemans and asking: 'And whereabouts in Yorkshire do you come from, Clemans?'

'Manchester, Sir,' he replied firmly.

'Thanks a bunch, Clemans,' thought I, and the general's raised eyebrows simply suggested: 'GOTCHA!'

Private Devon (not his real name) was one of 298 platoon's seven potential officers, so-called because they had received a higher standard of education than the average. It was made clear to them from the outset that they should clearly demonstrate officer potential throughout their twenty-two weeks' training and that they would be given plenty of opportunities to do so. Unfortunately Devon was bone-idle and at our weekly staff meeting Cpl Sid Bright, his very able section commander, regularly reported on his lack of both effort and enthusiasm. The result was that Devon received a number of warnings from Sid Bright, Jack Henderson or me. It all came to a head when the platoon was on parade dressed in PT kit for a session in Maida gym. Jack Henderson inspected them to discover that Devon was wearing a filthy civilian round-necked T-shirt – the issue Army PT shirts had a V-neck. An explanation was sought, whereupon Devon made the mistake of lying in an attempt to convince his immaculately turned-out platoon sergeant that he'd been issued with the rotting shirt he was wearing. Jack Henderson coolly ripped the offending garment from Devon's back and ordered him replace it *immediately* with the correct military version – a far more effective and relevant punishment than placing him on

Company Commander's orders. A few days later I was summoned to Peter Walter's office. As always he briskly came straight to the point. 'You'd better read this,' he said, holding out a letter which was neatly handwritten on smart paper with an embossed address in Farnham – it proved to be from Devon's father. Basically he had written that his son had accused my staff of unfairly victimising him and what did Peter intend doing about it? Knowing full well that Devon senior had only heard one side of the story, I asked Peter's permission to sort it all out myself. 'Right,' he agreed, 'just don't come back to me until you have!' I took the offending letter and telephoned the number on the headed paper. The lady who took the call admitted that she was Devon's mother and we arranged that I would pay a call early that evening to discuss the matter with Devon senior.

Turned out smartly (I hoped) in No. 2 Dress and equipped with the Platoon Book, I arrived at a large detached house situated in a very posh, wooded residential suburb of Farnham. I was met at the front door by a friendly looking lady who introduced herself as Mrs Devon. She ushered me in, explaining that her husband was due home from work at any minute and I accepted the kindly offered cup of tea. Devon's father appeared soon afterwards dressed in a pin-striped suit and sporting an Army Staff College tie. 'Oh dear,' I thought, 'this could be interesting.' But, having politely introduced himself and told me of his concerns, he asked me for my version of events. I showed him the Platoon Book, which revealed his son's consistent lack of any satisfactory progress, and I explained that I regarded Cpl Bright to be an outstandingly competent and fair NCO in whom I had complete confidence. I then drew his attention to the progress of the other six potential officers who were doing extremely well by comparison.

'Hmm, I see,' said Devon senior thoughtfully, and he then went on to request that I ask Cpl Bright to go easy on his son to allow him a break so he could catch up with the rest of the platoon.

'I'm sorry, Sir,' I replied, 'I think you know that I can't do that, but I will ensure that Cpl Bright is scrupulously fair in his dealings with your son.'

At that moment the door opened and the young man in question walked into the room as cool as you please – that is, until he spotted me when he stopped dead in his tracks.

'Sir, this is a perfect example of your son's attitude to his training – this evening he should be in barracks with the rest of the platoon cleaning his kit for an inspection and drill parade first thing tomorrow.'

'Thank you,' he replied, somewhat wearily, I thought, 'for taking the trouble to come here this evening to explain the situation – my wife and I appreciate it.'

I thanked them for their hospitality and left them and their errant son to it. The following morning Sid Bright was waiting for me as I stepped out of my car in front of the 298 platoon barrack block.

'Sir, we've got a big problem,' he said as he saluted me.

'OK, what gives?'

'Well, Sir, yesterday evening Devon skipped the kit cleaning and went home to visit his parents.'

'I know – I was there when he showed up.'

I went on to recount my conversation with Devon senior. Sid then told me what happened when his absentee recruit finally got back to the barracks later that evening. 'The rest of the platoon were extremely pissed off that Devon absented himself from the kit cleaning so when he got back they stripped him bollock-naked, covered him from head to foot with black boot polish and strapped him to the frame of his bed from which they'd removed the bedclothes and mattress.' I told Cpl Bright to get Devon cleaned up and to immediately parade him at the Company Office which is exactly where I went to relate the whole saga to my Company Commander. Peter was typically supportive and the reluctant recruit was quickly marched in front of him for one of the shortest interviews on record. By the end of the day the wretched Devon was no longer my responsibility nor that of the regiment. I have no idea what happened to him subsequently – he probably went on to have a lucrative career in the City.

Of course, as far as the Parachute Regiment was concerned, it was to be expected that a large number of recruits would fail to make the grade – after all it was a tough twenty-two weeks. On the other hand it was very satisfying to see those who had successfully completed their regimental training proudly formed up on Maida Barracks square for their passing-out parade in front of their equally proud mums and dads.

By the time I finished my two years at the depot I had 320 sport parachute jumps in my logbook. Luckily there were plenty of opportunities to indulge my passion for the sport thanks to the gaps waiting for the next platoon's forming up and during the time they were completing their basic military parachute course. One unexpected and memorable sport parachuting trip was organised by Ken who had arranged with Twentieth Century Fox to provide four jumpers to appear in their production of a film called *Fathom*, a comedy spy movie starring Raquel Welch as a glamorous agent called Fathom. Ken, Leigh Allison, Diana Parker and I were the team who flew to Spain for the filming and parachuting in September 1966. The deal was that we received no payment but we were each given a brand new Para Commander and however many jumps were required for the film. I remember boarding the BEA Comet at Heathrow wearing my full parachute rig of main and reserve as I didn't want to let it out of my sight – not something I'd recommend trying to do nowadays – but back then BEA didn't object. I can't remember what the plot was other than that we were supposed to be parachutists taking part in a competition where Fathom was a member of the US team. The drop zone was not too far from Malaga and was rock solid as both Ken and I were to discover to our cost. Every member of the cast and crew were accommodated in the same hotel with the exception of Raquel Welch, who was given star treatment on her own at a more luxurious place nearby. The first evening the four of us were sitting together in the restaurant, as we knew no one else, when we were approached by an absolutely delightful man who asked us if he could join us. He was genuinely interested in what we were doing and we were impressed when he said he was a member of the cast. He simply couldn't have been more modestly charming – he was Richard Briers and I remained a lifelong fan – it was a sad day when he died in 2013. For some reason Ken doubled as Raquel Welch – we were told it was because Diana was not tall enough – but he looked pretty stupid to us kitted out as he was in a silver lamé jump suit and a wig of long hair. On our fifth jumps for the film, Ken cracked a bone in his foot and I broke my leg – the DZ was particularly unforgiving. I was fortunate that there was an Alouette helicopter being used as a camera platform for some of the filming – Gilbert, the amazing French pilot who had done so much of the flying for the filming of *Those Magnificent Men and Their Flying Machines* and *The Blue Max*, landed right alongside me and, having been told of my injury, flew me in less than fifteen minutes straight to the hospital in Malaga where I got plastered – or at least my leg did. Two signatures in my logbook remain special reminders of an interesting trip – Richard Briers' and Gilbert's, the latter who wrote: 'Vous ferez mieux la prochaine fois,' or 'better luck next time!' *Fathom* certainly didn't justify a broken leg as far as I was concerned – it cost $2.225 million to produce, but it only took $1 million at the box office. Back in Aldershot my plastered broken leg provoked no sympathy – I was simply told to get on with the recruits' training as before.

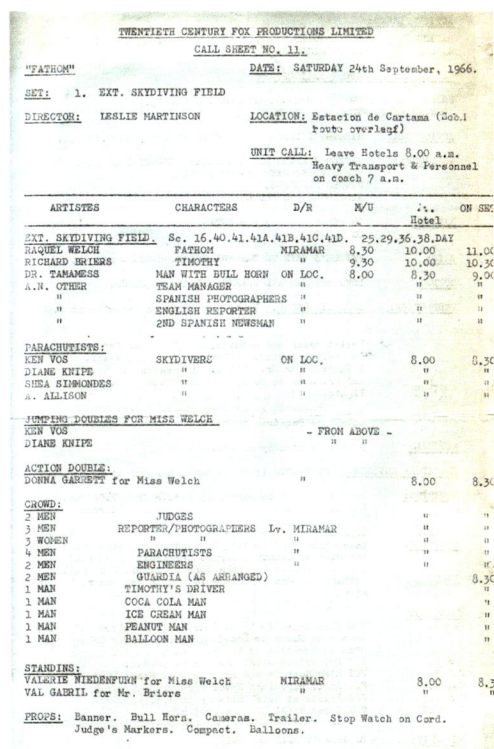

Fathom **poster and call sheet**

At about this time I splashed out on what proved to be the most reliable camera I've ever used – a Nikon F with a motor drive back – this I mounted on a helmet, allowing me use of my arms to 'fly' properly in freefall. A series of photos I took of Ken opening his parachute over Blackbushe in 1966 proved its worth.

After about eighteen months at the depot, Maurice Tugwell asked me where I'd like to be posted to after my time in Recruit Company had finished. When he explained that I hadn't been around long enough to be given command of the Red Devils, I requested a tour flying helicopters with the Army Air Corps. This was approved and soon afterwards I found myself at RAF Biggin Hill to undergo aircrew selection. I wasn't too worried about the aptitude tests but I certainly had concerns about my shortsightedness. The former presented no problems and I passed them OK before undertaking the medical. The form that I had to complete asked if I wore spectacles, to which I was honestly able to write that I didn't – but I neglected to admit to wearing contact lenses, which I had been doing since I joined the regiment. The doctor who conducted the eyesight tests failed to spot my lenses so I passed the eyesight examination successfully before it was discovered during the ear, nose and throat section of the medical that I was high-tone deaf. This was hardly surprising as it was obviously the result of all the time spent on the ranges without proper ear defenders – in those days we'd simply screw up pieces of 'four-by-two' weapon cleaning cloth and stick them in our ears. It was suggested that my high-tone deafness might not be permanent so I was cleared to drive to the Army Air Corps Centre at Middle Wallop for further interviews. These all went well, with the final hurdle afterwards being a visit to the RAF's Central Medical Establishment where the ENT specialist, a sour-faced woman named Dr Pearson, conducted further hearing tests. These, she told me without a glimmer of humour, I'd failed and that, as a result, there was no way that I could be permitted to fly turbine-engined aircraft. Well, Dr Pearson, I've got news for you if you happen to read this – my flying logbooks reveal that I've flown more than 2,000 hours in turbine-engined aircraft, mainly BN Turbine Islander, Pilatus PC-6 Turbo-Porter and Cessna 208 Caravan. However, all that comes later in my story, but back then the wretched woman managed to scupper my plans to fly with the Army Air Corps. Back in Aldershot in August 1967, when I'd finished my two years' training recruits, I received a posting order to join 1 PARA in Aden as Second in Command of B Company.

CHAPTER 11
1 PARA AND ADEN

The insurgency in Aden against the British Crown, the so-called Aden Emergency, lasted from late 1963 until British Military Forces finally withdrew in November 1967. By the time I had joined 1 PARA in early September, the Battalion, based in Radfan Camp, a tented facility located close to the airfield of RAF Khormaksar, had already been deployed for four actively exciting months with the expectation of covering the final withdrawal from Aden originally planned for January 1968. From a personal point of view it was disappointing as it proved to be only a three-month stint of active service – our departure date was brought forward to the end of November – and it was the longest period I'd had so far without any parachuting, military or sport, since I joined the regiment in 1963.

My erstwhile Company Commander at Sandhurst, Mike Walsh, was now the Commanding Officer of 1 PARA and my B Company Commander, Tony Watson, was a splendidly genial, laid-back officer who had been one of Mike's A Company subalterns in 3 PARA during the Suez operation in 1956. Tony was a delightful boss who delegated me plenty of responsibility and was relaxed enough to allow me to act on his behalf on a number of occasions when he was committed elsewhere. Our Company Sergeant Major was Gordon Burt, a star of Army cross-country running who was later commissioned and won a MC in Northern Ireland. Another memorable 1 PARA character of that time was Joe Starling, the much respected second-in-command. Joe was a real soldier's soldier who was always around when things got challenging, which was hardly surprising as he'd already won a MC as a young subaltern while serving in the Suffolk Regiment during the Malayan Emergency in the early 1950s. Joe's part in 1 Suffolk's success against the Chinese terrorists is well recorded in the excellent book, *Jungle Green*, written by Joe's Company Commander, Arthur Campbell MC. Some years later I acquired a copy of *Jungle Green*, which Joe kindly signed for me, and in an accompanying note he wrote: 'Arthur Campbell had a gift for writing as well as the military skills. Had he been castrated at birth he would have made Field Marshal.' In 1992 and some ten years after he retired as a Brigadier, Joe wrote his own book, *Soldier On!* This splendid volume of lively reminiscences, a number from his time as 2I/C 1 PARA, is a thoroughly enjoyable read and my copy is well-thumbed!

B Company 1 PARA was principally made up of three recruit platoons, straight from the Para depot in Aldershot, who had joined the battalion a day before its embarkation leave. With an average age of eighteen years and four months, they were employed on internal security operations within a few hours of arriving in Aden. They rapidly proved that they, like the rest of the 1 PARA toms, were a professional, tenacious and good-humoured bunch throughout the six months of this pretty grubby little campaign against two groups of insurgents – FLOSY (the Front for the Liberation of Occupied South Yemen) and NLF (the National Liberation Front). Towards the end of our deployment the situation had become most unpleasant with both groups taking on the other in attempts to become the dominant political force. We often unwittingly found ourselves as 'piggies-in-the-middle' of a volatile mess. After the first hairy couple of months, the Battalion's soldiering was given to manning of observation posts, checkpoints and patrolling, all of which enabled the Battalion to dominate the Al Mansura and Sheikh Othmann suburbs of Aden. The latter included our occupation of an old mission hospital transformed into a stronghold and unsurprisingly christened Fort Walsh. Based here we had in support a couple of armoured cars of the Queen's Own Hussars whose young troop commander one day thoughtfully (?) asked if I'd like to go with him on his vehicular patrol at first light the following morning. Not wishing to expose myself unnecessarily to potential insurgent sniper fire, I removed my red beret with its glinting silver cap badge and resolved to keep my head well down in the armoured car's turret as we pulled out of our stronghold. The young Hussar officer was obviously determined to demonstrate that he was made of sterner stuff as, to my amazement and that of the toms who witnessed it, he stood up in the turret and blew *Gone Away* on a hunting horn! When I told him about it Tony called it 'panache', and a few days later, as a result no doubt, he announced that he had challenged the QOH troop to a game of polo and would any of us like to volunteer to be a member of the B Company horse hockey team? It transpired that only Tony and Gordon the CSM had any recent equestrian experience with the result that I was among those 'volunteered' to be members – oh dear!

Tony was the only one of us who viewed the challenge with any degree of enthusiasm and he quickly organised our first training session – this entailed borrowing some South Arabian Army horses for some exercise along the beach. By the time I arrived at the stables the more docile looking of our chargers had already been allocated to the other team members and the one that was to be my mount was both gigantic and fearsome-looking. Don't get me wrong – I've always thought horses to be the most majestic of animals but this one regarded me with unexpected menace, which I found distinctly unnerving. I anticipated a battle of wills and so it proved. Much of what followed came about because our mounts had received minimal exercise during the insurgency and they were now ready to make up for lost time. I had barely managed to climb aboard before my steed, who obviously knew much more about where he wanted to go than I did, accelerated swiftly into a gallop towards the beach. On the approaches from up country into Aden the Battalion had set up a number of checkpoints of sandbagged emplacements surrounded by numerous coils of barbed wire to stop and search inbound vehicles to ensure that no dissident weapons and ammunition were being delivered into the area. I quickly realised that my galloping charger, over whom I was exercising absolutely no control, was careering along the beach heading straight for one of the 1 PARA checkpoints. The first coils of barbed wire seemed almost as high as my horse, who was clearly undaunted by this formidable obstacle. I survived his terrifying jump but finished up grimly clinging on around my charger's neck. It was in this configuration that he sailed over the next barbed wire obstacle, throwing me violently off into the sand in the process while the toms manning the checkpoint cheered Sir's pathetic horsemanship. Luckily (or unluckily, depending on one's point of view) one of the toms managed to grab the reins and a couple others, obviously hoping for more entertainment, helped me back into the saddle. I had no time to compose myself before the wretched animal launched himself over the barbed wire yet again with the same result. As I was flung into the sand I stupidly managed to hang on to the reins. I got to my feet just as my steed reared up on his hind legs and caught me a glancing blow with one of his front hooves across my forehead – this deposited me back into the sand once more. I now had little incentive to hang on to the reins any longer, so my equine adversary was able to charge off back down the beach in the direction whence we had originally come. Not only was I covered in sweat and sand but it was pointed out to me by the checkpoint commander that I was well-bloodied. I was therefore happy to accept his suggestion of a lift back to the Battalion's MI room where half a dozen stitches repaired the damage. The horse was subsequently found at the military hospital tied to a sign that said CASUALTY WARD, even if, ironically, he wasn't the casualty. The B Company polo team was quietly disbanded.

2i/c B Company 1 PARA

Radfan Camp

1 PARA checkpoints

Fort Walsh

Out of the blue one morning in early November I received a message from Battalion headquarters to report to 'Birdy' Martin, the Adjutant, who informed me that the CO wished to see me. Wondering whether it was to be an interview with or without coffee, I sought enlightenment.

'I believe he's got a posting order for you.'

'But I've only been in the Battalion for a couple of months,' thinks I, and, as I entered the CO's office and came across his unsmiling presence, I noticed the absence of coffee. He came straight to the point.

'I've had a signal from RHQ; they want you to take over as Adjutant of 4 PARA in February.'

He looked up to gauge my reaction.

'Who'll be my CO, Sir?' I replied, as the CO/Adjutant relationship in a TAVR battalion, which has no regular second-in-command, is very important.

'I understand it's to be David Callaghan,' was the answer. 'However,' he added, 'I'm fighting it as I want you to be my next Signals Officer.'

Not as good a job as Adjutant, thinks I, so: 'I'm sorry, Sir, but I'd rather like to go.'

A frosty silence was the result, followed by his declaration that I was being disloyal and that I should 'Get out!'

I saluted, turned about and left as quickly as I could. It was some time later that I learned that TFH had exerted his influence on RHQ to post me to be Adjutant of 4 PARA so I wrote to him thank him for being partly responsible and to express the hope that I could make the most of the opportunity. His reply was typically brisk and to the point: 'Dear Charles, I was not partly but wholly responsible for your posting as Adjutant of 4 PARA. Good luck, Tony Farrar-Hockley.'

I think we were all relieved when we learned that our handover of 1 PARA responsibilities to the South Arabian Army as part of the final British withdrawal from Aden was to be brought forward to the end of November. My own final memories of this wretched place were free drinks during the closing of the Officers' Mess at RAF Khormaksar on our last evening and feeling distinctly unwell early the following morning, when, as the last 1 PARA officer bringing up the rear of B Company, I saluted the GOC and the Brigade Commander to bid them farewell, before boarding the Battalion's final RAF Hercules flight Bahrain-bound. From RAF Muharraq we were flown home by civilian charter companies with the result that our flight arrivals were unexpected – having finally arrived back at Gatwick I remember a frustrated Tony Watson on the phone trying to contact anyone who could arrange some wheels to transport us back to Aldershot. Welcome home 1 PARA!

* * *

1 PARA's deployment in Aden earned all ranks a General Service Medal with a South Arabia clasp, and there was the bonus of a DSO for the CO, and well-earned MCs for Ted Loden, Hamish McGregor and Nicholas Emson, and a MM for Jimmy Duncan. Disappointingly there was only a Mention in Dispatches for Joe Starling, who surely deserved greater recognition for his inspired leadership and example. Finally we can but reflect on whether it was all worth the lives of three gallant 1 PARA toms, Brian Quinn, Colin Carver and John McIntosh – may they rest in peace.

Utrinque Paratus!

CHAPTER 12
4 PARA (V) AND THE RAVENS

Our earlier than scheduled withdrawal from Aden meant that 1 PARA were unable to move into their new home on their return to Aldershot as Montgomery lines would not become vacant until the originally planned date of February 1968. This resulted in the Battalion being sent on seven weeks leave during which, six days after we had landed at Gatwick, I was back in the sky over Thruxton for a jump from a Rapide from 11,000ft – my first for three months and the first of a dozen more I made before the middle of February 1968 when I journeyed north to join the 4th (Volunteer) Battalion of the Parachute Regiment (4 PARA (V)) as Adjutant.

The Permanent Staff, 4 PARA (V) 1968, with (front centre) CO David Callaghan, flanked by QM Paddy Byrne on his right and Adjt C S-S on his left

4 PARA (V) was then part of 44th (Volunteer) Parachute Brigade, with its HQ just off Sloane Square in London, and had been formed in 1950 with its parachute battalions then being the 10th (County of London) Battalion, the 12th (Yorkshire) Battalion, the 13th (Lancashire) Battalion, the 15th (Scottish) Battalion and the 17th (Durham Light Infantry) Battalion. Six years later the 12th and 13th Battalions were amalgamated to form the 12th/13th Battalion and in 1967 this battalion was in turn amalgamated with the 17th Battalion to form 4 PARA (V). The latter consisted of five companies

recruited from the best of the north of England – Battalion HQ & HQ Company at Thornbury Barracks, Pudsey between Leeds and Bradford, 'A' Company at Liverpool, 'B' Company at Oldham, 'C' Company at Gateshead on Tyneside and 'D' Company at Stockton on Teesside. The battalion had four regular Army officers, the CO, the Quartermaster, the Training Major and myself as Adjutant. We were supported by a cadre of regular Warrant Officers and Sergeants led by the RSM. The Commanding Officer was, as forecast, David Callaghan, who, having been Second-in-Command of 3 PARA, had been attached to the Kenya Rifles until he became CO of 4 PARA. I have to admit that I was a little nervous about meeting up with David again some five years after my faux pas during the 3 PARA drill competition, but my concern was totally unfounded as I couldn't have had a better CO – we were to become lifelong friends. 'You'll make some mistakes,' he had said, 'but don't make the same mistake twice!' Fair enough, I thought, then he added: 'And I have no problem with your freefall parachuting so long as it doesn't interfere with your job as Adjutant and hopefully 4 PARA (V) can benefit from the occasional freefall display.' This was particularly encouraging, especially as I'd just been elected to the Council of the British Parachute Association!

When I arrived in the Battalion the Quartermaster was Paddy Byrne, an outstanding character, as was Charlie Storey, the QM who later took over from him. Paddy had originally been an Irish Guardsman before transferring to the Army Commandos. In 1942 before the Dieppe Raid, LCpl Paddy Byrne was bodyguard to Lord Lovat, the CO of 4 Army Commando then based in Scotland. Paddy recalled being ordered by Lord Lovat to go to the QM's department to be issued with new battledress as they were to attend an important conference in London and the CO wanted LCpl Byrne looking as smart as possible. Paddy approached the Regimental Quartermaster Sergeant (RQMS) informing him that Lord Lovat had ordered that he be issued with a new battledress. The RQMS had obviously been having a bad day and, believing that LCpl Byrne was attempting to 'pull a fast one', he told Paddy to tell the CO to fuck off! Paddy reported back to the CO: 'Sir! The RQ told me to tell you to fuck off!' Both the RQMS and LCpl Byrne received sizzling bollockings from Lord Lovat for, among other things, simply wasting his time. Some two years later, on D-Day, Paddy was awarded a Military Medal for outstanding gallantry while commanding the Commando's Sniper Platoon. When, after the war the Army Commandos were disbanded, Paddy transferred to the Parachute Regiment and he finally became its senior QM as a Lieutenant Colonel.

Charlie Storey also had an interesting war. He served initially with 3 Army Commando during the Lofoten raid in Norway in 1941 before transferring to the Parachute Regiment not long after it was formed. As Platoon Sergeant of 7 Platoon, C Company, 3 PARA, he parachuted into Arnhem in September 1944 and, as C Company was the only 3 PARA unit to fight alongside 2 PARA, he was very much involved in the battalion's tenacious hold of their objective, the road bridge across the Lower Rhine. He even receives a worthy mention in *A Bridge Too Far*, Cornelius Ryan's excellent book about the Arnhem battle. But the bridge's defenders, having valiantly held it for four nights, were finally overcome to become prisoners of war. Ultimately Charlie and one of his comrades in arms managed to escape and, still wearing their Parachute Regiment battledress, they stole a German Mercedes staff car and drove it through friendly US lines to freedom. It was certainly a privilege to have known both these two stalwart, yet modest, parachute soldiers so well that they became good friends.

The next step was to do the rounds of the four rifle companies guided by David Higginbottom, my predecessor. It quickly became obvious that the 4 PARA (V) toms were a credit to the Regiment. They were all, of course, qualified military parachutists, apart from which they had also to complete the same battle fitness and small arms tests as their regular counterparts. All this coupled with their having to attend two weeks' annual camp, occasional Battalion weekend exercises and a minimum number of evening training parades at their local drill halls gained them an annual bounty in addition to regular rates of pay when they were on parade. This was in an era when the toms were paid in cash so almost inevitably many of them convinced their wives or sweethearts that TAVR soldiering was simply an unpaid hobby! However, and there's no doubt about it, whatever the 4 PARA (V) toms may have lacked in expertise they certainly made up for with their enthusiasm – it was good to be their Adjutant and I know that Colonel David felt a similar pride at being their Commanding Officer.

It took me no time at all to discover that there were plenty of freefall parachuting opportunities in the north of England and that there were also a small number of 4 PARA (V) toms who were committed sport parachutists. There was, however, only one other officer in the Battalion who had any sport parachuting experience of note and that was the Second in Command of B Company based in Oldham – he was Charley Mahon who was a barrister by profession in Manchester. We quickly became friends and, as you will learn, we shared plenty of interesting times together. The second two weeks of February and the whole of March 1968 were spent earning my pay as Adjutant and learning the job, but April was a very different matter with a dozen jumps recorded in my logbook. The first of these was as a guest jumper with the Red Devils into a show on Teesside Racecourse and, inevitably, jumping with the team became a regular occurrence whenever they had a display booking in the north of England and needed to make up the numbers. The following weekend I was invited to jump with the Northumbria Parachute Club, which operated at Sunderland Airport – it had been RAF Usworth until 1958, and later in 1984 the airport closed to become home to the Nissan Car factory. The key members were Sgt Kevin Milligan, Sgt George Russell, Cpl Vic Pollit, who were all 4 PARA (V) stalwarts, and Turner Fielding, who came from Wallsend and whose Geordie accent was so pronounced that initially I needed one of the other three to act as interpreter. They proved to be a splendid bunch and, after the four jumps I made that weekend dispatching students and following them out from the Flying Club's Cessna 172, they asked me if I would become the club's Chief Instructor, albeit part-time, and when I could fit it in with other commitments. As at that time they had no regular instructor we agreed on this arrangement and it proved to be an enjoyably fruitful association. After a couple of jumps at Halfpenny Green the following weekend, I continued to Netheravon where the Red Devils were instructing John Noakes, the 'action man' presenter of the BBC children's television programme, *Blue Peter*. The team had asked me to film John on his second, third and fourth freefall descents. Equipped with a heavy helmet-mounted Bolex H16 cine camera I exited the Rapide as swiftly as I could after John, but the ten or so seconds of freefall were barely enough time to frame him adequately on film. It was agreed that a longer freefall by John was required for me to obtain usable footage and, as the Red Devils were just about to leave for team training at Pau, the French military

John Noakes with C S-S and cine camera at Netheravon and photographed over Pau, France, by C S-S

parachute school, John and I were invited to join them. Luckily Colonel David gave his approval as he immediately saw that it would be great PR for the regiment. Had John not proved to have been as 'switched on' as he undoubtedly was we could never have achieved the excellent footage we did – after his three ten-second delays over Netheravon, Red Devils Chief Instructor Brian David and I progressed him quickly through a twenty-second delay, a twenty-five-second delay before our third and final filming jump over Pau – a forty-second delay from 8,000ft. The result of this final jump prompted Team Commander Peter Schofield to write in my logbook: 'Great camera job, Charles, thanks from THE TEAM.' Later that month I entered a 4 PARA (V) team of Milligan, Russell, Pollit and self into the Army Parachute Championships at Netheravon where we won the Cameronian Cup for the highest-placed TAVR team – the fact that we were the only TAVR team mattered not in the least!

In September the Battalion moved lock, stock and barrel to the Stanford Training Area in Norfolk for its Annual Camp. On arrival we discovered that 15 PARA (V), the Regiment's Scottish TAVR battalion, were based next door – inevitably the rivalry between the two battalions was intense. One evening Colonel David was invited to supper by the CO of 15 PARA (V) and it finished with the two of them being generously entertained by the whisky-drinking worthies of the 15 PARA (V) Sergeants' Mess. Their cherished malts took a hammering but so impressed were they with David remaining on his feet until the bitter end that the Pipe Sergeant escorted him back to our mess. The screeching drone of the pipes at three in the morning was not appreciated, particularly as I was the one who had to ensure that my boss was in a fit state to conduct the meeting he'd convened for all 4 PARA (V) officers at 8.30am the following day. As he hadn't appeared for breakfast, I left it as long as I could before banging on his door. A loud groan from within was the result. I had no alternative but to barge in and shake him into semi-consciousness.

'Colonel, the meeting with the officers is in thirty minutes.'

He rolled over and groaned. 'Tell 'em to fuck off!' was his instruction, so I left him to his slumbers and half an hour later walked into the anteroom where the battalion's officers were gathered expectantly.

'Gentlemen,' I announced, trying to make it sound convincing, 'the Commanding Officer's been called to an important meeting with the Brigadier, so this meeting is now re-convened for eleven o'clock.'

At 10.30am I banged on David's door again, which, on this occasion, woke him. 'What time is it?' he inquired as I entered. I told him and the sudden awareness of the 8.30am meeting which he now thought he'd missed caused immediate panic – his face was a picture.

'What about the meeting?'

I told him of my earlier attempt to wake him and that the officers had been gathering in the anteroom. I also told him that his response was to tell them to fuck off – an order that I'd carried out to the letter! It took him a good couple of minutes before he realised I'd been pulling his leg. He took it well, his warm grin of relief saying it all. I've always believed that this was when our firm friendship started, and, splendidly, it lasted until he died in 1995. During our stay at Wretham Camp we had an unscheduled VIP visit to the Battalion from the Minister of Defence and Colonel David asked if I could arrange a freefall parachute display for him. Charley Mahon and I were available but, as I explained to David, we had no aircraft as the AAC Beaver was not due to arrive until the day after.

'What about the Wessex helicopter which is bringing in the Minister?' he asked.

'If it's Royal Navy it won't be a problem,' I explained, 'but if it's RAF, forget it as neither Charley nor I are RAF freefall-trained, and we'd be using our own equipment, not the RAF's.'

David quickly fed this information to our Brigade Commander, Brigadier Pat Thursby, who obviously believed that 'rules are for fools, and for the guidance of wise men', because the following day Charley and I successfully exited the RAF Wessex for a jump from 6,000ft for the Minister, who seemed suitably impressed. I never did discover who said what to whom, but well done Brigadier Pat – the fact that he had recently taken over as chairman of the Army Parachute Association might have had something to do with it.

Soon after we returned from Annual Camp, Charley Mahon and one of his B Company soldiers, Cpl David 'Del' Delsoldato and I drove to Sunderland on a Friday evening for a weekend's jumping. Lee Bambrough, the flying club's owner, kindly agreed that we could stay in the clubhouse using our camp beds and sleeping bags. After enjoying a meal and a few beers in Sunderland we returned to the flying club to find the place locked up and in darkness. We found a tiny window that opened into the ladies' loo through which Del, being the smallest of us, managed to squeeze. I suppose it was almost inevitable that he also set off the burglar alarm. Half an hour later, two police cars and a 'Black Maria' arrived complete with flashing blue lights, blaring sirens and half a dozen of the local constabulary's finest who refused to accept the simple truth of our story. Thus we were arrested and driven off to Sunderland 'nick' in the Black Maria. We were then interrogated by a particularly aggressive detective sergeant. He gave the diminutive Del an especially hard time and to one of his questions it was Charley who quietly replied: 'It's OK, Del, you don't have to answer that.' Whereupon Del's interrogator spun round to face Charley: 'Oh really, Mr Mayhon,' he retorted, deliberately mispronouncing Charley's surname, 'and what do you do for a living?' 'I'm a barrister!' was Charley's quiet, but firmly spoken, response. You could have heard a pin drop. Even now I remain convinced that the police inquisitor actually wrote 'B-A-R-R-I ...' in his notebook before the penny dropped – and I'll remember his resultant double-take forever. After that he couldn't get rid of us quickly enough!

Early in 1969 I was able to stand down as the part time Chief Parachute Instructor of the Northumbria Parachute Club as 'Aussie' Power, a member of the Red Devils, retired from the Army to turn the club into a full-time sport parachute operation to be called the Northern Parachute Centre. It was also at around this time that I received a posting order from Regimental Headquarters, RHQ, appointing me team leader of the Red Devils vice Schofield with effect from a date early in 1971. My dream job in the regiment was now firmly visible on the horizon. Coincidentally this was timely as I had been toying for sometime with the idea of 4 PARA (V) having its own parachute display team and now there was no reason why this couldn't happen – apart from the possibility of it being vetoed by Colonel David. But this did not occur. Not only was David all for it, but he also suggested that the team should be called the Ravens as the Battalion's lanyards and DZ flashes were black and apparently ravens are well known for their flying ability.

But before the Ravens could take flight I received a call from the PR department of MOD who were assisting Anglia TV to produce a documentary about the Battle of Arnhem – 1969 being the 25th anniversary of the regiment gaining its most famous battle honour. I was asked if I'd consider making a couple of jumps on to one of the Arnhem DZs armed with a cine camera to provide a parachutist's eye view of a landing. I was also informed that Colonel David had already given his approval for me to be officially 'on duty', and, if I agreed (which of course I did), in four days' time I'd be on the same flight out to Düsseldorf as General Sir John and Lady Hackett. The previous year General Sir John Hackett GCB CBE DSO and Bar MC had retired from the Army after an illustrious career, his last job having been Commander in Chief of the British Army of the Rhine.

At Arnhem, as the 34-year-old brigadier commanding the 4th Parachute Brigade in the 1st Airborne Division, he'd served with distinction, was badly wounded and, having evaded capture for nearly five months, he finally escaped back across the Lower Rhine to freedom in February 1945. After landing at Düsseldorf and, as instructed, I made myself known to the General as I was to travel with him and Lady Hackett to Arnhem. We were met by about half a dozen senior officers from HQ BAOR who invited the General and Lady Hackett for lunch in the Officers' Mess, but the General politely declined, explaining that they had arranged to see some old friends who lived nearby – he gestured to me to join them in the staff car, which I did – it was the only time I was driven in a staff car with four stars prominently displayed front and rear! As we pulled away from the airport the General gave detailed directions to the driver before turning to me: 'I don't know about you,' he said, 'but Lady Hackett and I didn't fancy a stuffy meal in the mess, but we know a charming little restaurant down in the town and we'd be delighted if you would be our guest for lunch.' Of course I warmed to them immediately, and when he discovered that Arnhem had been the topic of my military history thesis at Sandhurst, he asked me if I'd like to have a personal battlefield tour with him when we arrived in Arnhem as the Anglia TV crew was not due until the following day. The tour started at the spot on the Ginkelse Heide DZ where he himself had landed and it proved to be the start of an extraordinary account of those dramatic days in late September 1944 and told with incredible lucidity, humour and modesty. We visited the famous Arnhem road bridge, the historic crossroads in Oosterbeek where the 10th Battalion of the Regiment was reduced to thirty soldiers and no officers, and the small hollow in the woods near the Bilderberg Hotel where the remnants of the 4th Parachute Brigade (about 60-strong) gathered on the fourth day and held off attacks by tanks and flame-throwers until dusk. Then, led by their gallant Brigade Commander, they broke out with fixed bayonets leaving their dead and wounded behind them before joining the diminishing divisional perimeter around the Hartenstein Hotel which housed General Urquhart's Divisional HQ for most of the battle. It was here on the seventh day that the Brigadier was almost fatally wounded. His quiet telling of the Arnhem story both for me and later for the television camera was intensely moving and an amazingly humbling, never-to-be-forgotten experience. The two parachute descents I made with a camera on to Ginkelse Heide the following day went according to plan, but they were a total anti-climax when compared to General Sir John's unique conducted tour.

Later the following month the Ravens made their first freefall display – the first of thirty-two the fledging team carried out that summer – this debut one from an Army Air Corps Beaver at the SSAFA Air Pageant at RAF Church Fenton. It was a successful descent from 9,500ft for which I was joined by Charlie M, Del and Mal Read, a trio who became regular Ravens. Things didn't always go according to plan. On the first Saturday in June we had been booked to display at the Rotary Club Gala in Highbury Park in Birmingham during the afternoon, followed by a second show two hours later at the Castle Donington High School Carnival with a final jump back into the Rotary Club Gala that evening. Logistically it presented a few problems, especially as the timings provided little flexibility. From maps provided both drop zones were plenty big enough and a Brummie skydiving chum was kind enough to conduct a recce of Highbury Park, while I checked out Castle Donington High School on the day as it was near East Midlands Airport, from where we took off in the Trent Valley Aviation Rapide flown by Bill Downes. John Fargin, the Battalion's RQMS, an ex-wartime airborne soldier, who had quickly appointed himself our most necessary and regular DZ controller, had obviously become tangled up in Birmingham's weekend traffic because when we flew into the Highbury Park overhead there was no sign of our bright dayglo target cross. And we also found to our horror that there were two show grounds with associated arenas, crowds and car parks each located on opposite sides of the park. Foolishly I had left my only copy of the DZ map with John so I was unable to identify which was our target DZ, especially as we had no ground-to-air radio communications. Then we saw a white target cross being laid out in the middle of the larger of the two arenas. The organisers had obviously been quick to appreciate the problem and, fortuitously, had found enough white material to improvise a target cross. I instructed Bill to run the Rapide in over the white cross for the first pass. The first four landed safely in the larger of the two arenas before we ran in for the second pass. I casually glanced across at the other arena to unexpectedly see our dayglo cross being pegged out in its centre – shit!

'Bill, can you give us another pass over the dayglo cross?'

'No problem,' he shouted back down the fuselage as he quickly appreciated the problem and realigned the Rapide accordingly. The remaining four of us exited the aircraft and landed around our dayglo cross. I was immediately aware that something wasn't quite right as a worried-looking John Fargin approached me.

'Is this the Rotary Club Gala, John?' I asked.

'I've no idea, Sir,' he replied, 'the traffic was appalling and I've only just got here. I found this arena and, as I saw you in the overhead, I laid out the cross.'

At that moment a worried-looking official appeared on the scene. 'Is this the Rotary Club Gala?' I asked him.

'No,' he said, grinning joyfully, 'this is the Boy Scout Festival – the Rotary Club Gala's over there!' He pointed to the other side of the park and the other arena.

Later that evening, having jumped into both the Castle Donington High School Carnival and for a second time into the Rotary Club Gala, the organisers of the latter entertained us generously and were wonderfully understanding of what had transpired. Subsequently I hadn't the heart to charge them full price, but I believe honour was satisfied when I sent them a bill that included a fifty per cent discount for the first display!

Fortunately only one other of the thirty-two displays the team made that summer didn't go according to plan and that was at the Bolton Cricket Club Gala in July. The result prompted the *Bolton Evening News* to record: 'RAVENS' FEATHERS ARE RUF-

FLED'. The wind had been somewhat gusty and the first three of the eight-man team to exit the Rapide missed the DZ. One of them was John Cooke, one of our regular guest jumpers, and on landing he had managed to drape his parachute canopy over a lamp standard in Bolton High Street – the *Evening News* subsequently took great delight in publishing a photograph of workmen disentangling the canopy from the lamp standard. As Bolton was Cookey's home town he became something of a local celebrity, particularly when he told friends that luckily for him the traffic lights in the High Street were green which allowed him to fly his canopy across the crossroads!

The following month the Battalion upped sticks and moved down to Penhale near Newquay in Cornwall for its Annual Camp. While we were there I renewed friendship with Lt Cmdr Digby Lickfold, a swashbuckling Navy helicopter pilot whom I'd last seen on HMS Albion in Aden in 1967 and who was now commanding a Naval Wessex helicopter squadron at the Royal Naval Air Station at Culdrose. Digby was very much a Navy character who was more than happy to allocate a number of his aircraft to us for helicopter training – especially when he'd learned that the RAF were unable to do likewise. Of course the Ravens needed similar so we jumped a Wessex twice on to Perranporth beach for the benefit of the holidaymakers and twice more into Penhale Camp itself for two displays for VIP visitors. Many thanks Digby and 707 Helicopter Squadron Royal Navy!

Once the Battalion had moved back to Pudsey, news of some plotting in Aldershot reached my ears. Peter Schofield, the Red Devils Team Commander, from whom I was due to take over in the spring of 1971, had, with his wife, established a profitable little business selling sport parachute equipment. Newcomers to the team were instructed to visit Peter's wife to be kitted out with Red Devils jumpsuits, team jackets, jump boots, helmets, goggles and gloves. Peter's wife then sent the invoice to the Team Commander. It was therefore in Peter Schofield's interest to remain Team Commander and if this happened my posting to succeed him would be unlikely. I was bitterly disappointed and wasted no time in expressing my frustration to Colonel David who couldn't have been more supportive, even when I told him that in the event of my not getting the job I had decided that I'd resign my commission. Peter Schofield played it cleverly. Realising that if he'd simply asked for an extension he would be unlikely to get it, he therefore told the regimental elders that, in his opinion, Shea-Simonds was not qualified to do the job. So Schofield was asked if he would consider extending as team leader until such time as a suitably qualified candidate could be appointed – of course he agreed, so I resigned my commission in the regiment with effect from February 1971. RHQ in turn agreed that I could remain as Adjutant 4 PARA (V) until then enabling me to complete ten years in the Army and eight in the Regiment. Whatever reservations RHQ may have had about my qualifications to lead the Red Devils, they obviously had none about my qualifications to lead the Ravens while remaining as Adjutant 4 PARA (V) – Colonel David certainly hadn't! Early in the new year the Regimental Colonel visited 4 PARA (V) and I was summoned before him – no coffee was offered while he attempted to persuade me to change my mind about my resignation, even suggesting that I might get a Company

Commander's job within a matter of months – in my view a highly unlikely carrot-dangling proposition. I explained why I had no intention of changing my mind before he lost control and almost yelled at me: 'You'll be back within a year, just you mark my words!' As there were just the two of us in the CO's office, I saw no need to raise my voice as I replied: 'Sir – my fucking pride wouldn't let me come back!' As I'd lost all respect for the man, I deliberately didn't salute him as I walked out. When I told Colonel David what had happened he was wonderfully sympathetic and he was delighted when I reassured him that he would have my fullest support for however long he remained my boss.

By the autumn of 1969 I'd established a sport parachute drop zone on the Bradford University playing fields behind Thornbury Barracks, on to which the Ravens parachuted regularly. We usually jumped from a Cessna 172 supplied by the Yorkshire Aeroplane Club based at Leeds-Bradford Airport or from a Cherokee 6 supplied by the Air Navigation & Trading Flying Club (ANT) based at Blackpool Airport. I was fortunate enough to have a splendid relationship with both organisations and I used both to provide aircraft for Ravens displays. Two experienced and valued guest jumpers with the team at that time were RAF Sgt Steve Silander, a V-bomber crew member, and Dick Reiter, an American based at the US Communications Station at Menwith Hill near Harrogate – and, because it was geographically handy for them, they took advantage of the Thornbury Barracks drop zone on a regular basis – it was good to have them on the team.

However, before the Ravens' display season started, we learned that the Battalion's 1970 annual camp was due to be held during June in Germany at Sennelager, which was itself not too far from Bad Lippspringe airfield, home of the Rhine Army Parachute Centre – excellent, I thought! Colonel David believing, like Napoleon, 'that time spent in reconnaissance is seldom wasted', decided that I should accompany him on such a visit to Germany. On the third day we were checking out the allocated training areas from the air using an Army Air Corps Scout helicopter. Having been airborne for about half an hour we landed to rendezvous with the CO's vehicle and driver to enable him to continue his recce on the ground. Meanwhile, I was tasked with flying back to Detmold where I had to attend a couple of administrative meetings later that day. Following our airborne progress on an aeronautical chart, I noticed that our route took us within two or three miles of Bad Lippspringe – an opportunity to visit the Rhine Army Parachute Centre was too good to miss, especially as its Chief Instructor was a good friend from our early sport parachuting days at Thruxton. He was substantive Lance Corporal, acting Corporal, local Sergeant Robert Sydney Acraman, who was definitely one of the sport's best-known and most entertaining characters. Hilarious stories about him are legion. There was the occasion at Netheravon when he let it be known that he was planning to ride a pushbike into freefall off the wing of the Rapide. Those of us who were fortunate enough to be on the load were soon almost crying with laughter as we witnessed our aspiring aerial cyclist struggling to manoeuvre his mechanical steed up on to the wing and thence into the fuselage – and all this accompanied by a brilliantly funny running commentary from our potential hero of the moment. Our pilot, a passed-over major in the Green Jackets, who was not exactly renowned for having a sense of humour, was inevitably alerted by the noise of the commotion growing in volume behind him. A groan of disappointment from all of us in the aircraft greeted the major's demand: 'Cpl Acraman, get that bike off this aeroplane immediately!' The result was that, sadly, Robert's planned freefall bike ride never happened – a pity, really, but it may well have been the catalyst for the stalwarts who, some years later, successfully rode pushbikes into freefall off the tailgate of a Shorts Skyvan. One of Robert's earlier jobs had been as a junior NCO in 63 Parachute Squadron RCT based in Aldershot where he'd been responsible for training those RCT volunteers wishing to serve in 63 Squadron to reach a standard of fitness to enable them to pass P Company, the selection process for joining airborne forces. One particularly strenuous part of selection was, and still is, the dreaded log race, which required teams of steel-helmeted candidates racing over the local training area carrying 60kg lengths of telegraph pole. From an undisclosed but probably devious source, Robert had acquired a police constable's pointed helmet, which became the badge of shame to be worn by some unfortunate miscreant in each of Robert's squads.

On one memorable occasion he led his log-carrying squad of sweating, blaspheming would-be paratroopers into one entrance of Woolworths in Aldershot, through the store and out the other end with one of them sporting a policeman's pointed helmet – and all to the startled amazement of the customers! So you can well imagine why I now asked the AAC sergeant pilot if we could make a diversion into Bad Lippspringe with the hope of seeing Robert. He kindly agreed and, as we made our approach to land, I saw a group of parachutists being checked prior to emplaning by the man himself. By the time the rotors had stopped turning I had donned my red beret and disembarked. The stick of jumpers, with Robert bringing up the rear, was walking purposefully towards where the Rapide was parked with its engines ticking over. Robert glanced in my direction and, apparently ignoring me, quickened his pace to catch up with the jumper at the front of the stick. 'Corporal Nivens,' shouted Robert above the engine noise, 'get your kit off and give it to Captain Shea-Simonds!' Less than five minutes later I was sitting on the floor of the Rapide and airborne in the climb to 5,000ft wearing a strange set of kit which included ill-fitting helmet and goggles, to make an entirely unexpected and unplanned parachute jump. Having landed safely, however, I'd already started to pack the luckless 'Jock' Nivens' parachute on the grass when Robert strolled over. 'Stop doing that, Sir,' he said, 'Corporal Nivens is quite capable of packing his own bloody parachute!' Having thanked my two benefactors for their unique brand of parachuting hospitality, I resumed my rotary journey towards Detmold, having spent less than ten minutes on the ground at Bad Lippspringe. It wasn't until later when I wrote up the jump in my logbook that I realised it had been my birthday – a great present, Robert, thank you!

When in early May I discovered that Whitbread, the brewer, was organising and sponsoring an unusual race for teams of three attempting to achieve the fastest time from the top of Blackpool Tower to the summit of the 2,000ft Snaefell in the Isle of Man, some sixty-five miles away, I was determined that 4 PARA (V) should enter a team in the aviation class – and, typically, Colonel David gave our entry his blessing. Apart from myself, the team would consist of Charley and Del, with regular Ravens Dick Reiter and Cliff

Lloyd as reserves and assisted by three motorcyclists, Eddie Vaughan, John Moon and Colin Murray, from 156 Regiment Royal Corps of Transport. The plan was for the three of us to use the lifts and stairs from the start at the top of the tower down to its base, then motor cycle pillions along the promenade to the airport, followed by the flight in a Cherokee 6 flown by Keith Whyham, CFI of ANT, to overhead Snaefell and finally parachute jumps on to the summit itself. During the day before the race we had fast prac-

The team: Cliff Lloyd, Charley Mahon, Eddie Vaughan, C S-S, John Moon, Keith Whyham, David Delsoldato, Colin Murray and Dick Reiter

tice runs on the bikes down the promenade to the airport. On the return runs we were flagged down by a friendly policeman who politely pointed out that the speed limit was 30mph. Later I discussed the speed issue with Charley, telling him that I was going to ask our motorcycle riders to ignore the speed limit on race day if they were happy to do so. I also suggested to Charley that he might like to defend us in court if we were nicked for speeding. He replied very firmly if that should occur, we were definitely on our own! On the following day all went according to plan with the three of us clinging desperately to our motorcyclists as we roared flat-out for six-and-a-half minutes down the prom. Our friendly policeman saw us coming – he stepped into the middle of the road to stop any conflicting traffic and waved us through! On arrival at the airport Keith already had the Cherokee 6's engine running while Cliff and Dick also had our parachutes prepared so we could easily put them on as we taxied out for take-off. The flight across the Irish Sea to the Isle of Man was uneventful enough, apart from Cliff and Dick briefing us on the wind speed over the summit DZ – earlier it had looked acceptable, but now it was decidedly marginal. Too bad – we were committed! Guided by the smoke direction on the summit and the forecast wind speed I had plotted an exit point from an aerial photo, but clear of the aircraft and hanging under my open canopy, I thought we might be too far upwind of the DZ, especially as, towards the end of our descents, it seemed to all of us as if we were below the summit. But mercifully a helpful last-minute updraft positioned us nicely for firm landings right on the DZ – the photo says it all! We recorded a total time of forty-six minutes from the top of the Tower to Snaefell's summit. We were placed third, beaten by a Red Devils team who knocked nearly ten minutes off our time having used a Skyvan, but the winners, who beat us both, were three ex-Parachute Regiment Army Air Corps pilots who simply flew a Scout helicopter from Blackpool Sands in front of the Tower across the Irish Sea to land right on Snaefell's summit. Afterwards we agreed among our team that we wouldn't be in any hurry to repeat our modus operandi and, interestingly, and, as far as I know, nobody's parachuted on to the summit of Snaefell since the race!

Decidedly windy! Charley, C S-S, Cliff and Dick and the summit drop zone of Snaefell, May 28, 1970

Two weeks later 4 PARA (V) moved to Sennelager for its annual camp and to discover, frustratingly, that the Rhine Army Parachute Centre was temporarily closed because Robert and his staff were competing in the Army Championships at Netheravon. This prompted me to search elsewhere for a German alternative where the Ravens could parachute during the one day off we had from soldiering. Having been told of a club based at a small airfield called Garbeck in the Ruhr, five of us drove there for a day's jumping. It was a very basic operation but we were made most welcome. They had two aircraft

– a Piper Cub, which could carry one jumper only at a time, and a Mouraine Rallye, a low-wing monoplane, which could lift three. Having checked our logbooks and licences, I was invited on the first lift with two friendly Germans and, as all went well, we were permitted to look after ourselves for the rest of the day. 'Relative work' is the discipline in sport parachuting which is, in simple terms, the ability of two or more parachutists to manoeuvre relative to each other, and even link up together during the time available in freefall – and the Ravens were grabbing every opportunity to practise this skill. As exiting the aircraft as close together as possible is important for the jumpers involved, I asked the local club members if it was possible to have two together on the wing before exiting the Rallye, but, as it quickly became obvious that RW was not a skill with which they were familiar, they said they didn't know. As Charley and I were keen to give it a go, we were soon practising positioning ourselves close together on the wing while still on the ground, when the lederhosen-equipped pilot strode across to us and firmly declared: 'Relative from ze Mouraine verboten ist!' Charley and I were unimpressed and determined to ignore him. Minutes later we were airborne and climbing to jump altitude and our wretched pilot launched into a non-stop commentary about the local landmarks while we were trying to concentrate on our planned relative work. Suddenly he gestured to an expanse of water below: 'Das ist der Möhne Dam!' he declared. 'And we bombed shit out of it in 1943!' was Charley's classic response. Thereafter our pilot said not another word and the twenty-second delay from 5,000ft went according to plan prompting me to write in my logbook: 'Great link-up with Charley M just before wave-off time.'

On the soldiering front Colonel David was well pleased with the way that the Battalion had performed during its test exercise, so much so that he granted our Padre's request to hold a service in the field at its conclusion. In a woodland clearing with all ranks of 4 PARA (V) gathered around him, our worthy, but somewhat earnest man of the cloth was determined to make the most of this heaven-sent (or was it CO-sent?) opportunity, especially when it came to delivering his sermon. His theme for the latter was that, while we were all 'ruffy-tuffy' paratroopers, he was pleased to see that we could all demonstrate care and concern when it was appropriate. 'For instance, en route to this location, a budgerigar flew into the back of the three-ton truck in which some of us were travelling. I was immediately impressed by the compassion extended to this bewildered little bird, etc, etc…' As I glanced around the assembled toms I noticed that there were some in the B Company corner of the congregation who were grimly trying to suppress their laughter – and not making a very good job of it. As Charley was their Company Commander and, as Adjutant, discipline was one of my responsibilities, I cornered him after the service.

'Bloody hell, Charley, can't you control your company?' I demanded of my clearly amused colleague.

'Well,' he replied, 'after the vicar got out of the truck, he didn't see what happened to the budgerigar next.'

'And what did happen to the budgerigar next?' I asked him.

'You just don't need to know!' he said, at which I decided, probably not very bravely, to leave it at that!

Once the Battalion had returned to Yorkshire it was time to think about what I was going to do once I had left the Army. I was determined that it should involve sporting aviation and, principally, parachuting. I reckoned therefore that it would be useful to learn to fly which, as recounted earlier, was something I'd already tried unsuccessfully to do in the Army – thanks again, Dr Pearson! But where should I go to achieve that aim? The Air Navigation and Trading Flying Club at Blackpool and the Yorkshire Aeroplane Club at Leeds-Bradford airport were the two contenders. I opted for the former as I had got to know the owner and CFI, Keith Whyham, very well from all the jump flying he had done for the Ravens. He had also become a good friend. He was a quiet, self-effacing, totally laid-back character and a natural pilot. On one occasion and having just got airborne during an instructional sortie, the starboard undercarriage leg had fallen off the PA 28 a few feet off the ground. Having burnt off four hours' worth of fuel and persuaded his student to climb into the back left-hand seat, he slid across to occupy the front left hand seat and alerted air traffic control to his intentions. During his approach to land on the grass, he stopped the engine, switched off the fuel and ignition to reduce the risk of fire, before clicking the starter a couple of times to rotate the propeller into the horizontal. He then carried out an immaculate dead stick landing, touching down initially on the port wheel, then in turn on the nose wheel as the speed decayed, before allowing the starboard wingtip to drop gently on to the grass, only removing a couple of inches of paint from the underside of the wing – this was the only further damage to the aeroplane. It was an outstanding example of skilful flying. As an instructor he taught by example with the minimum of fuss and making every sortie a thoroughly enjoyable experience. I made my first instructional session with Keith on July 11 during a positioning flight in the ANT Piper PA 32, Cherokee 6, to and from Pickering for a Ravens display for a gala at the Scarborough Ski Slope, and similar a month later to RAF Finningley for their air show and yet another Ravens display. However, most of the forty hours I flew during my Private Pilot's License (PPL) course was in a Piper PA 28 Cherokee 140, a docile four-seat, low-wing monoplane. On August 27 I had driven to Blackpool for an early start with Keith in PA 28 G-AVRP for a session on the circuit of exercises 12 and 13 – take-offs and landings. By this time I had achieved eight hours and twenty-five minutes of instructional time and felt that I was close to being sent solo. It was a beautiful day with blue skies and not a breath of wind. After forty-five minutes Keith simply said: 'I think that'll do, Man.' He called everyone 'Man' when he couldn't remember their names!

'Aren't you going to let me go solo?' I suggested cheekily.

'Well, that last one was a bit firm,' he offered, by way of explanation. I pointed out that the windsock indicated that the wind had got up, and that my last landing had been made downwind – so understandably it was on the firm side! He kindly relented and we taxied to the threshold of the runway, where, having given me a quick briefing, he got out and left me to it. The take-off, circuit and landing were all uneventful, prompting me to write in the remarks column of my log book later: 'Ex 14 FIRST SOLO!' as thousands of student pilots have done in the past, and will do so in the future. I taxied back to the apron, reported to Keith and asked him what was next. As he was about to go off and fly a couple of holidaymakers on a short pleasure flight around Blackpool Tower, he simply said: 'Well, you'd better go and fly another three circuits.' These luckily passed off without incident, as did the rest of the forty hours and five minutes of my course, with the exception of a couple of flights that could so easily have ended in disaster.

Every Thursday evening, throughout the summer and weather permitting, the Ravens benefited from 15 Flight Army Air Corps, based at RAF Topcliffe, generously providing us with a Beaver for forty minutes' flying time for parachuting. On this particular Thursday I'd already flown an hour-and-a-half of solo time at Blackpool and the forecast for the rest of the day looked good. The only way I could also get to RAF Topcliffe for our weekly parachuting was if I flew myself there, but how could I persuade Keith to let me, as a twenty-plus hours student pilot's licence-holder, do just that? John Sudbury, a chum who knew Keith much better than I did, said that I should wait until he got into an aeroplane for his next flight and ask him when he was strapping himself in. 'He'll say yes to anything then!' John suggested from his own experience and so it came about. Having cleared my planned flight with ATC at Topcliffe, but without telling them I was a student pilot, I put my parachute kit on the back seat of PA 28 Romeo Papa and took off for the forty-minute flight to my destination sixty-four nautical miles away on the other side of the Pennines. As three other members of the Ravens were waiting for me when I touched down, it wasn't long before we were all airborne in a Beaver for a quick parachute jump. Just over an hour after I'd landed at Topcliffe I was in the air again heading back towards Blackpool. It took me about fifteen minutes to realise something was wrong. In my eagerness to get away quickly earlier in the afternoon I hadn't taken the westerly wind into account, with the result that I had a tailwind outbound and now, during my return flight, a headwind was slowing my speed over the ground. At the halfway point I calculated that I'd be lucky to arrive back at Blackpool by the time it got dark! With about ten miles to go, I could see the lights on Blackpool Tower and those of the runway in use at the airport. I landed in the quickly fading light and taxied back to the ANT hangar, expecting Keith to materialise rapidly out of the gloom to administer a well-deserved bollocking. Like a naughty child, I furtively pushed Romeo Papa into the hangar and ventured into the clubhouse to face the music. Keith was behind the bar dispensing drinks to members and, as he saw me approach, he simply queried: 'Hi, Man, what kept you?' My apologetic confession was quietly accepted and thus I learnt about flying from that! I successfully flew my PPL flight test with Keith on October 26 and the licence itself arrived by post from the CAA a couple of weeks later.

During the three months of my flying training I was fortunate enough to have taken part in a UK milestone sport parachuting achievement. In the USA at that time, eight jumpers formed into a ring of eight in freefall and held for five seconds had become the minimum requirement for it to be defined as a 'star'. Now it was time for some star building in the UK by a TA team from the Royal Green Jackets. The first I knew about it was when Jim Crocker, a stalwart regular from Thruxton days, phoned to ask me if I'd like to be the still photographer for their star building attempts. Of course I would! Once again Colonel David was firmly 'on side' – maybe he felt that that the Regiment should be represented! We all met at Dunkeswell Airfield in Devon in mid-September with support from a Royal Navy Wessex helicopter from 846 Sqn based at RNAS Culdrose. The first four days were a write-off as a result of appalling weather that only started to break on the fifth day. The first two attempts netted two four-man groups. On the third lift the Wessex climbed through the cloud to run in for the drop at 11,000ft. John Beard, who was spotting, only caught occasional glimpses of the Dunkeswell runways through gaps in the cloud, but there's a very similar airfield four miles away which John only identified as he launched himself from the Wessex and shouted: "It's UPOTTEREEEEE……" After the team had only built a five-man, we all successfully landed on Upottery, closely followed by the Wessex that landed, picked us up and flew us back to Dunkeswell. The team's fourth attempt, which resulted in another five-man, was made after another interesting spot from John over solid cloud that stretched as far as the eye could see. We sank under open canopies through 1,000ft of opaque moisture until we came out over picturesque rolling countryside without an airfield in sight. Jim was the low man so we all followed him down to land close to a quiet road, along which a van appeared from around a corner. The van stopped as Jim stepped into the road to ask the driver if he could give us a lift back to the airfield.

'What airfield?' asked the driver.

The first UK Star. The team in order of entry: John Shankland, John Beard, Mike O'Brien, Jim Crocker, Guy Sutton, Tony Unwin, Terry Hagan, John Harrison. Cameras: Mark Miller (cine), C S-S (still)

'Dunkeswell,' Jim replied.

'Where be Dunkeswell?"

'Near Honiton,' Jim suggested.

''Oniton,' replied our local yokel, ''Oniton be in Devon, you be in Zomerzet!' Later that afternoon the team put together a six-man that was the best of the six attempts from the Wessex that day. Their enthusiasm remained untarnished, however, so three weekends later we all met again at Dunkeswell. This time the weather for the two days was perfect and, on the fourth jump from the South West Aviation Skyvan, the team built the UK's first 8-man star which was held for seven seconds. It was a splendid achievement – so much so that I chose my photo of the Royal Green Jackets Star to be on the cover of my book, *Sport Parachuting*, which was published early the following year (about which more later).

Colonel David was now into his last two months as CO when he summoned me into his office. 'Sit down. I want to talk to you about Bounty Night.'

This had all the hallmarks of David floating an idea for which he wanted my agreement. 'I understand the companies have each got it planned OK,' I replied hopefully. Surely he wasn't going to put a spanner into the well-oiled machinery of battalion tradition. Every territorial soldier was eligible to receive an annual bounty of some £100, (which in the late 1960s was not peanuts), provided he fulfilled so many training days in the year, attended annual camp, classified with his personal weapon on the range and achieved certain standards of physical fitness. In those days this sum of money was paid in cash on Bounty Night at each of the five company drill halls in Liverpool, Oldham, Pudsey, Stockton and Gateshead. And the occasion was, as can easily be imagined, an excuse for five of the most appalling alcoholic debauches held anywhere in the north of England in any one year.

'That's as may be,' he said firmly – here it comes, I thought – 'but this year, as it's my last, we're going to have a Battalion Bounty Night.' I sat there, literally struck dumb, as my mind raced to come up with legitimate reasons why this quite appalling idea should be nipped in the bud. But this Wise Old Pelican knew me too well. 'And it's no good your producing reasoned argument why it's not a sound idea – I've decided it's going to happen, so you'd better get together with the Quartermaster and the RSM and organise it – OK?'

'Right, Sir,' I said, 'but it's got all the potential for being a bloody disaster.'

He grinned, 'Yes, it has, hasn't it?'

Dear God, he was going to regret this, I thought, as I left his office, determined that it was not going to be on my account. Because of their collective sixty years-plus of regimental service, the joint reaction of the QM and the RSM was of even more shock and amazement than my own, but they also realised that protest was futile – the Commanding Officer had made up his mind. The RSM, an aggressive Scotsman with a square head totally in keeping with his position as coach to the undefeated Battalion boxing team, possessed all the tact of a herd of charging elephants. He briefed the permanent staff Company Sergeant Majors with uncompromising words. 'We'll get this bloody fiasco over without incident – OK?' They got the message and set about their various tasks with grim determination. At the same time Paddy Byrne quietly took on the task of finding a suitable location and briefing the Cook Sergeant Major on what culinary delights would be suitable for five hundred inebriated parachute soldiers. The RSM's suggestion of a barbed wire compound on the top of the Yorkshire Moors as the perfect venue was to the point, but not considered to be very helpful by a resigned QM who had himself decided that a red hot chicken curry was the easiest solution to the evening's food problem. Meanwhile I had contacted my opposite number in the 3rd Battalion in Aldershot for some music and he had very quickly organised the support of their dance band, led by the Band Sergeant whose glamorous wife was their singer.

The venue that was finally selected wasn't far off the RSM's original suggestion. Fenham Barracks, on the edge of Town Moor in Newcastle, was a rambling monument to the worst of pre-Victorian military architecture – a parachute battalion equipped to war establishment would have been pushed to have made a dent in its appeal and it had the marvellous advantage of having been disused for over a year – a certain amount of damage might therefore go unnoticed. Bounty Night itself was on a bitterly cold Saturday towards the end of October. In the late afternoon Newcastle was grey and cheerless as the trucks arrived on the square from five company locations. Echoes of numerous shouted words of command reverberated around the red-brick walls as the toms were directed to their allocated floor space for the night – the place was devoid of any furniture apart from a few tables, 6ft, GS (general service), transported up by the QM for the curry. By the end of the afternoon the actual bounty pay-off had taken place and the Battalion had dispersed into Newcastle with fat wallets and impressive thirsts. Fenham Barracks was now deserted once more with the exception of the 3 PARA dance band setting up its equipment at the far end of the old cookhouse building, the cook Sergeant Major stirring his vicious-smelling curry and the CO, QM, Adjutant and RSM all nursing private thoughts of impending doom. We didn't have long to wait. The realisation that our worst fears were justified dawned slowly. The first to enter the cookhouse soon after 9pm were three nurses from the local hospital – the only response to hundreds of invitations that had been sent to the female population of Tyneside by our Gateshead Company. Obviously the images of a Parachute Battalion invading the district to sample the fortifying effects of Newcastle Brown ale were enough to deter all but the brave trio who had just entered the building. The RSM welcomed them with all the charm of a caged orangutang as they took in their surroundings with eyes standing out like the proverbial chapel hat pegs. They were each given a drink which they sipped suspiciously as the 3 PARA dance band launched themselves into their first number.

Memories of my first All Ranks Dance in the Regiment came flooding back. All the officers, wisely minus our ladies, were resplendent in mess kit looking on while the toms, in various stages of drunkenness, took the opportunity to verbally give their superiors the wisdom of their military experience. One of them was goading a colleague, Mike, who was an outstanding swimmer with an impressively athletic figure, 'Whass the size of your chess, Sir?' Mike rose to the bait. 'Forty-nine inches – what's yours?' 'A large brandy!' was the triumphant reply.

I was less fortunate. One of my savages placed a hand firmly on my shoulder and, hanging on grimly, tried desperately to focus his eyes on mine. He failed dismally and ended up addressing my bow tie. 'Jer know, Sir, you're the best fookin' platoon commander I ever 'ad!' Whereupon he proved it by dramatically and violently throwing up all over the maroon and scarlet jacket of my mess kit. I was determined that my No. 2 dress shouldn't suffer a similar fate at Fenham Barracks. I was on edge when the first of the soldiers staggered in at half-past closing time. The three nurses, who had been dancing together in the middle of the floor, huddled nervously closer to each other. The curry was the first priority for the returning revellers and it was consumed with piranha-like efficiency with plastic forks from paper plates. The logic behind the latter detail was to dispense with any washing-up – reasonable in theory but, in practice, plastic forks, paper plates and chicken curry remnants were simply discarded on the floor. The QM, bless him, managed unseen to smuggle the three nurses from the building with their honour intact and, when he told me that this mission was accomplished, I mentally crossed one problem area off my list. By 1am the cookhouse defied description. The floor was a carpet of paper plates, plastic forks and broken bottles all tastefully swimming in curried chicken remnants and rice. The band played on valiantly with its glamorous vocalist singing her heart out in an effort to ignore the appalling scene around her. A few of the soldiers were dancing with no one in particular while others had simply slid down the wall and were sleeping in the debris. The majority were drinking and arguing seriously. Colonel David viewed the whole disastrous scene with fatherly benevolence and good humour and, perhaps, with sad thoughts of his impending departure to take up some soul-destroying staff job. I knew he'd miss the Battalion – the toms were in a deplorable state on this ill-conceived Bounty Night, but he adored them all in spite of it. I had no such thoughts. I was desperately trying to work out how this appalling shambles could be brought to an end without provoking a riot. Then it happened.

It was totally unexpected and its effect dramatic. A curried chicken carcass went whistling through the air and, horror of horrors, it hit the Band Sergeant's wife full in the chest. She uttered a strangled cry and the band stopped playing instantaneously. It all suddenly went deathly quiet. All eyes were on the now not-so-glamorous singer as the curry juice trickled down her ample cleavage and the tears, blackened by mascara, ran uncontrollably down her cheeks. I struggled to get to the band – the foul aftermath on the floor had become an evil-smelling skating rink. I finally made it and suggested to the Band Sergeant they should start playing again. 'You've got to be bloody joking, Sir,' he shouted angrily, 'look at my wife.' Poor girl – she was a real mess. Then I also got angry. It was disgraceful and I could only apologise. The band had been the only redeeming feature of the entire debacle. But its leader was understandably in no mood to accept my apology and the band started to pack up their equipment with grim resignation. Meanwhile the survivors of the revelry were either snoring against the walls or were filtering out through the doors. It was all over.

The following morning the Battalion was due to be on parade to be addressed by the Commanding Officer. It was to be the last occasion he would see them all together before his departure. As soon as I'd packed up my kit I sought out the Regimental Sergeant Major – I was still furious about the flying chicken, particularly as I knew that I'd have to write a formal letter of apology to my opposite number in 3 PARA. I was determined that justice should be done. 'Mr Bell, last night was a bloody disgrace – I want you to find out who threw the chicken before this morning's parade.'

'Right away, Sir.' He replied and strode off to find the culprit. Considering the state in which they'd ended the previous night, the Battalion didn't look too bad on parade that crisp, bright morning, though one or two were blinking uncontrollably in the weak winter sunshine. The Regimental Sergeant Major crashed to a halt in front of me – his salute was impressive. 'The Battalion is formed up – there are four hundred and seventy-six men on parade… SIR!'

'Thank you Mr Bell,' and, so that the toms couldn't hear, 'who threw the bloody chicken?'

'I've made intensive investigations, Sir,' he said, 'and I've had nae luck so far.'

There was nothing more to be said at that moment, but I was not going to leave it at that. I then handed over the parade to Colonel David. "4 PARA is formed up and ready for your inspection, Sir. There are four hundred and seventy-six men on parade.' I wondered if he remembered the drill competition of five years ago.

'Thank you, Adj,' he replied, 'I won't ask you to count them!' Of course he bloody remembered. Anyway he said all the right things to the assembled Battalion and they were finally dismissed to face their respective truck rides back to their various company locations. I suppose it could have all been very much worse, but, over the next few days, I continued in my quest to identify the chicken thrower – without success. The following week I received a terse note of acknowledgement to my apology from my opposite number in 3 PARA and later that morning there was a knock on my office door. It was John Fargin, the RQMS. We concluded our business and he made for the door. 'Just one more thing, RQ.' I said, and he stopped with his hand on the handle.

'Yes Sir?'

'Who threw the bloody chicken?' It was a shot in the dark, but there wasn't much that went on in the Battalion that he didn't know about. He stiffened perceptibly and I knew I was on target.

'I'm sorry, Sir, I can't say.'

'Come on RQ, don't be so bloody silly – of course you can say.'

He looked nervously around the room as if it was bugged. 'I'd rather not,' he replied.

But I had to know – it was becoming obsessive. 'OK,' I suggested, 'it'll be between the two of us and that'll be the end of the matter, I promise you – now who was it?'

He took a deep breath. 'Well, Sir,' he said, with a wicked grin, 'it was the Regimental Sergeant Major!'

David handed over to his successor soon afterwards and I was saddened at his departure – as far as I was concerned he would be a tough act to follow, and so it was to prove. I didn't have an easy time with the new CO 4 PARA – but that made my departure from the Battalion and the Army more bearable – best to leave it at that! The difficult part was disbanding the Ravens as no one could be found to take over from me – the *Yorkshire Evening Post* published an appreciative 'obituary' which in part recorded: 'They have earned a reputation for not letting the public down.' I settled for that! The Ravens' final display was at the request of the Sergeants' Mess who asked me if I could do a Father Christmas jump for the kid's Christmas tea party on December 19. Having agreed, I discovered that the Father Christmas outfit they'd acquired didn't include a beard, so I raided the MI room for a huge wad of cotton wool and the Orderly Room for a pot of Gloy glue to stick a phoney cotton-wool beard on to my face. I planned to jump from the Yorkshire Aeroplane Club Cessna 172 which was in parachuting mode and was thus minus the starboard door. By the time we'd flown the ten minutes from the airport to overhead Thornbury Barracks my beard had been blown asunder and had been transformed into a swirling cotton wool blizzard around the 172's cabin. I landed close to

C S-S as Adjutant, 4 PARA (V)   Letter from General Tubby Butler

where the kids were gathered, but sadly I think they were underwhelmed by the Father Christmas who stood before them adorned with grubby stubble instead of the customary bushy white whiskers. I'm sure my 'Ho, ho, ho' was not very convincing!

In January 1971 just before I left the Army and 4 PARA (V) I received a charming letter from Lt-Gen Sir Mervyn (Tubby) Butler KCB CBE DSO MC, one of the Regiment's characters and its Colonel Commandant. In it he wrote: 'Now that you are leaving the Regular Army I am writing to thank you for your services during your eight years in the Regiment, particularly your contribution to Free Falling in the Regiment as a whole and for the great success of the Ravens in the North of England.' It's treasured!

CHAPTER 13
GRINDALE FIELD

Ray Etchell was a talented sport parachutist and one of my chums at Thruxton in the 1960s until he was tragically killed in a car crash early in 1968. He had been a soldier in the Regiment until he transferred into the Army Catering Corps and, during the time I was regularly parachuting with him, he was a WOII running the 2 PARA cookhouse in 16 Parachute Brigade. I tackled him one day about why in heaven's name had he transferred from the Regiment to the ACC? He put me firmly in my place. 'During my time in the Catering Corps I've gained a number of useful qualifications in catering and hotel management which will set me up a treat when I finally leave the Army,' he informed me. 'What are you qualified to do when you leave – apart from being able to shoot people??' Fair comment! As I was about to leave the Army, Ray's wise words came to mind. Indeed, what qualifications had I got? A BPA Advanced Instructor/Examiner Rating, which was a result of 655 sport parachute jumps – 319 during my time in 4 PARA, together with one solitary military static line jump made during the same period. I never had any taste for military static line jumping, especially as I had experienced two interesting entanglements out of my grand total of thirty-four 7s/6d a day-type jumps – it was, quite simply, bloody dangerous – and probably still is. Military parachute pay has always been well earned. And as for my flying experience it was embarrassingly meagre – a private pilot's licence with only thirty-two hours 'in command' out of a total of fifty-eight. In spite of all this I had now committed myself to leaving the Army to start a business running an airfield and a full-time sport parachute centre. And now, after nearly fifty years, I must confess that at the time I didn't think of Sarah, my wife, and my two young children, Patrick and Lucy, nearly as much as I should have done – this confession and associated unreserved apologies are long overdue.

During the previous year a small sport parachuting operation had been established by Mal Read on a grass airstrip adjoining Flamingo Park zoo near Pickering in Yorkshire and, when we weren't jumping into the playing fields behind Thornbury Barracks, Flamingo Park provided a convenient alternative, even if some of the larger, open-topped animal enclosures had received unwelcome parachuting visitors on a couple of occasions. Mal and I briefly considered a joint full-time operation at Flamingo Park, but its proximity to the zoo and the rough one-directional airstrip made it far from ideal. Then two larger-than-life Scouse characters appeared on my radar. Bobby Francis and Ronnie O'Brien had both been in the Liverpool company of 4 PARA's predecessors, 12/13 PARA, and were both experienced sport parachutists. On learning of my plans they quickly expressed an interest in being involved. At the same time Iain McDonald, a recently qualified commercial pilot, had heard of a farmer and aviation enthusiast living in Grindale, a small hamlet inland from Flamborough Head. Watson Stuart, the farmer, had recently created a pristine grass airstrip on his land that might be suitable for the pleasure flying operation he was planning to establish. At fifty-five acres perhaps it might also be suitable for a sport parachuting operation? The farmer proved to be a delightful Yorkshireman and a real 'solid citizen', who was planning on learning to fly using his own airstrip if possible. Watson's brother-in-law, Des Stephens, was another splendid local farmer, who was already an experienced aviator having been a press-on wartime RAF Lancaster pilot. He was proud to have recorded substantially more night flying hours than daytime in his logbook thanks to all the operational flying he had achieved in Bomber Command.

Bobby, Ronnie, Iain and I, motivated more by unbridled enthusiasm than by carefully planned business approach, decided to set up a joint operation as a partnership on the newly christened Grindale Field, subject to approval from Watson Stuart, with whom we were able to negotiate a twenty-one-year lease. The wonderful support and encouragement we received from Watson, his lovely wife Joyce and their two vivacious teenage daughters, Jane and Debbie, were just what we needed in those early days. So it was all systems go, and we were in business as the Sport Parachute Centre with a leased Cessna 172 G-ARAV as our 'jump ship'. On February 7, 1971, Iain flew G-ARAV into our new base where Bobby, Ronnie and I swiftly removed its starboard door and emplaned to climb to 5,000ft to make the first official jump on to Grindale Field. Having landed, I changed seats with Iain and flew my first circuit and landing in G-ARAV. The following day Iain checked me out as a jump pilot – I had a derisory total of thirty-four hours' time as 'pilot-in-command'! Determined to rectify the situation and, taking advantage of a lengthy spell of decent weather, I flew another forty-two hours and made another forty-four jumps between then and the end of April.

Inevitably our operation attracted considerable local interest as headlines in the *Bridlington Free Press* of January 29, 1971, announced: 'Skydivers plan big thrills future for Country Airfield', and the *Yorkshire Times* of February 12 shrieked: 'East Riding "spacemen" fall for fun', both which may have prompted two experienced pilots to contact us. Chris Jackson was a dairy farmer in nearby Lebberston who had flown in the Royal Navy during his national service, while John Medforth, a heavy plant engineer, was building his own aircraft – a tiny Volkswagen-engined single-seat Taylor Monoplane. Both flew for us regularly and both became lifelong friends. One evening John and I were having a beer in the Timoneer, our 'local', on Flamborough Head, when John discreetly pointed out a cheerful, ruddy-faced character seated at the other end of the bar. 'Do you know who that is?' John asked quietly, and I had to admit I had no idea. 'It's Jim Lacey.' He said, but the penny only dropped partially. 'Not Ginger Lacey?' I suggested, before John took me over to introduce me to this legendary Second World War fighter pilot who had retired from the RAF in 1967 as a Squadron Leader and was now living near Flamborough Head. He is probably best remembered as having successfully shot down twenty-eight enemy aircraft during the war of which eighteen were accounted for during the Battle of Britain, making him the top scorer during the period of the battle, July 10-October 31, and during which he was also awarded the DFM twice. He also achieved fame for shooting down the Heinkel 111, which bombed Buckingham Palace on September 13, 1940, and to mark this victory the Irvin Air Chute Company of Australia presented Jim with his own personal parachute and it became a much-treasured trophy.

Jim having been presented with his own parachute by the Irvin Air Chute Company of Australia

In addition to his being an outstanding pilot and, as Jim was such a great character, it was inevitable that we would persuade him to get back into flying as one of our jump pilots. When our club members discovered that they had been flown to altitude by a Battle of Britain ace they were quick to ask Jim to sign the jump in their logbooks as indeed he did for me. One day he arrived at the airfield with the parachute presented to him by the Irvin Air Chute Company of Australia and asked me if I'd like to make a jump with it as it had never been used. I told Jim that I'd be privileged to but, as it hadn't been repacked in the thirty years Jim had owned it, we stretched it out on one of the packing tables to check and repack it. We immediately discovered that the canopy was made of silk and, while it probably would have opened satisfactorily, it almost certainly would have sustained unacceptable damage because of the inevitable deterioration of the silk canopy material during the thirty years since its manufacture. I explained all this to Jim before we carefully repacked his historic parachute. Sometime later Jim gave me a copy of the iconic photograph that accompanies these words. A favourite Jim Lacey story was from the time in 1968 when he was a technical adviser during the filming at Duxford of the acclaimed film, *The Battle of Britain*. The famous German fighter pilot, Adolf Galland, was also there as an adviser. When he was introduced to Jim he said: 'Ah, Squadron Leader, I am sure zat ve met during ze Battle of Britain.' Jim's instant response was a winner: 'Highly unlikely, I'd have shot you down!'

During 1969 I had been approached by publishers A&C Black, who asked me if I'd be prepared to write a textbook about sport parachuting. I agreed and in March 1971 *Sport Parachuting* was finally published; the only reason I mention it in these pages is that it gives me the opportunity to pay tribute to Major General Dare Wilson CBE MC who kindly gave me every encouragement during my writing of the book before he himself penned an erudite, perceptive foreword to it. In 1960, having served right through the war, Palestine and Korea, Dare was appointed to command 22 SAS where he was introduced to freefall parachuting. The sport quickly benefited from his energy, enthusiasm and managerial skills. It was while he commanded 22 SAS that he wrote a paper for Brigadier Michael Forrester, the Commander of 16 Parachute Brigade, suggesting the formation of the Army Parachute Association, an organisation that still thrives more than half a century later. Having handed over command of 22 SAS in 1962 he was elected the second Chairman of the British Parachute Association and, during his four years in office, he was largely responsible for having parachuting officially recognised as a sport and drafting the original BPA parachuting regulations. He retained an active interest in the sport until he died in 2014 aged ninety-five. We owe him much. His autobiography, *Tempting the Fates*, is a fascinating read.

The most important thing at this time was that almost immediately we started doing a satisfactory amount of business training ab-initio sport parachute students and it was also encouraging to note that more and more ladies were taking up the sport. It was in March 1971 that Jackie Smith made her first parachute jump at Netheravon and in 1978 she became our first World Ladies Parachute Champion – she will appear in these pages again. Meanwhile Jane, Watson and Joyce's elder daughter, made her first, second and third jumps at Grindale on her seventeenth birthday – as can be imagined, this gained us plenty of positive publicity. Another lady who started at much the same time was Les Pilmoor, another local farmer's daughter. Les progressed quickly until her twenty-first jump when, at the end of a fifteen-second delay, she had a stiff ripcord pull. Unable

The first BPA-approved instructors' course. Back: John Williams, Gerry McCauley, John Boxall, Stu Cook, Ray Perkins, Tony Rose, Alistair McMillan, Bob Burn. Front: John Norris, Mike Taylor, Bob Francis, C S-S, Iain McDonald (pilot), Ronnie O'Brien, Tracey Rixon, Dave Bennett

therefore to open her main parachute, she coolly and successfully activated her reserve and landed safely just off the airfield, albeit sustaining a couple of crushed vertebrae. She made a full recovery and now, after nearly fifty years, she has two grown-up daughters, and I remain good friends with her and her husband, Richard. It was in 1971 that the British Parachute Association introduced the concept of week-long residential instructors' courses and we held the first approved one approved by the BPA at Grindale. It was good to have a lady on that first course and that it was Tracy Rixon, a well-respected and experienced parachutist.

During the parachuting their led to the building of the first British eight-man star over Dunkeswell in 1970, we had established an excellent relationship with South West Aviation, which operated the Skyvan we used. In May, Norman Gould and Tony Gover, two splendid ex-Army Air Corps pilots, flew the Skyvan to Grindale for a week of big aircraft jumping. The weather was especially kind and during the nine days I managed thirty-seven jumps from 12,500 ft, with, disappointingly, our group's best performance only being six seven-man non-stars! On July 13, when we were back to just using the

Skyvan Week, Grindale Field, May 1971: Steve Marrozeki, John Middleton, Clive Rumney, C S-S, Sally Cain, Buzz Bennett, Jim Crocker and John Shankland

172, the weather didn't clear for jumping until early afternoon. I was on the first load following a student parachutist out from 7,000ft before I climbed into the pilot's seat to take over the jump flying. After only one load I taxied in to refuel. The duty instructor was Frankie Peel, an endearing Yorkshireman and one of nature's walking disaster areas. As I climbed out of the 172 Frankie appeared and kindly offered to do the refuelling, suggesting I took the opportunity to grab a quick coffee. The next load was ready to go by the time Frankie had finished the refuelling and consisted of Maureen Denley, who was due to make a static line descent from 2,500ft and was to be dispatched by Mike Taylor, an instructor who was working with us during his summer break from studying for his

Master's degree at the London School of Economics, and Clive Rumney, a teacher and very experienced visiting Australian jumper. Mike briefed me that once Maureen had made her jump, I was to climb to 7,000ft to drop him and Clive. Passing about 300ft in the climb I became aware that the 172 was losing power so I started a gentle turn to head back towards the airfield. I tried activating the carburettor heater – it just made matters worse. By now we had reached 450ft and the rev counter told me that the engine was losing power as it was now only giving me 2,000rpm instead of the required 2,500rpm. It was startlingly obvious that we weren't going to gain any more height and that from where we were it was unlikely that G-ARAV would get us back to the airfield. I had to lighten the load – and quickly. 'GET OUT!' I shouted. Mike ordered Maureen out and she, totally unaware of the emergency, coolly stepped on to the wheel ready for a student exit. 'GO!' bellowed Mike, whereupon Maureen threw herself back off the wheel. 'ONE THOUSAND, TWO THOUSAND, THREE THOUSAND, CHECK CANOPY…' She screamed as she disappeared under her deploying canopy in the slipstream. Mike remembers: 'I saw her main deploy, and, without pulling in the static line, I shouted to Clive, "Reserve!" I stepped out on to the step, looked aft at the tail, let go and pulled my reserve. I remember seeing the canopy deploy almost horizontally. I made a couple of swings under the fully inflated canopy, reached for the risers and landed. Clive landed just a little distance away. Interestingly, I was able to pick up my reserve kicker plate, which landed about 30 yards from me.' All three jumpers landed safely a few seconds later, albeit off the airfield. Alpha Victor and I, lightened of our parachutist load, now looked like we might have a chance of making the runway, in spite of the prop. finally stopping as we passed through 150ft, we came safely to a stop at the intersection of the two runways. I glanced down at my hands – they were shaking like a leaf. But the grass was especially green and the sky was especially blue. Even the birds stopped singing!

Then Frankie Peel appeared on the scene. 'Er, Charlie,' he started sheepishly, 'I think I might have used the wrong fuel.'

'WHAT?!' I shrieked, 'which barrels did you use?'

The awful truth was to be revealed as he confessed to using the fuel from the black and white barrels (Avtur), turbine fuel, which we'd been using for the Skyvan, whereas he should have used that from the green and red barrels (Avgas) for the piston-engined aircraft. I then realised to my shame that, as the pilot-in-command, it was my responsibility to ensure that correct fuel was in the tanks. A lesson well learned! Just over a year later Mike and I and twelve others were involved in a jump over Halfpenny Green airfield which went dramatically and very nearly fatally wrong – but that's a story for the next chapter!

A flying training facility was part of our plans for Grindale so I reckoned a flying instructor's rating was my next goal for which, to start the course, I needed an Instrument Meteorological Conditions (IMC) Rating and 150 hours' command time. I decided to undertake the ten-hour IMC course at Blackpool with old friends Keith Whyham and John Sudbury at ANT. Again the weather was kind and I managed the whole ten-hour course, which included a successful test with Keith, in the two days, July 19-20 – phew! Hopefully I could achieve enough flying to start my flying instructor's course by the end of the year.

In the meantime, Jim Crocker became the leader of our parachuting relative work group, affectionately known as the 'Hard-Ass Star Team' and whose aim was to put together the first British Ten Man star. Jim's energy and enthusiasm drove us relentlessly towards achieving our goal. We achieved the ten-man over Halfpenny Green from the Skyvan over the

The first British ten-man star. Back: Bob Higgins (11), John Middleton, Clive Rumney, Norman Gould (pilot), Steve Talbert, Sally Cain, Steve Marrozeki, C S-S. Front: Pete Gruber, Lou Johnson (camera), John Shankland, Jim Crocker, Mike Bolton

Lou Johnson records a Hard Ass Star Team eleven-man star over Dunkeswell, October 23, 1971

weekend of August 29-30 and numerous nine, ten and eleven-man stars during twenty-nine jumps from the Skyvan over Dunkeswell during two weekends in October.

By the end of the month I had enough P1 hours in my flying logbook to start my flying instructor's course. I chose the Yorkshire Aeroplane Club and was very fortunate to have been taught on the course by the CFI, Arthur Carvell. Arthur was a delightfully warm personality and a fantastic instructor, the latter as a result of his vast and varied flying experience. He had gained his RAF wings in 1939 and flew operational tours on Whitleys, Battles and Blenheims before being shot down in 1941, spending the rest of the war as a POW. After the war he instructed at Desford before leaving the RAF in 1953. Thereafter he became CFI of the Yorkshire Aeroplane Club. My first sortie of the course was Effects of Controls Pt 1 which I flew with Arthur on November 1, and between then and Christmas I flew a further nine-and-a-half hours with him. He was an absolute delight to fly with, meticulously demonstrating every detail of each exercise before cheerfully encouraging his luckless student to produce a similar performance. I have to admit to having picked up some sloppy flying habits since I had gained my pilot's license twelve months previously, but Arthur tidied up my flying with infinite patience and good humour, for which I'll always be grateful.

On Boxing Day I took off in the dark from Grindale at 5.30am in the Cessna 150 we'd leased as our training aircraft to fly south to Netheravon for a flying visit to see my mum and dad. I climbed through solid cloud to discover bright moonlight on top at 5,000ft. It took me thirty minutes to fly the thirty nautical miles to overhead my first reporting point at Ottringham – so with a ground speed of 60kts it was going to be a long flight! I soon established radio communication RAF Waddington – the duty controller obviously didn't appreciate being dragged from his slumbers at 6am, but in spite of this he couldn't have been more helpful, quickly identifying me on radar to monitor my progress southwards. After a couple of hours it became depressingly obvious that I shouldn't have had such a large mug of tea before I took off – I was busting for a pee but there was no suitable receptacle to be found. But I did have a torch and I discovered that by unscrewing the bulb end and removing the batteries, I had a sort of pee pot substitute! Of course once I'd filled it I had to empty it and I should have anticipated the result – I opened the window and the prop wash blew the contents of the torch straight back into the cabin and soaked me! The rest of the flight was incident-free. London Flight Information established what the weather was on the ground at Netheravon and RAF Lyneham kindly agreed that I could divert to land there, which I did following a precision radar approach and three hours, ten minutes in the air. And I hadn't seen the ground from start to finish.

It wasn't until the middle of February 1972 that I was able to resume my flying instructor's course and to enjoy three more sorties with Arthur. These were sadly the last I flew with him as the following month he suffered a debilitating stroke that robbed him of his speech. He was a much-loved character and his having to stand down as CFI was a bitter blow. I feel privileged to have learnt from him. That he was an instructor who had few equals is exemplified by the instruction he must have given his son Dudley who had a sparkling flying career in the RAF in which he flew for three years with the Red Arrows, was the Harrier display pilot and during which time he was awarded both a Queen's Commendation for the Air and an Air Force Cross. Alex Webster, another ex-RAF pilot, now became the CFI and inevitably there was a bureaucratic delay before he could assume the responsibility of running flying instructor courses, which he did in late April. Between then and when I finally passed my FIC test with Les Rackham on July 2, I had flown fourteen sorties (eleven hours) on my instructor's course with Alex, whom I didn't find as relaxed and as approachable as Arthur, but I finally had my flying instructor's rating and this led to my flying instructing for the next 41 years!

By the time I returned to Grindale having successfully completed the course, I discovered that Iain had been up to some skulduggery in an effort to form a limited company from the partnership and for his sole benefit. The only legal expert I knew and trusted was my parachuting chum Jim Crocker. From humble origins in the East End of London, Jim, with his razor-sharp mind and boundless energy, was making his mark in the legal profession so I phoned him for his advice. A meeting was set up for the following day and I had to borrow an aeroplane so that I could fly to Birmingham and collect Jim as it would have taken him too long to drive. Iain was represented by Mrs Wellit (not her real name), an imposing-looking country solicitor who was kitted out from head to toe in heavy tweed. Jim was also an impressive-looking individual, so it promised to be an interesting contest. Jim was introduced to Mrs Wellit and his opening line was a showstopper: 'Hullo, Mrs Wellit,' he said in the broadest Cockney accent he could muster, 'fancy a leg-over?' Mrs Wellit was, quite literally, struck dumb. Obviously nobody had ever spoken to her like it before. She simply had no idea what Jim was going to come up with next, which was, I'm sure, exactly what he intended. From that moment onwards Jim dominated the meeting, with the result that Iain was forced to buy out my share of the partnership and pay Jim's fee. Thus I finished my eighteen months at Grindale having made 306 more jumps, flown 190 more command flying hours, and gained a flying instructor's rating – but now out of a job!

CHAPTER 14
THOSE WHO CAN, DO – THOSE WHO CAN'T, TEACH

On June 23, 1972, the day after Jim's successful confrontation with Mrs Wellit, I flew him from Leeds back to Birmingham in a Yorkshire Aeroplane Club Cessna 172, and I subsequently arrived back at Leeds just before midday. During the return flight I decided to ask CFI Alex or his deputy CFI, John Fenton, if they might be prepared to offer me some work at the club as a part-time flying instructor while I sorted myself out. As I checked in on my return John appeared and asked if I could spare him a few minutes. Once in his office he announced that, because of Arthur Carvell being permanently grounded, the club had a vacancy for a full-time flying instructor and would I be interested in the job? This offer and its timing were almost too good to be true – of course I was interested! He went on to explain that, as the club had no shortage of part-time instructors at weekends, my job would essentially be from Monday to Friday – this made it even more appealing as it meant that I could continue jumping with Jim and the team on Saturdays and Sundays. I accepted immediately and it resulted in my enjoying three splendidly fulfilling years – I started the job three weeks later, during which time I'd sold my house in Bridlington and, having obtained the necessary mortgage, purchased similar in Leeds into which I moved with my loyal, devoted companion, Boomerang, a Jack Russell/Doberman cross who had come from Les Pilmoor's dad's farm in Hunmanby. Meanwhile, my wife had taken Patrick and Lucy to stay with her mother and in due course, very sadly, this became a permanent arrangement.

My colleagues at the club were a delightful and experienced bunch of aviators who were amazingly supportive in spite of my only having held a flying instructor's rating for less than a month. Deputy CFI John Fenton became a staunch friend. We quickly discovered that we had Uppingham and the Army in common – John had been in Intake 1A at Sandhurst in 1947, before being commissioned into the Royal Tank Regiment with whom he had served in Korea. He left the Army in 1953. After seventeen years with BBA, the family business in Cleckheaton, John, who had gained a flying instructor's rating in 1966, left to become, with Alex Webster, a director of the Yorkshire Aeroplane Club. John was a fascinating, larger-than-life character for whom there were never enough hours in the day to allow him to indulge in all his enthusiasms. He was a first-class instructor to those who really wanted to learn, but he was intolerant of indolence and pomposity and of those who failed to make the most of their god-given talents. He was an inspirational boss. The part-time instructors had all flown in the military. 'Bodger' Davies, a British Airways captain, had flown Sabres in the RAF; Dr Clive Hayter, a professor of physics at Leeds University, had flown Mosquitoes in the Far East; Steve Lerche, an independent flying instructor, had flown Hurricanes in the Western Desert; Stan Greaves, a local insurance broker, had been shot down flying a Wellington during the war and found himself incarcerated in the same POW camp as Arthur Carvell; while Dr Tony Glover, who'd flown in the Fleet Air Arm and had shot down a Japanese Zero in the Pacific, was our local CAA-approved doctor. John briefed me before my first visit to Tony to renew my flying medical: 'As you're one of our instructors, Tony won't charge you, so take a bottle of whisky with you to give him as payment for your renewal after which you'll be expected to stay to down a couple of tots with him!' And so it came to pass!

The weekend before I started at the club I drove to Halfpenny Green airfield for a weekend's relative work parachuting with the Hard-Ass Star Team. Saturday, July 15, provided perfect weather and the jump in question was my third of the day. The one before had been a work-up jump from the visiting Islander which had arrived earlier from Stapleford so that it could fly in formation with DH89A Rapide G-AHAG. The aim of the jump was to attempt to build a fourteen-man star from 10,000ft with six of us to exit the slower Rapide momentarily first, while the remaining eight of us were to exit the formating Islander simultaneously to fly across to the first six who would hopefully build a firm six-man star base. Jim briefed the Islander pilot to formate echelon starboard to the Rapide at the same level about twenty-five yards away and about ten yards behind. The Islander pilot was unknown to us but he arrogantly assured us that he'd done plenty of formation flying so it'd all be no problem – with the benefit of hindsight, perhaps, that was when the alarm bells should have started to ring – but they didn't. The climb of the two aircraft to jump altitude was normal. I was to be fourth out of the Islander with Sally Cain, Mike Taylor, Mike Bolton and a visiting American, Doc Goodman, behind me. On the run in over the airfield to drop I glanced across at the Rapide as its first jumper was climbing out on to the wing, at which time, relative to us, it started to lose height. As we in the Islander started to move back down the fuselage towards the open door space, I ignored the Rapide and tried to concentrate on keeping as close to whoever it was immediately in front of me. Seconds later, 'READEEEE… SEEEETTT… GO!'

We dived out into the slipstream. Instantly there was something solid a few feet below me – instinctively I curled up and missed it – whatever it was. Sally reacted similarly and also missed whatever it was by a whisker. The result was an eight-man star but there were people missing. Hanging under my open Para-Commander I only counted ten other canopies – where were the missing three? Was it the Rapide that Sally and I nearly hit? Clearly something was not right. Jim and I landed not too far from each other so I shrugged off my parachutes and ran across to him and blurted out what I'd seen – at this stage those in the Rapide were unaware that anything had gone wrong. Initially Jim and I were only able to account for eleven of us until we spotted a lone canopy way up high. We were still two adrift. We then witnessed the Rapide coming in to land with fabric fluttering from the top of its fuselage. We got to the Rapide just as the engines were shut down. In those days we all wore French Paraboots that had thick soles and elasticised laces, the latter which were expensive to replace – if an ankle injury occurred on landing it was easiest to cut the laces to remove the jumper's boots. We found Mike, who was seventh out of the Islander, lying on the floor of the Rapide, with two broken wrists and a cracked pelvis caused by his crashing through the fuselage roof. He must, understandably, have been badly shaken – all he could say was: 'Don't cut me fucking boots off!' He later recorded: 'As I came out of the door I just saw the thing there and couldn't do much about it. I put my hands up to protect my face and crashed through the wood and fabric roof, and landed inside. My legs were through the door. Instinctively I decided to clamber back inside the aircraft and stay with it. The pilot looked round and wondered what on earth had gone on. I put my thumbs up to indicate to him that I was reasonably OK, and he proceeded to land.'

DH 89A Rapide G-AHAG after the incident – the potentially lethal radio aerial is clearly visible!

Meanwhile, the Islander had landed and jumper number fourteen, Doc Goodman, climbed out having decided not to jump as he'd seen that the Islander was losing its formation position as the Rapide was drifting across below. He had tried to stop Mike from jumping but he was already on his way. Mike Taylor's jump was equally dramatic. He exited the Islander immediately behind Sally before straddling the Rapide just in front of the tail plane and actually riding it for a few moments. Mike later wrote:

> *Everything happened extremely quickly. I just remember hitting the roof of the Rapide and automatically hanging on. My left leg had been broken at the femur, tibia and fibula on the edge of the roof. I just remember lying on the roof, facing forward with my arms outstretched, holding on. There were bits of fabric flying around from the hole I made and the hole that Mike Bolton made (although I didn't realise at the time that Mike had plunged through the roof into the aircraft). Between the two holes was the stiletto-like radio aerial which thankfully we didn't hit – had either of us done so we'd have been skewered.*

I distinctly remember thinking, 'well, I can't stay here,' and looking behind me seeing how close the tail plane was. I was wearing a chest-mounted reserve which luckily hadn't burst open on impact with the aircraft. The next thing I can recall is easing myself over the side and tucking myself into a ball thinking I was bound to hit the tail plane. Amazingly, I found myself in freefall and in one piece. I must have fallen to around 6,000ft when I felt myself feeling very dizzy and near to blacking out. I therefore deployed my PC, which opened perfectly.

His landing two miles away in a corn field with a smashed femur and broken tibia and fibula must have been horrendous. It didn't take us all long to appreciate that if the Islander had been about ten feet further forward relative to the Rapide at least five or six of us would have smashed horizontally across the Rapide's upper wing, which would have been catastrophic. The Islander pilot couldn't get away fast enough to return to Stapleford – of course he undoubtedly knew that he should have broken away as soon as he realised that he was unable to hold formation with the Rapide, especially as the latter inevitably slowed as its jumpers exited. I wrote in my logbook: 'An eight-man bust by Nev waiting in slot. Just missed Rapide, Mike Bolton didn't and Mike Taylor bounced off it, a miraculous escape by the both of them.'

Even the birds stopped singing!

Mike Taylor had his left leg in traction for sixteen weeks and later, with one leg shorter than the other, he finally got back into parachuting. He continued jumping until 1979 when another nasty parachute landing forced his retirement. He subsequently wrote: 'Would I do it all again? Absolutely! Sport parachuting was the greatest, with the greatest people it has been my privilege to meet.' Mike Bolton made a full recovery, only hanging up his French Paraboots (with the laces still intact, no doubt) in 2015, having made well over 5,000 jumps. Well done him!

On my first day in my new job on the following Monday, my baptism of fire was eight instructional sorties totalling four hours and fifty-five minutes' flying time. As I was soon to discover, this was not unusual. I was immediately into an amazing routine averaging about forty hours a month of instructional flying and chalking up half a dozen jumps or more during most weekends. Flying instructing proved to be both challenging and rewarding. Of course there were a few students who had enough confidence and ability to finish the forty-hour course and gain their private pilots' licences with seemingly little effort, while there were also a few students who didn't find flying a light aircraft in the least bit easy, but they struggled on regardless. In the latter category was a delightful Yorkshireman, John Fothergill, whom I remember with great affection. He had absolutely no aptitude for flying, but he possessed a dogged determination to carry on. I really enjoyed flying with him, with the first challenge being to try to get him to relax – he tended to grip the controls vice-like as if his life depended on it and, as John Fenton suggested, he was probably the only pilot who managed to get both ailerons down at the same time – for the uninitiated, this is a mechanical impossibility! Most student pilots who learn to fly over many months will, on average, make their first solo flight having flown between ten and fifteen hours dual with an instructor. Dear John Fothergill took forty-seven hours to achieve this milestone. I was genuinely thrilled when he finally pulled off three acceptable landings in succession, but, to be doubly sure that he was safe enough to send him off on his solo, I took control of Cessna 150 G-ATHV – for some reason John's favourite 150 – and flew it on to final approach low with full flaps and plenty of power. 'You have control, John,' I said, while being prepared to unscramble any mess he might make of it. But surprisingly he didn't. He applied more power, sorted out the change of trim and eased the 150 up to the correct final approach flight path, after which he managed his fourth acceptable landing of the day. I called air traffic control: 'Leeds, Golf Hotel Victor, we're changing pilots – Mr Fothergill's first solo.' I briefed him to do one circuit and landing and, if he remembered, to pick me up afterwards. As I had got into the habit and before I shut the door I always said: 'And don't bend it!' I watched him line up and take off. A few minutes later I nervously I witnessed him turn Hotel Victor on to final approach – but I needn't have worried. He finished his circuit with a very reasonable landing – mercifully none of the dozens of students I've sent solo have ever put a mark on the aeroplane they've flown for this milestone flight. Later back in the clubhouse I congratulated him as I handed him his first solo certificate: 'Well done, John, next session we'll consolidate on the circuit with a go at cross-wind landings.'

'Nay lad,' he replied, 'that's it.'

'What do you mean – that's it?'

'All I ever wanted to do was to fly an aeroplane on me own – and now I've done it!' He thanked me profusely and shook my hand before walking out of the door and we never saw him again. He'd set himself a personal goal that he'd successfully achieved, but I have to say I missed the challenge of flying with him, and apart from that he was such a charming man.

But just occasionally the job wasn't so rewarding. One day a Rolls-Royce pulled up outside the club and a very large ruddy-faced man alighted together with a pimply stricken youth who, it transpired, was his son. I was on duty behind the counter in the flight office when they entered. He approached me and with a foghorn of a voice demanded: ''Ow mooch to teach lad 'ere to fly?' Having hastily multiplied the going hourly rate by forty, being the minimum number of hours needed to complete the course, I gave him a ballpark figure. He immediately produced a thick wad of notes to open an account before telling us to let him know when it needed topping up. Meanwhile the sad-looking son hovered despondently in the background and never said a word. A couple of days later I started flying with the young man in an attempt to teach him and this was difficult right from the start as his monosyllabic grunts lacked even the remotest vestige of enthusiasm. Perhaps my communication skills – or lack of them – were to blame. I sought advice from John Fenton who flew with the young man on his next lesson. John encountered a similar lack of feedback or effort from him. When I flew again with my reluctant student it was for Exercise 6 – straight and level flight. I demonstrated this to him by establishing the correct attitude, power and trim, after which I suggested: 'You have control.' But he made no attempt to do so. It wasn't any lack of confidence that was the problem, it was simply that he just wasn't interested. 'I have control,' I told him and I flew us back to the airfield. After landing I cleared the runway and pulled the mixture control knob out to shut down the engine. In the ensuing silence I turned to him and, seeking enlightenment, I asked: 'Do you want to learn to fly or not?' 'No, I don't really.' He was obviously close to tears. Back in the club I arranged for a cheque to be made out to his father for the amount he was still in credit, and, when he arrived to collect his son, I handed it over as I informed him that his son just wasn't interested in learning to fly. It was a sad, embarrassing moment and I couldn't help but feel sorry for the young man – but what an opportunity he'd missed. I was learning quickly that there was more to flying instructing than simply telling the student, 'pull for up and push for down.' In this context, George Bernard Shaw's maxim, 'Those who can, do – those who can't, teach,' springs to mind, but I'm convinced it doesn't apply to flying instruction. A reasonable amount of flying skill is required by the instructor if his demonstration of any exercise in the syllabus is to have any credibility. In the 1970s I was hugely fortunate in being able to instruct full time and be paid a reasonable salary for so doing while only holding a private pilot's licence. Most flying clubs paid their instructors a set amount for every instructional hour they flew – the problem with this arrangement was that the instructors in those clubs tended to get airborne even if the weather was not suitable for instructing. For instance, for the early exercises of effects of controls, straight and level and climbing and descending, it's important for the student to have a visible horizon as a datum. I was therefore delighted at my being employed as a salaried flying instructor by an organisation that recognised the importance of suitable weather for instruction.

Meanwhile, Jim had been on the hunt for a bigger aircraft for the Hard-Asses to jump from and had discovered Flight One, an aerial survey company based at Staverton near Gloucester, which was operating an ex-RAF Scottish Aviation Twin Pioneer that proved to be ideal as it could lift sixteen skydivers – as we were now being called – a descriptive Americanism that was replacing the term 'sport parachutist'. The first weekend of many using the 'Twin Pin' was at Halfpenny Green in early September when we managed eight jumps (skydives!) from 12,000ft. The third of these was my 1,000th jump and we put together a ten-man star. Having the Twin Pin regularly available enabled us to climb to 12,000ft every time and this certainly improved our performances – this was exemplified by a new British record, a star that twelve of us built on November 14. My logbook reveals that I made 126 skydives from the Twin Pin in the two years 1972/74, all from 12,000ft or more. It was a great aeroplane for the job, but what we didn't appreciate at the time was that Jim gave Flight One a charge over his house to give them a guaranteed number of flying hours – an amazingly generous gesture. Eventually Flight One's support of skydiving wound down as the company eventually decided it wasn't economically viable. While the Twin Pioneer operation was in full swing I discovered that John Fenton was cast in the same mould as David Callaghan, my CO in 4 PARA, when he enthusiastically approved of my idea of establishing the Yorkshire Aeroplane Club Sport Parachute Wing with a drop zone at Green Gaits Farm handily located less than half a mile north of the Leeds-Bradford Airport boundary. In turn YACSPW became the genesis of the Leeds Bradford Free Fall Club.

Lou Johnson took this photo of a nine-man star over Halfpenny Green on September 10, 1972. Clockwise from Dick Reiter in blue and yellow, John Shankland, Jim Crocker, Dave Waterman, Neville Hounsome, Sally Cain (breaking wrists), Steve Talbot, Buzz Bennett and C S-S

Bob (Biff) Burn exits the Twin Pioneer (photo by Pete Dickerson)

1973 was to prove to be an interesting year. For the second year I was elected to be vice-chairman of the Council of the BPA; I was selected to be the UK delegate to the Commission Internationale de Parachutisme (CIP) of the Federation Aeronautique Internationale (FAI) and I became editor of the BPA magazine, *Sport Parachutist*. Vice-chairman of the BPA was not a very demanding job, especially as Lawrie St John was a delightful man and an energetic chairman. Being the UK CIP delegate was a very different ballgame because for the most part the other nations' delegates were hugely experienced skydivers with whom it was always interesting and stimulating to share views and ideas about competition rules and regulations, the latter being our prime function. If they weren't experienced skydivers it soon became obvious. The US delegate at that time was Norm Heaton, an entertaining tobacco-chewing hillbilly from Oklahoma whose skydiving experience was somewhat limited. At one technical meeting he made a particularly crass suggestion whereupon three or four delegates quickly and firmly put him in the picture. He was sitting close to where there was a telephone in the corner of the room – he was aware that everyone was looking at him as he picked it up: 'Operator, gimme hell, everyone else is!' But he was always good fun, unlike one of the Scandinavian country's delegates who, we soon discovered, only had two static line jumps to his credit. This gentleman was blessed with no sense of humour and the skin of a rhinoceros as he could never understand why any technical suggestion he made was almost always ridiculed. As relative work was about to be adopted as a CIP/FAI competition discipline it was good to be involved at this level as a member of the relative work sub-committee of CIP from its inception – the other members were Eilif Ness (Norway), Bert Wijnands (Holland), Richard Charter (South Africa) and James F Curtis III (USA). We worked well together and we soon became staunch friends. For three years my dear chum John Meacock had been doing a great job editing the BPA magazine, but he found the job was not compatible with his ownership and operation of the thriving Peterborough Parachute Centre. I was to remain editor for the next eight years – the job was to prove very rewarding as I was communicating with so many interesting contributors from around the world.

Meanwhile, Jim had fixed up what proved to be the Hard-Ass Star Team's last outing by entering a European Ten Man Star Competition to be held in Innsbruck over three days in early March using a Twin Otter as the jump ship. Our principal rival was the German team, Walter's Vögel, led by a talented skydiver and pilot, Walter Eichhorn, whom I later encountered again in the display flying world when he regularly flew one of the few remaining ME 109s. Unfortunately the weather wasn't very co-operative with the result that we only managed two competition jumps. We only scored two nine-man stars but it was enough to beat Walter's Vögel, who finished just one point behind us. Two other vivid memories of the weekend remain. The first was witnessing skiers enjoying their sport at higher levels on the mountains on either side of us as we skydived past them into the Innsbruck valley. The second was an incident that could have had fatal consequences. It can easily be appreciated that plenty of lateral separation between skydivers before they deploy their parachutes is vitally important. This is achieved by each skydiver turning 180º before flying away for a few seconds before parachute deployment. At the end of one of our practice skydives, such separation between two of the team hadn't been achieved. As Neville, affectionately known as the 'Egg Man' (he was as bald as a coot), opened his parachute, Thommo, one of our reserves, plunged into Neville's deploying canopy. Neville literally had no idea what hit him as his main parachute, now resembling a bundle of washing with Thommo inside it, fell past him. Instinctively he pulled his reserve parachute handle as Thommo fought his way out. Having successfully extricated himself, Thommo deployed his main parachute normally and landed safely. Neville landed not far away under his reserve, still none the wiser as to what had occurred.

'Fuckin' 'ell, Thommo,' shouted the Egg Man, 'did you see that?'

'Fuckin' see it? – I was fuckin' in it!' was Thommo's swift response, which said it all!

The Hard Ass Star Team, winners of the European Ten Man Star Competition, Innsbruck 1973. Back: Jim Crocker, Jon (Willy) Williams, Dick Reiter, Sally Cain, Mike Chapman, C S-S. Front: Neville Hounsome, Dick Miskin, Pete Gruber, John Shankland

Back in the UK, Jim had met Arthur Haycox, who owned Endrust, a car rustproofing company, and whom he successfully persuaded to sponsor the team. From now on we became the Endrust Skydivers and our first outing in this guise was at the first British RW Nationals. This time it was our turn to get beaten by one point, so we missed out on being the British team at the first RW World Cup to be held later in the year at Fort Bragg in the USA. As someone pointed out at the time: 'Who was it who said, "Losers are important – without them there can be no winners?" Answer: a loser!' Thus we accepted being losers, but Jim, with encouragement from Arthur Haycox, pressed on with an alternative plan for the Endrust Skydivers to get to the USA – he entered us into the ten-man star 'Turkey Meet' planned for the Thanksgiving weekend in late November at Zephyrhills in northern Florida. Jim described it to Arthur as 'the biggest international skydiving competition in the world'. By this time I'd flown more than 600 hours of instructional flying at the Yorkshire Aeroplane Club and John Fenton was happy to for me to take three weeks' leave to enable me to be an Endrust Team member for the competition.

At Pop's Place. Back: Neville Hounsome, Rod Rodriguez, Thommo, Jim Crocker, Paul 'Pop' Poppenhager (in the door), Dick Reiter, C S-S, Bob Higgins and Clive Rumney. Front: Biff Burn, Bobbie Francis, Mike Bolton, Sally Cain, Yarpy Pullen, Nod Bourne, Mike Chapman and Jon (Willy) Williams

There were fifteen of us on the trip – the twelve of the Endrust Team and three supporters. Having flown into Miami, our first port of call was Indiantown, a hundred miles north, and home of the South Florida Parachute Centre, or Pop's Place, affectionately so-called after its founder and owner, Paul 'Pop' Poppenhager. Pop was, and at the time of writing, still is, one of America's skydiving characters. At the age of nineteen in 1954 his first jump was as a young soldier in the 82nd US Airborne Division. He had founded his thriving parachute centre in 1960 and by the time we knew him he'd accumulated 5,500 jumps and a similar number of hours' flying time. He was also a qualified parachute rigger and aircraft engineer. Jim's choice of Pop's Place for our eight-day training camp was inspired – Pop, his family and Rod Rodriguez, his second-in-command, all couldn't have been more welcoming and supportive. The only problem was the centre's aircraft that Pop or Rod flew for us – the Beechcraft Model 18 – the Twin Beech. It wasn't ideal because it had a small door and we knew that for the Turkey Meet itself we'd be mainly be jumping from DC 3s – a much larger aircraft with its larger door offering a substantially easier exit. On arrival Pop asked us what time we'd like to start jumping the next day, to which Jim replied that, as we were all staying at basic club accommodation on the airfield, we'd like to get airborne for the first lift at 7.30am – I think Pop was surprised when he turned up the following morning at 7.15am to check out the Twin Beech to find us all standing there with our kit on ready to go. The weather was perfect and we averaged five jumps a day from 10,000ft for the next eight days.

For us Brits an unexpected event occurred on our sixth day, November 16. Just before take-off for our first jump after lunch Pop said we might be lucky enough to witness something of the immediate post-launch flight of Skylab 4 during our climb to altitude. Indeed, to see Skylab climb dramatically up through the clouds from our Twin Beech viewpoint, albeit many miles from Cape Canaveral, was especially memorable. I'm sure we all had different memories of this part of the trip – a painful one for me was my continued inability as fifth out to get a clean dive exit through the small door of the Twin Beech. I regularly bashed my right shin on the sill of the door and after three or four days my leg was a bloody mess that Pop's wife kindly kept bandaged for me. Jim did an exceptional job as our leader so I didn't dare tell him in case he dropped me from the team! And then there was the extraordinary orange grove spraying operation run by two brothers flying a North American B-25 Mitchell from the 7,000ft (1.3-mile) grass airstrip. To witness a twin-engined Second World War bomber thundering up and down at 10ft spraying the orange groves was unforgettably impressive. I asked one of the brothers why they eased the nose wheel off the grass so soon after they started their take off run – surely this extra drag slowed their getting airborne? I was informed that, as it was the last nose wheel tyre they'd got, they were trying to make it last as long as possible – no wonder they seemed to use every inch of the 7,000ft runway to coax the old bomber into the air. On a number of occasions during our lunch break Sally and Willy used to disappear off the drop zone for twenty or thirty minutes – we were all too polite to ask them what they were up to, but Pop had no such inhibitions, so he asked them where they went. Sally replied that, because it was so hot, they'd been for a swim in a nearby creek to cool off. 'Hell,' said Pop, 'that creek's full of alligators!' 'Oh,' Sally replied innocently, 'I wondered what all those logs were doing there!'

Thommo was the only member of the team who was accompanied by his wife as he had recently finished a ten-month spell of enforced separation at Her Majesty's pleasure. Now, to make up for lost time, they were staying together at the Seminole Inn a couple of miles down the road in Indiantown itself. Having enjoyed an early breakfast at a local café each morning he'd walk out to the drop zone to be ready for the first load. Unusually one morning he was late on parade and Jim soon started looking anxiously at his watch. Then we all heard the rapidly increasing wail of a police siren moments before we saw the police car itself, whose blue flashing lights added to the spectacle. With an enhanced squeal of brakes it came to an abrupt halt only a few feet from where we were all standing. And who should get out of it but Thommo… and he was handcuffed to the local Sheriff! What on earth had he got up to this time, for Chrissake? Thommo was the master of the practical joke and this was one of his most memorable, even if he and the Sheriff – with whom he'd shared breakfasts in the local café – hadn't been able to keep straight faces for more than about twenty seconds! After eight memorable days and, before we said cheerio to our new-found friends at Pop's Place, we had both Pop and Rod make a skydive with us so we could award each of them a thoroughly well-deserved Hard-Ass Star Team T-shirt. And so we journeyed north for the competition itself at Zephyrhills 150 miles away.

At Zephyrhills. From left, Jim Crocker, C S-S, Mike Bolton, 'Pop' Poppenhager, Sally Cain and Jerry Bird

On arrival at this Mecca of skydiving we registered and were informed that we were the only team from overseas, before then discovering that 41 other teams had entered the competition. We then sought out the legendary Jerry Bird, the well-respected pioneer and exponent of ten-man speed. He'd generously agreed to give us some coaching, especially on how to exit the three different aircraft types to be used for the competition. The impressive line-up was one C-46 Curtis Commando (sixty skydivers), one Lockheed Lodestar (twenty skydivers) and three Douglas DC-3s (thirty skydivers each) and, happily from my point of view, all had bigger doors that the Twin Beech. Jerry also jumped with us on four of our eight practice jumps and this resulted in more useful 'Birdman' advice. Our first practice jump was from the C-46 and it proved to be something of a culture shock for the Brit contingent. Soon after we got airborne we were aware that a number of 'funny' cigarettes were circulating among the other fifty skydivers who were sitting on the floor around us. Having been forewarned about the dangers of skydiving while under the influence of any form of illegal stimulants, we had no problem in refusing to participate ourselves. As I previously hadn't had the opportunity to have a look at the cockpit of the C-46 I made my way forward to the flight deck during our climb to altitude. I discovered the two pilots with their feet up on top of the instrument panel sharing a 'funny' cigarette between them! Maybe all this contributed to the amazing carefree carnival atmosphere of the event – or maybe not! Our three stalwart supporters managed to fix themselves up as members of an American team just as Pop, Rod and their wives arrived from Indiantown to cheer us on, as did Arthur, our generous Endrust sponsor whom Jim introduced to Jerry Bird. Not having had the benefit of knowing how Jim had described the Turkey Meet to Arthur back in the UK, Jerry thanked Arthur profusely for now turning the competition into a truly international event. Fortunately Arthur was delighted so we reckoned his continued sponsorship of the team was a strong possibility. The competition was successfully completed over the two days of the Thanksgiving weekend with our having made one jump from the C-46, one from the Lodestar and three from DC-3s. We scored two 9s and three 10s with the latter averaging 38.9 seconds – all this was enough for us to finish in a creditable fifteenth place and one ahead of the US Army Parachute Team, the Golden Knights who after four rounds were in medal contention, before, on their last jump, they only scored a seven. Unsurprisingly Jerry Bird's team, the Northern Turkey Stars, deservedly won the competition with five ten-man stars that averaged 24.38 seconds – well done them! And huge credit was due to the organisers, judges, manifesters and pilots for a brilliantly run contest with more than 2,000 competition jumps being made in the two days. During the five days we spent at Zephyrhills, the runaway success of Richard Bach's delightful 1970 book, *Jonathan Livingston Seagull*, was a regular topic of conversation – it had sold more than a million copies by the end of 1972 and had remained at the top of the *New York Times* bestseller list for thirty-eight weeks in 1972/73. *JLS* quickly became an iconic inspiration to the skydiving community, sparking off any number of motivational T-shirt designs. I returned to the UK with a *JLS* tee shirt that simply pronounced: 'PERFECT SPEED IS BEING THERE!' Amen to that!

Back in Yorkshire and into 1974 the club had taken on some new students. Tom Banks had a share in the ex-Ken Vos Scintex Super Emeraude G-ASMV which I hadn't seen since Ken stayed with me in Bahrain during his epic flight in her to Australia in 1965 (see Chapter 9). I thoroughly enjoyed instructing Tom in this delightful little aeroplane. Graham Walker and Robin Colvill were members of the popular Yorkshire comedy band the Grumbleweeds, and they both started their PPL courses with us at much the same time. It was often hilarious flying with them – occasionally they'd impersonate a well-known

The pretty little ex-Ken Vos Scintex Super Emeraude

showbusiness character as they communicated on the radio with air traffic control, much to the latter's amusement. Before I took Harry Hepplewhite on his trial lesson I routinely asked him if he'd flown before and he replied that he'd done some flying in the RAF during the latter stages of the war. After this first lesson he decided to embark on a PPL course so I asked him to produce his service flying logbook the next time he came to the club. What his logbook revealed and what he modestly hadn't told us was that he'd flown more than 600 hours in Spitfires! He quickly gained his PPL and soon afterwards he was flying regularly for our parachuting operation. Another wartime RAF flying veteran was Geoff Crawford, a local businessman, who'd finished the war as a rear gunner on a Coastal Command Sunderland, a lonely job that he admitted he hadn't enjoyed one bit. In due course Geoff gained his PPL and purchased a brand-new Cessna 172 on which I checked him out. After one of his first solo trips in this smart new aeroplane he came into the flying club, handed me the keys and asked if we could look after them for him. He then thanked me for giving him back his confidence. 'Please use the 172 whenever you want,' he suggested, 'and just top it up with fuel when you get back.' It was a generous gesture indeed.

In April it was time for the Endrust Skydivers to return to Innsbruck for the second European Ten Man Star Competition. Regular team members Jon Williams and Sally Cain couldn't be with us as they got married that same weekend – we reckoned this was a pretty lame excuse for their absence. Jeff Lancaster and John Partington Smith, two members of the previous year's Brit team, replaced them. John PS was a talented artist and imaginative cartoonist who had started to produce the brilliant *Superfly* series of cartoons for *Sport Parachutist*. They were both genial characters and excellent skydivers so they slotted in well. It was a much bigger event this time with ten teams competing over three rounds with a Twin Otter again providing the aircraft support. In spite of indifferent weather it was an enjoyable contest with Icarus, the French team, performing consistently well to win the gold; Endrust, one point behind, took silver, and Viking, a composite Scandinavian team, won the bronze. At the end of the competition it remained for us to enjoy a fun jump attempting to build a 'snowflake' formation, but the worsening weather only allowed the Twin Otter to run in at 8,000ft. We stepped out into a snowstorm and, unable to see the ground, we opened our canopies and found ourselves a couple of miles upwind of the airfield over every hazard known to skydiving – the raging Inn River, a busy dual carriageway, an electrified railway, high-tension cables and all accompanied by a wind, the speed of which was climbing rapidly up the Beaufort scale. Luckily we all found somewhere to land safely, apart from Mike Chapman who finished up in the Inn River and had to cut away his main canopy lest, inflated, it dragged him underwater and drowned him. Fortunately he made it to the river bank, after which he was rushed to the local hospital to be thawed out. Even the birds stopped singing!

Then, a couple of months later, Jim bowled me a really fast ball – he asked me to teach him to fly. I agreed reluctantly – I was concerned lest he treat the whole operation too light-heartedly as we'd had so many laughs skydiving together. But I had underestimated my good friend, Jim Crocker. He applied himself to learning to fly with total commitment, whether it was on the ground studying for the written exams, or in the air where he was determined to fly each and every exercise as accurately as he possibly could. For starters he flew two instructional sorties with me on June 23 (two hours and five minutes), one on June 26 (one hour and ten minutes) and six on June 27 (four hours and fifty minutes), after which I sent him solo. And in the evening of that third day he joined Dick Reiter and I to parachute into the Parkway Hotel Leeds for a display for the Headingley Round Table – phew! He wrote in my parachuting logbook: 'Many thanks for a fantastic flying day which will ever be remembered – FAR OUT! JC.' Jim was undoubtedly an exceptional student and it was incredibly rewarding teaching him to fly. Years later he kindly wrote to me: 'Absolutely no doubt about it, you were a fantastic instructor. You even told me so. After dead-sticking a C-206 into a tiny field in a vicious crosswind en route from Sibson to Kidlington in 1982 you sent me a message saying: "Well done, a credit to your instructor"!'

The DH89A Rapide, which was then based at Halfpenny Green and regularly used for parachuting, was G-AGJG, the same aircraft from which I made my first sport jump at Thruxton in 1963. Since then I'd always had great affection for this iconic 1930s type and its classically elegant de Havilland lines and I longed to actually fly her myself. Fortunately I was encouraged in this ambition by my good chum and well-respected jump pilot, Bill Downes, who was immensely experienced on Rapides – he'd even flown one to Florida by way of Iceland, Greenland, Newfoundland and the eastern seaboard of the USA. But first I needed to add a twin rating to my licence. In those days there was no set syllabus to be flown to gain a twin rating – all that was required was sufficient twin flying under instruction to enable the candidate to pass the twin flight test with an examiner. As at that time the club didn't have a suitable twin-engine aircraft available, Steve Lerche, who had agreed to instruct me, was able to borrow a PA-30 Twin Comanche from Sherburn in Elmet. I only flew two one-and-a-half-hour sorties with Steve before he declared that I was then ready for the test. Knowing what I've learnt since, this three hours of twin instruction was ridiculously inadequate. Flying a twin presents no problems when both engines are functioning normally, but if one of the engines fails the asymmetric situation that faces the pilot is likely to be tricky – especially when the aircraft is fully loaded. Today the CAA requires six hours of twin training to be completed before the test can be taken and I do not consider this to be unrealistic. Soon after my second training sortie with Steve I successfully flew the twin rating test with

DH89A Rapide G-AGJG at Halfpenny Green, August 3, 1974

C S-S and the 'office' of G-AGJG

Alex. Three weeks later, and clutching my newly issued twin rating, I drove to Halfpenny Green to be checked out on the Rapide by Bill. After an hour of familiarisation and circuits, he kindly let me fly my first parachute sortie in this historic aeroplane – I felt hugely privileged. I immediately suggested that I be permitted to fly her up to Leeds for a week's skydiving flying for the Leeds Bradford Free Fall Club and, in spite of my very limited experience on type, this was agreed for early September.

Above left: the Endrust team at the World Cup, South Africa: top, C S-S, Yarpy Pullen, Guy Sutton, Jim Crocker; middle: Dick Reiter, Dave Waterman, Mike Chapman, Alan Skennerton; bottom: Robin Mills, John Partington Smith.
Above right: on exit from a DC-3 (C S-S in yellow and red)

In the middle of August, John and Alex once again generously gave me time off to be a member of the British team for the second World Cup in Ten-Man Speed to be held at Wonderboom near Pretoria in South Africa. As the competition was an experimental World Cup rather than a more prestigious World Championships, the BPA was unable to fund us, so we were of necessity self-financing. While we were still essentially the sponsored Endrust Skydivers, we were a composite team with JPS, Dave Waterman, Robin Mills and Alan Skennerton from the 1973 Brit team joining the squad. There were fourteen teams in the ten-man event with support from five immaculately maintained DC-3s from the South African Air Force. With the drop zone being 4,200ft above sea level and the jump height being 10,000ft above ground level, mild hypoxia and harder landings caused problems, witness Jerry Bird who broke a bone in his foot – he continued skydiving anyway, relying on supporters to catch him at the end of each jump. After ten practice jumps we had achieved some reasonably timed tens, but disappointingly we scored an occasional nine. Unfortunately this was reflected in the final results of the eight-round competition itself – the first four teams scored consistent tens, 80 points, with Jerry Bird's Wings of Orange the winners, while we finished in fifth place having scored 78 points. On our second jump Sally got bumped on exit which started a nosebleed. By the time she approached the star her face and goggles were covered in blood, so much so she could hardly see – 9 points! Jim grabbed Willy after we landed and instructed him to take Sally (now Mrs Williams) to show her (still covered in blood) to the judges. He then told me to accompany him to lodge a protest with the international jury in an attempt to persuade its members to grant us a re-jump. I tried to explain to Jim as firmly as I could that we'd be wasting our time as the competition rules clearly stated that if the team exited the aircraft they would be judged – as a member of CIP's RW sub-committee I'd been involved in drafting these rules! But Jim was not to be deterred. He dictated his protest to me and I wrote it out as neatly as I could before it was handed to Chuck McCrone, the delightful American who was president of the jury. Later Jim and I were summoned to appear in front of the jury and Jim immediately launched himself into an impassioned plea as to why we should be granted a re-jump.

Chuck halted Jim in mid-sentence: 'Tell me, Mr Crocker, are you a lawyer by any chance?'

'Well, as a matter of fact I am,' our revered leader replied.

'I thought so,' said Chuck, before he delivered the damning verdict: 'Protest denied!'

It was the only time I ever witnessed Jim being totally at a loss for words.

In early September I flew the G-AGJG from Halfpenny Green to Leeds for a Rapide week for the now well-established Leeds Bradford Free Fall Club. It resulted in seventeen parachute sorties and another ten hours' Rapide time written up in my logbook – all vividly memorable! Instructing at the Yorkshire Aeroplane Club had so far given me the opportunity to fly a number of different aircraft types – twenty-five to date – some of which were simply Certificate of Airworthiness air tests for Yorkshire Light Aircraft, the maintenance organisation that was our next-door neighbour on the airfield. I particularly enjoyed flying the Super Emeraude, a Zlin, a Chipmunk, a Piper Cub and different variants of Auster and Beagle Terrier. At the end of one instructional sortie the student was taxiing us back to the club and, as we passed Northair, the local Cessna agent, I spotted an immaculate-looking Cessna 188 AGwagon crop sprayer parked in front of its hangar. I commented on how smart it looked, at which my student announced that it was in fact his and that he was looking for someone to fly it back to his crop-spraying operation at Sutton Bank. This was too good an opportunity to miss. 'I'll fly it up there for you,' I suggested.

'Have you flown an AGwagon before?' he queried.

And, as I was familiar with the Cessna 180/185 tail-dragger types, I couldn't imagine that the aircraft in question was too different; I fibbed outrageously when I told him I had.

'Excellent,' he said, 'I'll check the weather at Sutton Bank when I get back and if it's OK can you fly it up later today?'

'No problem,' I replied, thinking, 'that'll give me a chance to have a quick look at the flight manual if I can find one.' By the time I'd received the call to say that it was all systems go, I'd found that the cockpit and instrument layout was typical Cessna 180/185 and that the power plant was a 230 hp Continental 0-470-R flat six engine. The latter suggested that, as the aeroplane had no chemicals in the hopper and only half a tank of fuel, it was relatively light – so I cautioned myself to be careful of the torque on take-off by applying the power gently. Even so, she fairly leapt into the air in much the same way as a lightened Cessna 185 would have. The forty-minute flight was thoroughly enjoyable and I was lucky enough to pull off a reasonable landing on the grass at Sutton Bank, aware that the AGwagon's owner would almost certainly be watching – he was!

'How was it?' he asked as I climbed out.

'Oh, much the same as any other AGwagon,' I replied as nonchalantly as I could, mightily relieved that all had gone according to plan – another type, number 25, in my logbook!

On the skydiving front it was good to have the DZ at Green Gaits Farm on the doorstep. I remember dear Keith Whyham turning up in the ANT Cherokee Six to fly skydiving chum Nick Cullum on a photographic sortie for Aerofilms, his employer. When they returned I asked Keith if he could drop Nick and I over Green Gaits Farm. Before he set course for Blackpool he kindly gave us 9,500ft and I was able to photographically capture a relaxed Nick over the Yorkshire countryside – see photo above. On another occasion an Army Air Corps Beaver taxied on to our dispersal and shut down. I wandered over to greet the pilot, in this case one Staff Sergeant Nick O'Brien. It transpired that Nick was also ex-Parachute Regiment and an experienced skydiver who later finished a colourful Army career as a Major – he will appear again in these pages. But on this occasion he hadn't expected a skydive – some equipment was found for him and, an hour after he'd arrived in the Beaver, we were airborne in the 172 for a totally unexpected jump for him on to Green Gaits Farm. It proved to be the first of countless occasions when we've shared the sky together.

Back in 1972 the BPA Council had decided that there was a need to employ a full-time national coach/safety officer and the Sports Council subsequently agreed to provide grant aid assistance for the appointment. Initially in 1974 two experienced parachutists – Doug Peacock, a RAF PJI, and Bob Hiatt, an accomplished competition parachutist, had both applied for the job. But in due course they both withdrew their applications, leaving the job up for grabs once more. Perhaps, I thought, I should consider applying myself as I couldn't see myself remaining as a full-time flying instructor forever – in spite of working with such a great team at the Yorkshire Aeroplane Club. Not only that, I certainly wasn't instructing to build flying hours to pave my way to becoming an airline pilot – I couldn't imagine a less fulfilling profession; it certainly wasn't for me. Another important consideration was that in January 1975 the BPA had moved its offices from London to Kimberley House in Leicester. There was no way I could have worked in London, but the possibility of being based in Leicester caused the BPA NCSO job to beckon persuasively, so I submitted my application in April 1975.

Early that month also saw a number of us accepting an invitation from the Irish Parachute Club to skydive with them in the Emerald Isle. Six of us, including Nick Cullum and Dick Reiter, were due to fly out in our usually available Cessna 206 – not this time, however, as it was in the hangar for maintenance. Fortunately one of the club members kindly let me have the use of his very smart retractable Cessna 210 Centurion for the weekend while John Sudbury was to fly the ANT Cherokee Six across from Blackpool with Jim and four more jumpers. I read back the clearance: 'Golf Alpha Yankee Charlie Lima is cleared to Dublin, Delta White Two, Pole Hill, climbing to Flight Level Four-Zero; Squawk Four, Four, Zero, Six.'

'Roger, Charlie Lima, you're cleared for take-off – the surface wind three four zero at one zero knots.'

'Roger, Charlie Lima.' I released the brakes and we were on our way! Charlie Lima quickly impressed us – with her turbo-charged 310 hp Continental 10-550 engine she was soon tramping along at 155kts to gobble up the 170 (nautical) miles to Dublin in an hour and ten minutes. Having cleared customs we then headed for Edenderry airfield twenty-five miles away to the south-west and the home of the Irish Parachute Club. The weather had unkindly deteriorated and, on a special VFR clearance out of the Dublin Zone not above 1,000ft and with ridiculously poor visibility, I lowered both first stage of flap and the undercarriage to slow Charlie Lima to a sensible speed given the conditions. I then asked Nick, who was also a pilot, if he'd fly our trusty steed while I concentrated on the map reading. After fifteen minutes all the landmarks indicated that we'd arrived but below us there was nothing other than a huge field with a caravan parked in a corner – half a dozen figures were waving vigorously – at us perchance? There was no windsock – well, actually, there was, but as we discovered later, it was just a pole from which dangled a naked metal hoop. The sock bit had obviously blown away! I set up to land down the length of the field. Everything looked good as I sank towards the inviting green turf so I anticipated a gentle landing – wrong! I hit terra firma firmly – crash – airborne again – wallop – and another leap before I regained control. What an appalling surface – it made the strip at Flamingo Park look like Heathrow. And when John Sudbury arrived in

Before the first Irish Star was attempted. From left: Dick Reiter, Jim Crocker, C S-S, Charlie Hayden, Jim Keery, Brian Jackel, Mick Flaherty. Kneeling: Noel Larragy and Mike Chapman

the Cherokee Six he fared no better. Initially it appeared as if he was to be blessed with a perfect arrival – but it looked exactly like ours felt! At the second bounce back into the air, the baggage locker door located just behind the engine flew open to deposit a couple of bags on to the grass. John inadvertently pressed the transmit button as he exclaimed: ''KIN 'ELL!' The weather continued to deteriorate as we waited for the Irish Parachute Club's 172 to show up. Finally the sound of an aero engine getting louder dragged us away from our coffee to witness the 172 appear low over the surrounding trees. The direction of its approach to land was identical to John's and mine but this time the landing of the 172 was so sweet that it gently kissed the grass, causing not the slightest hint of vibration from the undercarriage – amazing! Of course we sought an explanation from Charlie Hayden, the 172's pilot: 'It's simple,' he informed us, 'you've just got to land to de left of de mark.' 'De mark' was a line showing the landing direction that had been burnt in the grass with petrol the previous summer – naturally it had become grown over to virtually disappear during the subsequent months – so much so that Charlie had to lower himself on to his hands and knees to point it out to us – six inches to the left on the approach and John and I would have been OK! It was good to be in the land of my shamrock-loving forefathers. The cloud gradually dispersed from the middle of the afternoon so we were able to start parachuting. The IPC members all wanted to jump from the Cherokee Six but John pointed out that he could only take four in the Six until he'd burnt off some fuel. Minutes later Mick Flaherty, the Chief Instructor, appeared with four students – all five were kitted out ready to go. 'Sorry, Mick,' said John, 'I can only take four, and there are five of you!' 'Dat's OK,' replied Mick, and, with a massive dose of Irish logic, 'one of dem's on de static line!'

Later we made his day, however, when Jim, Dick, Mike and I took him up to 9,000ft in the Six flown by John for us to build the first Irish five-man around him. Warm, generous Irish hospitality that evening accompanied the celebration of this new Irish record in Paddy McCormack's bar in Edenderry where Guinness was the only thing on the menu! The highlight of the following day was to be an attempt to build the first Irish star with IPC members Mick and Noel Larragy joining Jim, Dick, Mike, Jim Keery, Brian Jackel and I with three of us in the 172 and the remaining five in the Cherokee Six. As the 172 had no radio, a comprehensive and necessary briefing took place. It had been decided that Charlie Hayden would lead after he'd levelled off at 9,000ft – the latter being a realistically achievable height for the 172 with three jumpers on board. Soon we were airborne and climbing away from the field with John flying the Six and holding formation with the 172. When we reached 9,000ft we were at least five miles away from the field and our intrepid 172 pilot showed no sign of levelling off, with the result that John in the Six was finding it more and more difficult to hold formation with the 172 slowing as it was as Charlie continued to climb – 9,500ft, 10,000ft, 10,500ft and, finally, having been airborne for about forty-five minutes, the two aircraft were wallowing at about 11,000ft about a mile from the airfield – good enough for government work: 'READY, SET, GOOOOO!' Of course, and in polite language, the skydive failed to achieve its aim. We'd been airborne for so long in two aircraft with no doors with the result that we were all bitterly cold and, I suspect, suffering from mild hypoxia – the end result came as no surprise. I was livid. I let fly at Charlie as soon as he'd landed.

'Charlie, you were briefed to level off at 9,000ft – what the bloody hell were you playing at?!'

'Well, de 172 was going up so well I decided to keep goin'!'

To which, of course, there was no answer! In any event it had been an hilariously enjoyable weekend and so typically and wonderfully Irish that I promised myself I'd return – which I did the next year. Having thanked our splendid hosts and bid them our fond farewells, we had an uneventful flight home. Across the Lancashire coast I called our home base ATC: 'Leeds, Golf Charlie O'Lima's estimatin' de LBA when de little hand's on de eight and de big hand's on de six!' It was catching, you see!

Soon after our Irish adventure I received notification from the BPA that it would be pleased to appoint me as the Association's first full time national coach and safety officer with effect from July 1. Of course I was delighted, but I wasn't looking forward to telling John and Alex, my fantastic bosses at the Yorkshire Aeroplane Club. It had been such an amazing three years, during which I find recorded in my logbooks 1,145 hours' flying instruction and 412 skydives. My flying logbook also records that Boomerang clocked up more than 600 hours as a passenger during the same three years! By prior arrangement with Leeds air traffic control, my last day as a flying instructor at the club started at 8am before they opened, when they allowed me to let my hair down in Cessna 150 G-ASYP. My logbook simply records: 'Granted Freedom of the Airfield – created 3 new runways!' Later that morning, John, with infinite kindness and generosity, said as we shook hands: 'Our loss is BPA's gain – the job's tailor-made for you!' It was an emotional moment.

CHAPTER 15
BPA NATIONAL COACH AND SAFETY OFFICER

Having been a BPA Council member for eight years, I was luckily well up to speed with all the discussions there had been about the desirability for the Association to employ a full-time national coach and safety officer, and a paper had been submitted to the Sports Council seeking grant aid in support of the appointment. The paper originally envisaged the job being split between two people thus:

National coach

a. Preparation of syllabi for, and supervision of, instructor courses and associated examinations.
b. Coaching of national teams for World Championship and other international competitions.
c. By periodic visits, supervise the standard of instruction, safety and equipment at affiliated clubs.
d. Liaison with the Sports Council and other bodies on matters of coaching and development.

National safety officer

a. Technical adviser to the chairman of the BPA Council.
b. Permanent technical member of BPA Safety and Training Committee.
c. Permanent technical member of the Parachute Riggers Committee.
d. Liaison with the Civil Aviation Authority, the Armed Forces and parachute manufacturers.

Taking on both responsibilities might have seemed daunting, but at the time I could only see them as interesting challenges. Between jobs Boomerang and I moved house from Leeds to Cosby – a quiet village some seven miles south of Leicester, and already members of the BPA staff were well-established in Leicester at Kimberley House. The secretary-general was retired Squadron Leader Bill Paul who had been a RAF PJI when I'd first met him at No 1 PTS at RAF Abingdon in 1962, while the assistant secretary was his wife, Dorothy, with Helen Day and Suzie Bates as the cheerful juniors – all four gave loyal service to the Association. Also located in Kimberley House on the floor below BPA were the offices of the British Gliding Association. Bill Scull, its long-serving national coach, rapidly became a good friend who, in my early days in the job, assisted me no end, principally by putting me in touch with a number of useful contacts, especially within the Civil Aviation Authority. The BGA also acted as the secretariat for the Royal Aero Club and, as I was now also the BPA representative on the RAeC Council, this was, from a personal point of view, was a very convenient arrangement. Within the BPA itself I was responsible to its elected Council, but I reported directly to the chairman of the Safety and Training Committee, who throughout my three years as NCSO, was Jim Crocker and who was thus effectively my boss and I was fortunate that this was so as he couldn't have given me more support or encouragement. Having also regularly attended meetings of the Safety and Training Committee I knew most of the sport's Chief Instructors and I looked forward to visiting them at their clubs in due course. For example in July and August, my first two months in the job, I visited the North West Parachute Centre at Cark; the Hereford Parachute Club at both Shobdon and at their summer camp at Land's End, St Just; the Peterborough Parachute Centre at Sibson; the Northumbria Parachute Club at Sunderland; the Border Ventures Parachute Club at Brunton; the Eagle Sport Parachute Centre at Ashford; the Lashenden Sport Parachute Club at Headcorn; the Peak District Parachute Club at Ashbourne, and the RAF Sport Parachute Association at Weston on the Green. At the latter, RAFSPA also hosted the National Style and Accuracy Championships where, apart from being Meet Director, I flew thirty-five lifts in a Cessna 185 G-AYNN which we hired from Britten-Norman on the Isle of Wight. Parachuting at these clubs I made a total of thirty-nine jumps in the two months and clocked up thirty-seven hours' flying time, the latter mainly for jumping but occasionally for flying to and from the more remote clubs. And throughout all this Boomerang was my stalwart companion – such was his renown that I soon got used to arriving at a club or centre where, more often than not, Boomerang was recognised and welcomed before I was! While I would be on BPA business, I was determined that my visits to clubs and centres should not be seen as inspections to police their activities, so on arrival I always asked the Chief Instructor if there was anything I could do to help him. The result was that a useful relaxed two-way exchange of information and ideas usually followed as happened during my visit to the Hereford Parachute Club's summer camp at Land's End, St Just. Fortunately the journey to Cornwall by air was made possible by John Fenton lending me his Robin 400/180, a delightful French four-seater light aeroplane which, for mathematical convenience, cruised at 120kts or two nautical miles a minute.

The club's Chief Instructor was Johnny Boxall, an ebullient, larger-than-life character, who had arranged a skydiving programme of jumping every morning on to the airfield, followed every afternoon by the more experienced giving parachute displays on to local beaches. The latter were well-publicised in advance – club member Mike Farrell did a fantastic job cruising around the seaside resorts each day with loudspeakers on the roof of his car blasting out notice of each afternoon's display. The jump aircraft in use was a Rapide belonging to and flown by Viv Bellamy, one of the real characters of postwar light aviation – during 1941 Viv and my father were both Fleet Air Arm sub-lieutenants together in 755 Naval Air Squadron flying Blackburn Sharks at RNAS Worthy Down so I received an especially warm welcome from him. I awoke very early the following day and it was such a glorious morning that I decided to have a look at Land's End from the air. On my return I couldn't resist the temptation to wake up the club members camped on the airfield with a low-level pass over their tents. Viv admitted later that he wasn't sure whether he'd enjoyed my 'Lycoming-powered alarm clock' or not! The first of the two displays in which I participated with Johnny's team was on to Sennen Cove beach. I followed Johnny out of the Rapide and watched his Irvin Delta II Para Wing only partially inflate below me. Wisely he didn't spend too much time trying to untangle the mess, which he cut away before successfully deploying his reserve only to land in the sea. The rest of us threw off our kit and ran to Johnny's aid. Luckily he was in shallow water so we had no difficulty retrieving both him and his cut-away canopy after which we threw ourselves into the sea to cool off. Meanwhile, the girls had gathered up our helmets and wandered among the holidaymakers to try to persuade them to contribute to their collection for the 'Needy Boys of Hereford'! Johnny's Para Wing malfunction later prompted a useful discussion on why it had failed to deploy properly, something which was occurring all too often. It was at this time that there was a move away from the use of the wonderfully reliable Para Commander to it being gradually replaced by a number of more radical aerofoil designs – canopies that provided inherently faster forward speeds coupled with slower rates of descent. The Irvin Delta II Para Wing was one such design with the Strato Star offering a more reliable alternative. The main problem with these canopies was to ensure that they were designed with a system that slowed their deployment to an acceptable level. Credit must be given to the Red Devils who test-jumped a number of different designs that often resulted in appallingly hard openings. The Delta II Para Wing employed an interesting means of reducing the opening shock. During the packing of the Para Wing a strip of webbing about 4ft in length was wrapped in colour-coded stages around similarly colour-coded groups of suspension lines. During Para Wing deployment the lines would – hopefully – be released in sequence to prevent bone shaking opening shocks. It took Johnnie five Para Wing malfunctions and associated cutaways before the penny dropped and he finally decided to get rid of the thing. Unfortunately the system was hugely unreliable and it soon disappeared into oblivion. The wrap can be seen flying behind the Para Wing in the photo on the facing page.

My first 'Ram Air' canopy – so called because air rammed into its open leading edge gave it its aerofoil shape – was a 1975 five-cell design manufactured by Para Flite, a US company that christened it the 'Strato Star'. It quickly became the most popular parachute of the late 1970s and a taste of things to come in spite of it initially being equipped with a means of slowing its deployment appropriately referred to as 'ropes and rings'. Passing through a number of large rings stitched around its periphery was a near-60ft length of nylon cord (the rope), the open ends of which were attached to the pilot chute. The latter pulled the rope from its stowage on the canopy's bag to slow the canopy's deployment – when it worked! If the length of rope was not stowed meticulously it was liable to knot, which in turn could sometimes cause an adrenalin-pumping malfunction as it did during a visit I made to Sibson soon after I'd returned from Land's End. Four of us opened our canopies at the end of a skydive from 7,000ft – my 'ropes and rings' Strato Star failed to fully deploy – I only had about thirty per cent of useful canopy. It was an easy decision to cut it away and open my reserve. I then saw my Strato Star, now with tension released, fully inflate itself and fly away from me. Nick, who was flying the 185,

Left: the Irvin Delta II Para Wing; right: my slider-equipped Stato Star

looked down as we opened to see five good canopies – something of a surprise as only four of us had exited the aircraft. Soon ropes and rings also disappeared to be replaced by the now ubiquitous 'slider'. This amazingly simple design consisted of a square of nylon with a large grommet in each corner through which the suspension lines were passed before the slider was slid up to the top of the lines and the latter stowed on the bag. On deployment the slider slowed the canopy inflation as it slid down the lines – see the photo above. The slider-equipped Strato Star soon became the canopy of choice for most experienced skydivers, even for Richard Bach, author of *Jonathan Livingston Seagull*, who in a letter wrote to me: 'Jumping's the same as flying, I think – safety and control. I'm crazy about my Strato Star because you can control it so well. No more drifting helplessly into fishponds (my last round jump!)'

Involvement with the National Parachute Championships – both style and accuracy (sometimes called 'classic') and relative work, together with club competitions, soon became an enjoyable part of the job. At the Nationals I was always the Meet Director being responsible for all basic organisation – especially having to make the sometimes difficult weather-based decisions, but, as with club competitions, I'd often fill in as a judge or pilot as necessary. I was always fortunate in having the support of an enthusiastic and able bunch of volunteers without whom these competitions simply couldn't have happened. Style and accuracy were first Nationals for which I was responsible and were hosted over ten days by the RAF club at Weston on the Green in late August. We were able to complete the competition with three days to spare with the sixty-four competitors having made 637 jumps between them. We used three aircraft – a Cessna 185, a Cessna 210 and a Cherokee 6 – and we flew eighty hours between five of us. It was good to be able to fly all three types but, with the need to change from one aircraft type to another speedily, it was important that essential pre-flight checks weren't rushed. One of our flying team had just changed from the Cessna 185 to fly the Cherokee Six and had forgotten in his haste that the Six was restricted to only carrying four jumpers when it was full of fuel. Assisted by the curvature of the Earth and the generous length of Weston's grass runway, he only just got airborne over the boundary hedge with five jumpers on board. Memorably it was an enjoyable competition with two dedicated and determined competitive parachutists, John Meacock and Tracy Rixon, deservedly becoming Men's and Ladies' Champions respectively.

Boomerang guarding the Cessna 185 at Weston on the Green, August 1975

My next commitment was to be head of delegation of the British ten-man and four-man teams at the First World Relative Work Championships to be held at Warendorf in Germany after a training camp at Bergerac in France. Dave Waterman captained and coached the ten-man team while Ray Willis did likewise for the all RAF PJI four-man team. The training jumps in France were from the huge Soviet Antonov AN-2 biplane for the ten-man team or the Broussard for the four-man team – neither was a satisfactory option as, for the Championships, Luftwaffe Bell HU1-D helicopters were to be used with right-hand door exits. The AN-2 had a left-hand door exit. At Warendorf at one of the numerous briefings, the door issue prompted a spirited exchange between the Australian team captain and Austrian chief judge Franz Lorber with the former giving the latter a particularly hard time about the decision to use the right door exit on the HU1-D. Franz patiently explained that the matter was out of his control as the pilots of the Hueys would not alter their decision. More Oz unrest followed whereupon Franz announced firmly: 'All teams vill use ze right-hand door, except ze Australians who may use ze left-hand door – but it vill be closed!' A round of applause for the chief judge's words of wisdom effectively ended any further discussion. His ruling can't have caused the Australian team too much concern, however, as they finished in silver medal place in the ten-man event, with the US teams winning gold in both the ten-man and four-man competitions. The US ten-man team members were a dedicated bunch who'd made more than 400 jumps together led by Al Krueger, a charismatic, talented skydiver, who had lost his left arm serving in the US Airborne in Vietnam. He had been fixed up with a hook as a replacement so his team inevitably became Captain Hook and the Sky Pirates. Al Krueger proved to be an inspirational leader and his team were popular winners. Unfortunately our two British teams didn't achieve the results they might have done had they had more training jumps together – it was a lesson for the future. The competition, which included the first and only World Championship in ten-man speed, had been very well organised, so none of us could have anticipated that the closing banquet could have developed into such an appalling shambles. There had been little communication about the event beforehand and, because of the necessity for tight security to keep out unwanted supporters and hangers-on, it took well over an hour to permit bona fide competitors and officials to gain entry into the military dining hall where a magnificent-looking buffet had been laid out down the entire length of one wall. There was no team seating plan, but there was an overly generous supply of all manner of booze laid out on each of the tables, thus the teams who were first to enter had more than enough time, not only to decimate the alcoholic contents of the bottles provided, but also to replenish stocks from the yet-to-be occupied tables. Eventually all those who were entitled to attend had persuaded the officialdom on the door of their status and were eagerly awaiting start of the festivities. There appeared to be no master of ceremonies, so there was no announcement about the format for the evening. My memory of the occasion includes hearing what sounded like a whistle blast. This instantaneously prompted 250 or so skydivers, most of whom were thoroughly well-lubricated, leaping to their feet and descending on the buffet like a plague of ravenous locusts – the tables were literally stripped bare of everything edible within a matter of a few seconds. To make matters worse, the members of the gold medal-winning US delegation sat at the table they'd found for themselves, patiently waiting for both recognition of their fine competitive achievement and food – but neither made an appearance. Regrettably it wasn't skydiving's finest hour!

Accident investigation, occasionally in conjunction with the Air Accidents Investigation Branch of the Board of Trade, was an interesting responsibility of my job. The extraordinary incident at Ashbourne that October was a case in point. I had just landed at the end of a skydive over Sibson when John Meacock ran over to tell me that Derrick Orton, chief instructor of the Peak District Parachute Club at Ashbourne had phoned to say that there had been a fatal accident at the club and would I phone him back. This I did, for a mightily relieved Derrick to inform me that mercifully no one had been fatally injured after all, but there had been some serious fractures. I immediately drove to Ashbourne to assist in the investigation of this unique accident. On the third lift of the day Cessna 182 G-ARWL had taken off with a student lift to be dispatched by potential instructor Derek Schofield. The first student jumped without incident. The aircraft made a second pass over the DZ at 2,500ft and the second student, Stuart Avent, was given the exit command. While moving to the exit position he slipped between the

The Cessna 182, and student, under canopy – and on the ground. Photos: Eddie McBride

wing strut and the starboard oleo leg. He hung vertically from the strut before letting go. The main parachute deployed at this stage, tangling itself around the starboard oleo leg. Derek Schofield initiated the hang-up procedure, ordering the pilot, Ken Miller, to climb before starting to chop the canopy away with a knife. Some fifteen seconds later Stuart Avent lost sight of the 182 and, having thought he'd been cut away, activated deployment of his reserve parachute, which opened normally. This deployment stalled the aircraft, pulling it into an inverted nose-down position. The engine stopped and the aircraft, with the instructor, pilot and third student still aboard, descended, rotating slowly, suspended beneath the second student and his inflated reserve canopy. The aircraft struck the ground on the edge of the airfield in this position – see the photographs above. Ken received a broken jaw, Derek two broken femurs, while the third student, Frances Ives, broke both her ankles – injuries from which they all recovered fully. Stuart landed uninjured. My recommendation that all aircraft, normally requiring an exit from the wheel, be equipped with an approved jump step over the wheel for all static-line descents, was swiftly adopted. And we managed to get membership of the legendary Caterpillar Club for pilot Ken Miller, who had not intended to make a parachute jump, but whose life had been saved by the use of a Irvin parachute or one of Irvin design!

Running week-long BPA instructors' courses that were hosted by the larger clubs or centres were another feature of the job I found both fulfilling and enjoyable, always reminding myself of the seven P's – Proper Prior Planning Prevents Piss-Poor Performance! Here again it would have been impossible to undertake the task without the vital support and enthusiasm of a number of very experienced club chief instructors, among them John Meacock at Sibson, Jim Sharples at Shobdon, Geordie Laing at Netheravon and Doug Peacock at Weston on the Green together with other splendid characters – George Long,

Don McCarthy, Dave Howerski, Ronnie O'Brien, John Hitchen, Dave Hickling, Johnny Boxall and Dave Prince to mention but a few. I'd already been able to complete the first editions of both the *BPA Instructors' Manual* – inspired by the teachings of Brian Bellas (see Chapter 9) – and the *BPA Display Manual* before I started the job and, of course, these have become comprehensively more valuable as they have benefited from a wealth of experience of others over the past forty-plus years. Inevitably there were some interesting moments. On a course at Sibson I was flying John's Cessna 180 on a sortie with one of the potential instructor (PI) candidates practising dispatching others on static-line jumps. The PI shouted 'Cut!' And I closed the throttle as the 'student' was ordered on to the step. It was at this instant that the PI lost control of the static line, which flew out into a loop around the pretend student's neck. Luckily the latter was actually an experienced jumper who spotted the problem at the same moment as I shouted 'STOP!' It was only then that the PI realised just how alarming the situation was – had it been a genuine student, strangulation might well have been the result, instead of a simple course failure.

One of the candidates who attended the third instructor's course I ran was Terry Patton – invariably known as 'The General'; he was a 'reet' larger-than-life Yorkshire character who had found himself serving as a conscripted soldier in North Africa at the end of the war. One sports afternoon he persuaded a chum to join him for a camel ride in the desert. Having had a swift camel riding lesson from the Arab proprietor of the local Rent-a-Camel company, they set off across the sand imagining themselves to be latter-day Lawrences of Arabia. After an hour or so they stopped for a fag break, after which, on remounting, the General's hired camel refused to move. However much straining and shoving they both applied, the wretched animal remained sitting motionless in the sand. Spotting some parched scrub nearby the General had a brainwave – they built a bonfire around his reluctant 'ship of the desert'. A match was applied and its sudden awareness of the flames prompted the camel to get swiftly to its feet, at which precise moment the Adjutant happened to appear in his jeep – the General was immediately placed on a charge to be marched in front of his Commanding Officer the following day. '17532821 Private Patton T is charged with conduct prejudice to good order and military discipline contrary to section 69 of the Army Act in that he did wilfully set fire to a camel.' The CO struggled desperately to restrain his laughter while the General stood poker-faced in front of him. He couldn't get rid of him fast enough: 'Admonished – march out!'

Now, thirty years later and on the third day of the course, the General asked if he could have a word with me in private. I just hoped he wasn't going to confess that he'd set fire to something. A written exam was one of the syllabus requirements and it was about this that the General approached me. Quite simply he was of a generation who, because of the war, had received little or no education and, in his case, he'd never learnt to read or write. It wasn't that he was trying to duck out of sitting the exam, but naturally he didn't want the other candidates to learn of his embarrassing situation. I told him to phone in the following morning to tell me that he'd have to take his wife into hospital later that day and could he sit the written exam that evening? I let it be known that I'd granted the General's request and that evening I privately gave the General the exam orally, which he passed with flying colours. Likewise he passed the rest of the course and he subsequently became an excellent instructor – it was good to have been able to assist him in the way I did.

At the CIP meeting in Paris early the following year, the Relative Work Sub-Committee put together rules for an eight-man sequential event similar to those used for the four-man event. This came about because of the general lack of aircraft suitable enough to support ten-man speed. Many, including myself, were sorry to see the end of ten-man speed, but the proposed sequential alternative certainly offered exciting challenges. The tests became the completion of pre-determined formations in specified sequences during working times of fifty seconds' freefall time for eight-man and thirty-five seconds for four-man from 11,500ft and 9,000ft respectively. Each completed formation in the sequence scored one point and each could then be repeated if working time was still available. CIP gratefully accepted Richard Charter's generous offer to organise a World Cup in South Africa later in the year to evaluate the event, and Eilif Ness from Norway was

The CIP RW Sub-Committee: Curt Curtis (USA), Richard Charter (RSA), Eilif Ness (Norway), Bert Wijnands (Netherlands), C S-S (GB)

appointed chief judge. Curt, Bert and I agreed to support Richard and Eilif at the World Cup in every way we could to ensure that the new sequential concept worked successfully and was ready for the planned RW Championships in Australia in 1977.

But 1976 was a Classic events year so I still had the National Championships to organise in June. Additionally the Competitions Committee had appointed me head of delegation of the British team for the World Style and Accuracy Championships to be held in September at Guidonia near Rome. The 1,050 jumps made during the week of the Nationals at Shobdon produced Red Devil Scotty Milne as Men's Champion, with John Meacock as runner-up, and with Sandy Murray as Ladies' Champion, and Jackie Smith as runner-up. Regular NW Parachute Centre jump pilot Chris Benyon's enthusiasm is especially worthy of mention. Because Shobdon weren't sure when the AVGAS fuel tanker was due to arrive to top up the airfield tanks, I'd phoned the pilots who were to fly in with the visiting jump aeroplanes to ask them to arrive with as near full tanks as possible. Chris excelled himself. Not only had he topped up the Cark Cessna 182 with fuel at Halfpenny Green on his way to Shobdon, he'd also filled a scrounged fifty-gallon drum that he'd lashed to the aircraft floor. Then, during the competition, he only stopped flying when it was necessary to refuel. I've no idea of how much flying he'd done on the third day, but he was making numerous successive passes over the DZ to drop one jumper at a time in the individual accuracy event. He must have been in robot mode because on one sortie late in the day and having dropped each of his load of four jumpers, he went round for a fifth time with no jumpers on board – I called him up on the radio and suggested he landed and took a break!

At the end of June the Emerald Isle beckoned again when an invitation from the Irish Parachute Club arrived to request that I help them run a week-long RW seminar to coincide with their summer camp at Farranfore Airfield, now named Kerry Airport. Yorkshire businessman and enthusiastic skydiver Steve Swallow kindly agreed that we could use his Cessna 206 if he could join in the fun and benefit from some instructional flying in the aeroplane to and from Farranfore as he was approaching the end of his PPL course. In the bar during the evening of our arrival one of the Irish club members whom I'd met the previous year asked me: 'Are ye goin' fur yer PPA while yer here, Charlie?'

I sought enlightenment. 'What's PPA?'

'It's Parachuting Piss Artists,' was the startling response, and I was proudly shown the badge – a glass of Guinness surmounted by a parachute with the initials PPA underneath.

'And what do you have to do to qualify?' I asked nervously.

'Well, only one jump, but ye still have to be standin' at de bar when de sun cooms up de next day!' I declined to accept the thoughtfully offered invitation with as much good grace as I could muster!

The following morning there was ample evidence of failed PPA qualification attempts from the previous evening – there were loudly snoring bodies cocooned in sleeping bags all over the hangar floor. I suspect that most of the Irish skydivers spent considerably more on PPA attempts than they did on skydiving, with the result that performance of the latter suffered proportionately. But they were a wonderfully generous and entertaining bunch. On the third day there wasn't a cloud in the sky but the wind speed increased quickly to excess of the limit, even for experienced jumpers. I suggested that we should put the parachuting on hold until such time as the wind speed had decreased substantially. A suitable announcement was made to that effect, but this concluded with an instruction that all the students should get their kit on. It was only after the first four students had landed some three-and-a-half miles away that all parachuting was finally put on hold. It was immediately decided that we should fill the two aircraft with jumpers, less parachutes, sitting on the floor and fly west for twenty or so miles to land on

Inch Beach, a magnificent four-mile stretch of sand on the Dingle Peninsula. Here most of us, soon joined by a group who'd arrived by car, enjoyed a swim in the sea before we were all delightfully entertained by some of the girls dancing to violin and accordion ceilidh music, played by some of the more talented parachute club members – it was an enchantingly memorable alternative to jumping out of aeroplanes and wonderfully Irish!

For the Classic World Championships, Bergerac in France was once again selected as the training camp venue. The delegation of both men's and ladies' teams proved to be a dedicated and competitive bunch who worked hard under coach Doug Peacock,

Doug Peacock's camera records Bob Hiatt at opening time over Bergerac

himself a massively experienced style and accuracy jumper. Robin Mills exemplified the group's splendid team spirit when Chris McGuire, one of the ladies, had an unpleasant malfunction from which she cut away before landing safely, but somewhat shaken, under her reserve. Robin quickly recovered and untangled her main which, together with Chris' reserve, he repacked – and all before Chris had downed a coffee and regained her composure. Robin also had an entertaining personal rivalry with Scotty Milne, culminating in an ice-cream-eating competition organised by fellow Red Devil Dickie Bird, and which was seriously contested between them. What Robin didn't know was that Scotty was hugely proud of the trophy he'd won earlier that year for winning an eating competition against one of the Red Devils' sponsors – so for those of us in the know Scotty was odds-on favourite. Robin had no chance and was beaten by a multi-coloured tutti-frutti mountain – and Dickie Bird won a few francs. Having completed our training camp, we then drove to Guidonia in Italy for the World Championships themselves. Here Bob Hiatt deservedly became our hero of the competition in the Individual Accuracy event. There were scheduled to be a total of eight rounds and after the fourth Bob had hit the 10cm disc four times, but at a painful price of a torn knee ligament on the fourth. He persuaded the medics to bind up his leg and re-entered the competition later the same day – two more dead centres were the result. But in spite of his valiantly carrying on, he could only score 3 and 2, just a wretched one centimetre from the bronze medal – it had been a stoic effort.

Back home at Leicester airfield in October it was time for the Relative Work National Championships for which we had an Islander and a Cessna 185 G-AYNN that we'd hired from Bembridge. The latter provided me with my only enduring memory of the event. On the fifth day of the competition I was flying Symbiosis, one of the four-way teams, in the 185, for a jump from 9,000ft. My report of the incident records:

> *Up to approximately 8,000ft the engine behaved normally with a reduction in boost to about 20in, while the mixture was leaned accordingly. Then suddenly, and without any prior warning from the instruments or gauges, there was a sharp report from the engine; the windscreen immediately started to be covered by oil and the engine developed a loud metallic clatter. Unsurprisingly, and without prompting, the parachutists immediately exited the aircraft. I closed the throttle fully, leaned the mixture to cut off, fully coarsened the pitch and turned off the ignition and fuel. I informed Leicester ATC of the engine failure and then of my intention to carry out a dead-stick landing on the grass to the left of runway 28. This was carried out without any further incident or damage to the aircraft.*

Even the birds stopped singing! Subsequent investigation revealed that the little end coupling on the connecting rod had failed, and the rod itself had smashed an interesting-looking hole in the crank case – see the interesting photo below.

In early October and only a few days before I was due to fly out to South Africa for the World Cup in Sequential RW I was informed that Eilif Ness was unable to be chief judge and I was asked by Richard Charter if I would take his place – I wasn't entirely happy about agreeing but it seemed there was nobody else who could take it on at such short notice, and Jim Crocker and the BPA encouraged my acceptance. I was acutely aware that the World Cup had to be successful for a World Championships in Sequential RW to be held the following year, but luckily I was to have working with me a splendid team of judges representing ten of the nations competing. Oudtshoorn in Western Cape province was selected by the organisers to be the venue as it boasted more sunshine than California and an annual rainfall of less than 9in – we had considerably more than that in the two weeks we were there. So much so that it was clear that elimination of drought could be easily be achieved by organising an international RW competition! With all teams accommodated in the local Holiday Inn and South African Air Force support of four DC3s and five Kudus (the latter a sort of South African Cessna 185/Beaver cross), the competition was well run and, in spite of the appalling wet weather, six rounds of each of the four-way and eight-way events were just completed in the time available. A constructive post-meeting of four CIP members, six judges and a representative of each of the 19 nations competing produced enough useful input for the RW Sub-Committee of CIP to tidy up the rules at the next international meeting scheduled for early February 1977 – the World Championship to be held in Australia was now definitely ON! The final piece of entertainment at Oudtshoorn was the dance fiasco which was best described in the local paper under the headline: 'Parachute party girls row'.

> *OUDTSHOORN* – *A row was brewing between parachutists and a local dominee* here yesterday over the honour of the town's young girls. The Rev W F Liebenberg took strong exception to advertisements calling on 300 'pretty girls' to join visiting skydivers at a dinner-dance organised by the owner of an Oudtshoorn ice-rink. Speaking from the pulpit, Mr Liebenberg exhorted the girls not to attend the dance for the sake of their principles. Later he warned a catechism class that he would refuse to confirm any girl who disobeyed and he gave the class permission to tell others that all offenders would be censured by the church. The parachutists reacted with anger and disbelief. Officials said the dominee's warning amounted to an insult both to the parachutists and the organisers of the event. Championship director Mr Rod Murphy said in a statement: 'The championship committee was not involved in the organisation of this dance. It was organised independently by local townspeople and in fact few of the skydivers attended. If, in fact, the statements attributed to Mr Liebenberg are true, then they must be seen as an insult not only to the contestants themselves but to the International Aviation Federation who awarded this event to South Africa.' Mr Liebenberg visited the championship headquarters at the Oudtshoorn Airport yesterday where he denied attacking the morals of the competitors. He had the highest esteem for*

---

* A dominee is a Dutch Reformed Church priest.

the jumpers, he said, and it was not up to him to pass judgment on them. He said he believed Oudtshoorn's young girls would have been 'cheapened' and led into temptation by attending the dance. He did not like dancing. Asked whether the church would take action against young girls who attended parties this week, Mr Liebenberg said that this would depend on such factors as the girls' manner of dress and whether there was an abuse of liquor. Mr Mike Genniss, a member of the United States team who attended the dance, said yesterday: 'The whole thing is quite amusing. What does the guy expect us to do?' Mr Genniss said that were only about 20 parachutists at the dance and no single girls. 'We went inside, had dinner and drinks, and went home. It was a bit of a drag really.'

The only person who didn't see the funny side of it all was the wretched dominee himself.

A couple of weeks after I got home, my dear friend Richard Charter, who was chairman of the Parachute Committee of the South African Aero Club, sent me a kind letter in which he wrote: 'I think you played a major role in Sequential RW development by achieving the excellent judging result that you did at Oudtshoorn, and, what is more, at such short notice too. I sincerely hope that you enjoyed your function as chief judge as it is also my intention to advise the CIP meeting of your capabilities in this regard, and hopefully you will be saddled with this job again in the future.' Thanks a bunch, Richard!

1977 saw the familiar round of the CIP Meeting, National Championships, club competitions, four instructors' courses, editing four issues of *Sport Parachutist* and an occasional display where I was fortunate enough to have been invited along as a guest jumper. The display with the Guards Parachute Team into Hyde Park from an Army Air Corps

With the Guards Parachute Team into Hyde Park and with the Ansells Paramen into the water at Staunton Hall

Scout helicopter was particularly memorable as it couldn't be repeated today. The operation of single-engine aircraft over central London is no longer permissible, but in July 1977 it wasn't a problem. We took off from the park itself to gain altitude flying up above Oxford Street before turning back to exit the Scout over Kensington Gardens. The views of London during the parachute descent into Hyde Park were unforgettable. On another occasion I joined the Ansells Paramen for a display into the lake in the grounds of Staunton Hall near Ashby-de-la-Zouch for a Cheshire Homes Gala. A water jump is always an enjoyable experience, but the subsequent drying of all the equipment before repacking of both main and reserve parachutes is never quite up to the same level of enjoyment!

During late 1977 my father was having a few health problems, which prompted him to ask me if I could join him at Carton Industries, the family packaging business in Durrington, near Amesbury. In spite of the fascinating time I was having working for the BPA, I felt I had to accede to his request, but it wasn't an easy decision to have had to make. I gave the BPA six months' notice to leave their employ at the end of April the following year. It was then that I handed over to Doug Peacock, whose qualifications for the job were impeccable. Doug was a good friend who had given me considerable support as his predecessor – he went on to do the BPA proud. As likewise did Pete Sherman, who in turn took over from Doug. Pete, a larger-than-life personality, had been one of Dare Wilson's protégés in 22 SAS and a member of Dare's high-altitude skydive record-breaking team of 1962. So for my part I just felt hugely privileged to have been the BPA's first full time national coach and safety officer.

CHAPTER 16
CHIEF JUDGE 1977, 1981 AND 1983

Richard Charter's hope that I'd be saddled with the job of chief judge came about the following year when CIP landed me with the role for the World Sequential Relative Work Championships to be held in Queensland, Australia. The key players from the host nation were Claude Gillard, the larger-than-life president of the Australian Parachute Federation and their CIP delegate with the splendidly efficient pair of Dave Millard as meet director and Donna Berthelsen as organiser. Halfway through November after a stop-start jet-lag-inducing flight I finally arrived late in the day at Brisbane Airport where Donna was there to meet me. She was kindness itself and, during supper at a local restaurant, she told me that she'd 'volunteered' me to be chief judge at the Queensland parachute championships at a small airfield near the town of Caloundra some sixty miles north of Brisbane. She added that it also meant a very early start the following morning. I was so jet-lagged that I remember little of the drive there. It was just getting light as we drove along a rough track through some pine trees to get to the airfield when two kangaroos boing-boinged their way across in front of us. We pulled up at the Ramblers Parachute Club hut to encounter a post-party scene of total devastation from the night before and exemplified by one loudly snoring body laid back in a deck chair. He was still clutching an empty Fosters 'tinnie' and wearing the quintessential cork dangling bush hat pulled forward over his eyes. The corks were obviously having little effect as flies were marching resolutely in and out of his open mouth. I immediately felt reassured that I'd now arrived properly in Australia!

Apart from hosting the Queensland championships, the venue was also being used by most of the World Championship teams as a training camp. For this it was perfect as the ubiquitous DHC-6 Twin Otter, this one operated by Trans Australia Airlines, was the same aircraft also to be used for the World Championships. While at Caloundra, Brits Dane Kenny, Jackie Smith and I were delighted to have been invited by Roger Hull to take part in a skydive with the US team, Mirror Image. Roger, an ex-US Navy fighter pilot, was an exceptionally talented jumper with a computer-like mind who was always dreaming up imaginative skydiving challenges. This time he'd come up with what he called a 'sixteen-way orbital transmutation' – at least that's what is written in my logbook! We had to build four different four-man formations flying on the same level before one jumper from each formation flew clockwise to the next formation, and another jumper then made a similar move – the planned result would have every jumper making one move with each having been in all of the four formations. We walked through, or 'dirt dived' it numerous times before we took to the sky and 14,000ft to attempt it for real – and we very nearly completed it, but we simply ran out of freefall time. It was an intoxicatingly breathtaking skydive and I remember it so well – even the birds stopped singing! I've always believed that parachute judges are likely to enhance their credibility if they are seen to be active skydivers – so many thanks for that one, Roger.

Fast-forward to the Queensland Agricultural College at Gatton, sixty or so miles west of Brisbane and venue for the championships themselves. The scene is one of the college's lecture theatres for the chief judge's briefing held to the accompaniment of a thunderstorm venting its displeasure outside. It was almost to be expected that the Australian team captain would seek clarification of one of the rules and inevitably he was vociferously unhappy with my interpretation. I turned to Bert Wijnands, now chairman of CIP's RW Sub-Committee, for his support and Bert, bless him, confirmed my clarification. More Oz unhappiness followed and it was getting boring. It was time to make a stand before the whole thing slipped from my grasp. 'Gentlemen,' I announced, as firmly as I could, 'you're all just going to have to accept our clarification and that's it…' and at that precise moment there occurred a timely rumble of thunder and a spectacular flash of lightning – it was too good a chance to miss, so I pointed heavenwards, '…and He agrees with me!' Roars of laughter quickly brought the briefing to a swift conclusion.

Gatton proved to be an outstanding venue with the grass airstrip, drop zone, catering facilities and accommodation all within easy walking distance of each other. The competition itself was well organised with Dave Millard insisting that the jumping day started at 5.30am and finished at 6.30pm. Every time the sole Twin Otter landed it was filled with minimum fuel with the props still turning – and while the next load of jumpers were emplaning. The full competitive programme was thus completed with a day-and-a-half to spare. The team of judges representing fourteen of the nations competing did a fantastic job and I was fortunate indeed to have had Lorrie Young, an experienced judge from the USA, as my assistant chief judge. This was the last RW World Championships to have been scored in real time by judges using telemetres (high-powered binoculars), with the result that we only had one opportunity to get it right. I remember only one occasion when we got it wrong. The team from the Federal Republic of Germany were well in medal contention when, uncharacteristically, their fourth-round exit from the aircraft was a disaster from which they were unable to recover – this effectively put them out of the competition. The Dutch four-man team, captained by Bert Wijnands, were the next to jump. The moment they landed, Bert threw off his parachute equipment and ran over to find me in the judging area. The adrenalin was obviously still flowing as with considerable excitement he blurted out: 'Charlie, those people marched through my country in 1940, but you've got to give them a re-jump!' Once he had caught his breath he explained that there had been communication confusion between the flight deck crew and the German team who were keyed up and ready to go by the door. Bert's explanation convinced me that the confusion in the aircraft came about through no fault of the German team. I walked across to where they were packing their parachutes and found their team captain. I told him that they'd been awarded a re-jump and that they were on a thirty-minute call. They were profuse in their thanks. 'Don't thank me,' I said, 'perhaps you should thank Dr Wijnands.' Their re-jump score put them back in medal contention and they finished the competition in well-earned second place. But at the prize-giving their being presented with silver medals caused some embarrassment. They were standing rigidly to attention, waiting to be called forward. Claude Gillard made the announcement: 'And the silver medals go to the German Democratic Republic!' The Federal German team didn't move. Dave Millard whispered something in Claude's ear – his reaction was a classic: 'Oh, shit, no,' he corrected himself, 'you guys are the Federals!' I can't be sure whether the resultant cheers were for Claude's cock-up or for the Federal German team's splendid achievement.

At the Championships dinner that evening I was sitting at a table with the rest of the judges when two members of the German team came over to where we were sitting. 'Charlie, ve have a small presentation to give to you.' I stood as I was handed a fabulous book, *Blick aus dem Zeppelins*, of aerial photographs taken from Zeppelins 1929-1933. In it was written: 'With compliments and special thanks to Charlie Shea-Simonds, chief judge at the 2nd WPC/RW at Gatton, Australia, 1977. The National Team of Germany, FR' and signed by all fifteen members of their delegation. It was a very kind and thoughtful gesture and I was genuinely touched, but it was difficult to come up with a suitable response. 'Thank you all so much for this magnificent book, and thank you for being such a sporting team.' 'Ja, ve believe in ze sportsmanship,' one of them replied, 'not like zoze people over zere!' He pointed to the noisy and none too well-behaved Canadian team at the other end of the room just as Kelly Dunn, their outrageous leader, received a well-aimed piece of apple pie and custard in the face. It could have been straight out of a Laurel and Hardy movie and I struggled desperately to maintain my composure. The bottom line, however, was that it had been a hugely successful World Championships

Australia, New Zealand, Canada, Norway, USA, Holland, Germany and the UK are represented in this post-championships skydive over Gatton – C S-S top right in blue and white. Photo: Jacques Geilen

and I was privileged to have been chief judge. The positive atmosphere of the event exemplified itself to me during the last couple of days at Gatton when an international head of delegation load was organised with nine of us from the eight nations participating. Brit judge Bob Burn and I represented the UK, with Claude Gillard (Australia), Rande Caldwell (New Zealand), Uwe Beckmann (Germany FR), Buzz Bennett (Canada), Eilif Ness (Norway), Hein Cannegeiter (Holland) and Bill Ottley (USA), plus Dutch photographer Jacques Geilen joining us to record the jump. Initially it built steadily with seven of us joining the formation in our planned positions. Unfortunately Bill Ottley slipped below and was unable to get back up to our level before Uwe Beckmann closed too hard on the group and collapsed it spectacularly – see Uwe top-left in the photo on the previous page. It was an unusually enjoyable skydive, which prompted the thought that there is no other aviation sport in which international participation can be shared so intimately, so I was delighted when Jacques' colourful photograph finally arrived in the post to provoke memories of international skydiving chums. At the CIP meeting in early 1978 France was chosen as the venue for the 1979 World RW Championships and the German FR CIP delegate and good friend Uwe Beckman was proposed as chief judge. As this was the first RW Championships to be judged using video, and as Uwe had video judging expertise (which I hadn't), I was very happy to support the proposal.

Netheravon Airfield, then home to 7 Regiment AAC, the Army Parachute Association and the Joint Services Parachute Centre, was only five miles from where I was now living and working in the family business. I had, therefore, plenty of opportunities for both flying and skydiving at this historic military grass airfield – a situation I was able to enjoy for the next thirty-five years. By 1978 both APA and the Red Devils had retired their aged and much-loved DH89A Rapides and were now operating BN2A piston engine Islanders; I was soon checked out to fly them. At that time the Red Devils were regularly operating theirs from the grassy expanse of Queen's Parade – a temporary airstrip and DZ located conveniently close to their Aldershot base. Flying the Islander in and out of Queen's Parade was always something of a challenge and I was fortunate that Roger Mills, a BA Concorde Captain and Red Devils Chief Pilot, had conducted my Queen's Parade check ride so comprehensively. Pilots either loved flying the BN2A Islander, or hated it – personally I loved flying it!

The 1978 World Style and Accuracy Championships were held in Zagreb, Yugoslavia, and, as it was during my first year working in the family business, I felt I had to give Zagreb a miss – something I've regretted ever since as it provided the most exciting competition result in British skydiving history. Jackie Smith had joined the Army in 1969 and in 1971, having been seriously bitten by the skydiving bug, she became the first female Red Devil and later she went on to earn the right to wear the coveted Red Beret of Airborne Forces. During her five years as a member of the team she had become a talented competition parachutist and was a member of the British style and accuracy team in Hungary in 1974 and in Italy in 1976. But at Zagreb she excelled herself. Flying her well-used but much loved Strato Star she scored two dead-centres (DCs) on the first day of competition – the dead centre of the target was a 10cm disc located in the middle of the electronic scoring pad. On the second day she notched up another five DCs followed by a further two on the third day – a formidable total score of nine DCs from nine jumps. Then the weather broke. Jackie then had to endure three days of hanging about waiting for suitable weather so she could make her tenth and final jump. Her nearest rival, Cheryl Stearns of the USA, had scored 2cm on one of her nine jumps so it all depended on their last jumps. No pressure then! Finally she was airborne in the Antonov AN2 for her tenth jump from 2,500ft. After the first four jumpers had exited on individual passes over the DZ there was a lengthy hold as an injured jumper received medical attention – a situation of which Jackie was unaware. After some twenty-five minutes of circling the DZ the aircraft ran in for the most thrilling skydiving challenge of her life. Flying in under canopy towards the centre of the target she reached for the disc and hit the disc firmly with her left heel. She glanced across at the electronic readout on the screen, a moment's delay before it lit up: 0.00. Not only had she become World Ladies' Accuracy Champion, she'd become the first person, male or female, to score ten dead centres out of ten jumps at a World Championships. It was a truly magnificent achievement by a lovely lady who had trained so resolutely and so tenaciously to deservedly become the World No 1 in this event. Her splendid modestly written and often hilarious book, *Marooned*, is a must-read for anyone interesting in the history of skydiving, especially in the 1970s and 1980s.

At the 1979 BPA AGM I was re-elected to the Council of the BPA after which I attended the CIP meeting in Arnhem, Holland, where Michel Rogovitz, the French delegate, was asked to update the delegates present about plans for the World RW championships to be held later in the year at Chateauroux in central France. We were all amazed when we were informed that the organiser had felt it necessary to change the CIP/FAI-approved rules to make give the competition more spectator appeal with canopy handling to be incorporated into the competition. The suggestion was totally out of order especially when we'd had a successful World Cup and World Championships to prove the concept and the rules for the four-way and eight-way events. It was gently pointed out to Michel that his willy-nilly changing of the rules without the approval of CIP/FAI was a non-starter. He then dropped a bombshell by stating that, in that case, the French organisers had no option other than to withdraw their bid to host the World Championships. The French delegation obviously reckoned they had us over a barrel as who else would be prepared to put in an alternative bid with only seven months to go? Who indeed? It all went very quiet. It was clearly time to have some fun with the French, even if it dented the entente cordiale. I stood and, addressing Horst Brandl, the president of CIP, announced: 'President, the French delegate should know that they cannot just change the rules for these championships as they see fit, and so, to solve the impasse which faces us, the British Parachute Association is prepared to host the event during the dates already agreed and in accordance with the CIP/FAI approved rules. It will be a "no frills" championships to be held at Netheravon Airfield, home of the British Army Parachute Association. Islander aircraft will be used with officials and competitors being housed in basic military accommodation with Army catering available on the airfield.' I was frantically making it all up as I went along. 'And I am confident sponsorship will be available for the event from our two military parachute manufacturers, which will ensure that we are able to guarantee that the entry fee will not exceed $200 per competitor – are there any questions?' I sat down quickly before there were. From one side of the room there was applause initiated by my RW Sub-Committee colleagues and from the other side of the room there were mutterings from the Eastern Bloc countries' delegates as the KGB interpreters translated what I'd said into a number of different languages. It was starting to sound like the Tower of Babel so Horst wisely declared a coffee break to allow a period of cooling of the proceedings. I was immediately approached by Michel and the other three of his organising committee. 'Charlie, you are bluffing aren't you?' he queried. 'I couldn't be more serious,' I replied as firmly as I could. 'It's outrageous that you lot are trying to hold us to ransom in this way.' I turned and walked quickly away, trying to keep a straight face. Actually I liked Michel and I felt there was a good chance that he could persuade his colleagues that they should to agree to abide by the CIP/FAI-approved rules. Having had a huddled discussion in the corner between the four of them, Michel quietly announced that they would run the championships in accordance with the CIP/FAI-approved rules after all. It was a close-run thing and I never did reveal to Michel that I had been bluffing – phew!

Back on Salisbury Plain I was dreaming up ways to obtain some interesting sporting aviation-orientated PR for the family business – a company specialising in manufacturing protective packaging. I persuaded good friend John Laing, at that time the charismatic chief instructor of the Army Parachute Association, to skydive with one of our cardboard containers while I took the photographs. His solo jump went well so we recruited Wally Wallace for the next attempt when the two of them had the box flying between them. With the caption '…FOR FREEFALL PROTECTION' we used the photo on the 1980 company calendar – whether it prompted any sales is debatable, but at least the participants enjoyed themselves!

On arrival at Chateauroux for the third World RW Championship in August the British team, of which I had been appointed head of delegation, found an unpleasant surprise awaiting them. While the French team were enjoying the facilities of a modern three-star hotel located close to the airfield's main entrance, we found ourselves accommodated in a decaying Napoleonic barracks some three miles away with Jackie, as the only lady on the team, finding herself in a separate block from the rest of us. Not unreasonably, feelings were quickly running high. Then Jackie appeared visibly upset having fled her barrack block. She had gone to the washroom for a shower and come across a crowd of naked French soldiers who waved their penises about and suggested she join them in the showers. We all packed our kit and drove to the aerodrome where I sought

The Brit delegation at Chateauroux with the silver medal-winning Symbiosis seated in front: Geoff Sanders, Will Grut, Jackie Smith (alternate), Rob Colpus and Dane Kenny with C S-S extreme right

out Michel Rogovitz – he could see that I was bloody furious, so he did as he was told when I ordered him into my car. Without speaking I drove him to the barracks where I frostily showed him around the place as I explained Jackie's unnerving experience. 'And is that how you treat World Champions in France?' I demanded. 'Mon Dieu!' he exclaimed. 'C'est affreux – je suis vraiment désolé!' He went on to admit that he hadn't actually been to the visit the barracks before the competition, but he could well understand why I was so upset and he assured me that he'd sort out more appropriate accommodation by the end of the day – which, to be fair, he managed to do. In spite of this unfortunate hiccup, Symbiosis, the Brit four-way team jumped exceptionally well to deservedly finish in silver medal second place while the eight-way team finished in a creditable fifth place. At the next CIP meeting early the following year Michel Rogovitz publicly apologised to the British team for the way in which they had been allocated sub-standard accommodation at Chateauroux – it was most gracious of him to do so and I was happy to thank him for it. At the same meeting Uwe Beckmann reported that using video for judging at Chateauroux had proved successful and he recommended its use at future World Championships and this was agreed. Personally I was delighted by this decision because, at the same meeting, I was approached by Jim Hooper, the boss of Zephyrhills, who asked me if I would consider being chief judge for the 1981 World Championships to be held there following a successful bid from the United States Parachute Association to host them. I was happy to agree. While I was employed by the BPA I had married again and I hoped that I'd make a better job of it this second time around. Anita is a lovely lady who, while I was at Gatton for the World Championships, had given birth to my second son, Philip. It was at about this time that this marriage also broke down irretrievably, and for which, yet again, I must be held responsible – too much flying and skydiving. Once again humble apologies are due, this time to both Anita and Philip.

In 1980 the World Championships in Style and Accuracy were held in Kazanlak, Bulgaria, at the end of August and I'd been selected by the BPA to be head of delegation. This time it was a men-only team as no ladies had been able to compete at the Nationals. Competitors and officials were accommodated in the town in a brand-new hotel built specifically for the Championships as the organisers were obviously out to impress everyone. The airfield was about three miles out of town set in an remote area of countryside noted only for growing roses with, of course, aircraft support being provided by a fleet of Antonov AN2s, the aircraft used by the Eastern Bloc countries for a seemingly infinite variety of tasks. We soon identified the organisation's secret policeman, a permanently morose-looking individual who soon demonstrated he was clumsily inept in doing his job. Halfway through the event I found Daisy, our little interpreter, in tears, so I asked her what the problem was. Convinced that it was bugged, she refused to talk about it in our team tent, so we went for a walk around the DZ where she explained that the organiser's secret policeman had tasked her with finding out how many members of our team were in the military. I replied that I had no idea, but I told her that I would find out and let her know. Our passports had been taken from us when we arrived at Kazanlak, so they must have quickly discovered that Red Devils Scotty Milne, Dougie Young and Deke Wright were employed as 'Government Officials', while policeman Paul Slaughter's passport described him as a 'Police Officer'. If they couldn't work out for themselves that the three Red Devils, with their smart appearance, polished boots and 'short back and sides' haircuts, were in the Army, I certainly wasn't going to tell them. The next day I told Daisy that I had been unable to find out which members of our team were in the military but that I had discovered that Paul was in fact a secret policeman who was there to keep an eye on the rest of us. Later she reported that the organisation's secret policeman was well pleased with what she'd been able to find out!

On the subject of interpreters, one memorable moment occurred during the judges' briefing when chief judge Buzz Bennett stopped for his interpreter to translate but she remained silent.

'Why don't you translate?' queried Buzz.

'Because it's not important,' was her reply to cheers from the judges, to which Buzz could only retort: 'EVERYTHING I say is important!'

In the Brit team tent there was always a mug of tea on the go for welcoming visitors, one of whom was Di Rutledge who was New Zealand's sole representative at the event. So, rather than her sitting as the only inhabitant of the Kiwi tent, we adopted her and she became a good friend of ours from then on based in our tent. Thirty-seven years later Di and I renewed that friendship and I now owe her a huge debt of gratitude for all the proofreading of this book she's done so conscientiously. The Brit team had a very successful competition which can be summed up in the words of a letter I wrote after the event to TFH, who was by this time Colonel Commandant of the Parachute Regiment:

Di Rutledge with her disc

The Regiment was represented by Deke, Scotty, Dougie and C S-S

I am writing in my capacity as head of delegation of the 1980 British Parachute Team at the recent World Parachute Championships in Bulgaria to say how proud and thrilled I was to have Sgts Milne and Wright and Cpl Young as members of that team. They proved themselves to be great sporting ambassadors for our country and the results achieved by Milne and Young reflect tremendous credit to both the Regiment and the British Parachute Association. I am delighted to be able to enclose copies of extracts from the individual score sheets. These results cannot express the excitement before the last round of the Individual Accuracy Event where Young was placed first equal with nine consecutive dead centres and Milne fourth with a 1cm total. When Young scored 1cm in the final round and Milne scored a another dead centre, it was then necessary for them to have a jump-off against each other for the bronze medal! Milne's cast-iron will and vast experience prevailed but Young's performance was really just as satisfying!

That just about says it all! Later I wondered if TFH as Colonel Commandant had remembered meeting Scotty during a visit to 1 PARA by the Prince of Wales who in

1977 had been appointed Colonel-in-Chief of the Regiment. The Battalion was about to emplane for an airborne exercise and Scotty, who was then the Mortar Platoon Sergeant, was already wearing both main and reserve parachutes and standing in front of a massive weapons container. The latter must have contained a 81mm mortar tube, a couple of mortar bombs, his personal weapon, twenty-four-hour ration pack and, very probably, a tube of Smarties. It was certainly well over the RAF maximum weight for a weapons container and the Prince of Wales, who had just successfully completed his military parachute course, was quick to spot it. Scotty was introduced by the CO 1 PARA, whereupon the Prince of Wales asked him if he could see how heavy it really was. Scotty agreed and the Colonel-in-Chief struggled to lift it off the ground before remarking: 'Sgt Milne, that really is a very heavy weapons container!' To which Scotty, without thinking, replied: 'Well, Sur, if yer want ta run with the big dogs yur gotta learn to pee high up the wall!' His Royal Highness was highly amused, but TFH obviously wasn't, as he commented: 'That's not quite the way I'd have put it, Sgt Milne!'

1980 ended with my responding positively to a suggestion from Jim Hooper that Bert Wijnands and I visit Zephyrhills to learn of his plans for hosting the World RW Championships scheduled to take place in October 1981. So at the end of December Bert and I met up with Jim and, apart from discussions about the CIP requirements for the suitability of the centre to be the venue for the Championships, we managed to make a few skydives – most of those I made were assisting Dane Kenny in his inspired coaching of three youngsters in the finer skills of relative work. During the DC-3's climb to altitude for my second skydive on December 30 I found myself sitting opposite a lovely-looking young lady who, with another group, was due to exit the aircraft on the pass over the DZ before ours. We grinned at each other as she got to her feet and moved towards the door – I watched her group exit before it was our turn on the DC-3's next pass over the DZ. During canopy deployment after an uneventful skydive I saw that I was going to land on the far side of the airfield and close to where another skydiver, who had landed before me, was searching for something in the grass. I recognised her as being the young lady who had been sitting opposite me in the DC-3. I asked her if I could help and she told me she had lost her 'Cookie Monster' (a Muppet character from TV's *Sesame Street*), her mascot, who had always jumped with her tucked under the chest strap of her parachute harness. We were unsuccessful in our search so we walked back to the parachute club together, during which time I discovered that her name was Julie Hanks, that she lived in Bristol and was then enjoying her fourth skydiving holiday at Zephyrhills. Four days later Cookie Monster was found and he and Julie were happily reunited. And as, dear reader, you will soon discover in the pages that follow, this gloriously enchanting, amazingly talented lady and I have shared some fantastic skydiving and flying adventures during the thirty-six years since we first met.

Back home and it was into the new year for a fulfilling start at the BPA AGM where I was elected to be chairman of the Association. At the incoming Council Meeting I suggested that consideration be given as to the desirability of my continuing as UK CIP delegate, BPA's Royal Aero Club representative and editor of *Sport Parachuting*. The BPA

Council asked me to carry on with the first two jobs but they felt that I should stand down from the latter. I reported this in my last editorial in the April 1981 issue:

> *BPA Council has decided, very fairly, that I should not continue as editor of SP while chairman of the Association. I have done the job for eight years (forty-nine issues) so it's probably time for a change, but I shall be sad that it's coming to an end. The job has given me much pleasure, has been very rewarding and has made me many friends, particularly those BPA members who contribute regularly and who really make the magazine what it is. I shall also miss dealing with Fishers, who print the SP – they have been fun to work with and have always done a totally professional job. Thanks sincerely to all who have made the job of editor such a stimulating and satisfying commitment.*

In February a team of us had organised the BPA's hosting of the 1981 CIP meeting at Bisham Abbey near Marlow on the Thames. It all went well and it was here that I was officially appointed chief judge of the World RW Championships at Zephyrhills. Julie arrived home in Bristol in March so we crammed in plenty of flying and skydiving together during the next eight months. In June we jumped from a Tiger Club Tiger Moth and a Stampe into the Bletchingley Village Fete for her 106th jump and her first display. She just missed the playing field and planted her size-six jump boots into the hallowed turf of the local bowling green. In August we jumped together over Shobdon during which time I took a photo recording Cookie Monster enjoying a skydive. Julie recorded in her logbook that it was CM's first jump since his accident in Florida!

Julie and Cookie Monster over Shobdon, August 1981. Photo: C S-S

Don Henry was a delightful American who, as a US Marine Corps pilot, had flown Corsairs and B25s in the Pacific during the war. I had met him at Redhill in 1980 and, when he learnt I was due to be in Florida the following year, he'd very kindly invited me to St Augustine to fly his Lycoming-engined Stampe. This was a good excuse for Julie and I to take few days' break before we had to be at Zephyrhills – she had kindly agreed to accompany me to be the chief judge's secretary. Apart from flying Don's interesting

Stampe with a prop that rotated in the opposite direction to the Gipsy Major engine usually found in a Stampe, Julie and I flew an immaculate little Piper L4 Cub belonging to a chum of Don's, before we also flew the club's beautiful Great Lakes 2T biplane which, with its 180 HP Lycoming engine, was a delight to fly. On our second day at St Augustine we flew the Great Lakes in formation with Don in his Stampe low level for the forty miles up the coast for lunch at Fernandina Beach. It was a memorable two days of laid-back American sporting aviation epitomised by Don's wonderfully generous hospitality!

C S-S and Julie flying the Great Lakes 2T biplane out of St Augustine

On October 6, having completed the 160-mile drive to Zephyrhills, we arrived in mid-afternoon to find that preparations for the World Championships had yet to be completed. Mercifully one of the first people we met was Lowell Bachman, my American Assistant chief judge, and what a stalwart character he turned out to be. Owner of Para-Gear, the largest sport parachute equipment company in the world, Lowell proved to be a modest, softly spoken tower of strength and I was unbelievably fortunate to have him as the most loyal second-in-command I could have wished for. Together we quickly set about trying to make the judging and video facilities fit for purpose with Julie dutifully typing the growing list of things that needed to be done. In spite of all the feverish activity going on we managed three skydives with an international cast of friends – these demonstrated that at least the routine jumping operation was up to speed. The international panel of judges were an experienced bunch from whom I selected good chum Buzz Bennett of Canada to be the four-way event judge and John Butterworth from New Zealand to be the eight-way event judge – their considerable expertise proved essential. But before the competition could start there was, inevitably, the garish razzmatazz of a grand opening ceremony complete with an all-female marching band providing the music for cavorting cheerleaders and prancing majorettes. And throughout the proceedings a Piper Cub flew in wide orbits overhead towing a banner that exhorted the two American teams by spelling out: GO FOR IT USA NO 1 – GOLDEN KNIGHTS & MIRROR

IMAGE. Curt Curtis, who was sitting next to me, remarked: 'Charlie, there you have an example of American sportsmanship!' In spite of all this the results scored by the judges produced worthy winners with the American Army Parachute Team, the Golden Knights, winning gold medals in the four-way event, that in which our own Symbiosis deservedly won the bronze medals, while the US team, Mirror Image, won the gold in the eight-way event. With the competition over it was time for the presentation of the trophies and medals and Mike Collins, the Command Module Pilot on Apollo 11, did the honours after which he was persuaded to make his first free jump from 12,000ft and in a ten-man star at that! Later that evening he was the Guest of Honour at the closing

Lowell Bachman and C S-S

Guest of Honour, Mike Collins

banquet held at the local Holiday Inn where all the competitors and, it has to be said, one or two of the judges also, were, having survived ten days of competition stress in a sun drenched dust bowl, ready to party big time. By the time it came to the speeches the assembled multitude was thoroughly well-lubricated and, as a result, were ready to start flinging the bread rolls. Having been suitably introduced, the Command Module Pilot of Apollo 11 rose to his feet and slowly surveyed his audience – he had about fifteen seconds to get it right, then: 'Gentlemen,' he announced firmly, 'I really don't know what I'm doing down here amongst all you DERELICTS!' It was brilliant and it brought the house down. From then on he held us in the palms of his hands with some thought-provoking words that inspired us all in much the same way as his splendid autobiographical book *Carrying the Fire* continues to do. It was a fitting end to the 1981 World RW Championships at which, in spite of a few hiccups, I felt privileged to have been chief judge. In a subsequent letter dear Lowell eloquently put some of these hiccups into perspective: 'You and Julie certainly had more than your fair share of problems, but the nice thing about man's mind is that one forgets the small problems and only remembers the good. In closing I have to recall a statement you made and now I wonder to whom it applies – you, me or both. "It's the price you pay for all your past sins in parachuting".'

At the 1982 BPA AGM I was re-elected chairman of the Association and both here and at the subsequent CIP there were some political 'rumblings in the jungle' gathering momentum. In 1948 the South African government had initiated Apartheid, or formal racial segregation, about which, very reasonably, most of the world became increasingly uncomfortable. It wasn't until 1977, however, that Commonwealth heads of state decided that some form of political pressure ought to be applied. At their meeting at Gleneagles in Scotland it was agreed that 'sport is an important means of developing and fostering understanding between the people, and especially between the young people, of all countries.' In spite of this statement the Commonwealth presidents and prime ministers present at Gleneagles agreed, as part of their support for the international campaign against apartheid, to discourage contact and competition between their sportsmen and sporting organisations, teams or individuals from South Africa. The result of this was that the British Sports Council announced that it would not grant-aid any British team competing in any international competition in which South African teams were also participating, although it was accepted that teams could not be prevented from competing. At the 1982 CIP meeting there was no bid to host the World Championships in 1983 so it was decided that the Bureau of CIP – consisting of the president and the first and second vice-presidents – should select the venue if bids should materialise. By this time I'd been elected second vice-president of CIP.

In early June the South African Aero Club presented a comprehensive bid to host the World Championships in Sun City in the Republic of Bophuthatswana with, for the first time ever, a zero entry fee – all the teams had to do was to get there thanks to the generosity of Sol Kersner, the owner of the opulent Sun City leisure complex. Very reasonably, an answer was requested by the end of September – with three days to go before this deadline the Austrian Aero Club submitted an alternative bid of which the only detail was a costly entry fee. A frantic round of international telephone conversations followed and, with the BPA Council's seven to two approval, I voted for acceptance of the South African bid as did Uwe Beckmann, the first vice-president. It was a decision which, because of its political implications, did not meet with universal approval. Richard Charter immediately contacted me and managed to persuade me to be the chief judge, about which more to follow. By the end of 1982 I'd completed fifteen years as a member of the BPA Council during which time I'd been editor of the BPA magazine, *Sport Parachutist*; three years as the BPA's first national coach and safety officer; eleven years as UK delegate to CIP; chief judge of the RW World Parachute Championships, Council member of the Royal Aero Club since 1974, and finally two years as chairman of the Association – 'jack of all trades, master of none' perchance! In any event I decided to stand down as a BPA Council member at the end of 1982 and as CIP delegate at the end of 1984 to make way for a younger generation of skydivers; after all, I'd just been accepted as a member of POPS – the Parachutists over Phorty Society – to which the hilarious letter from Top Pop and dear chum John Cooke will testify!

POPS UK

★ PARACHUTISTS ★
OVER PHORTY SOCIETY

Broughton House,
Field Broughton.
Nr. Grange over Sands.
Cumbria.
Tel Cartmel 545.

March 12th 1982.

Dear Mr Simons,

Further to your application to join our exalted organisation. I first checked your credentials (and found them wanting), I then placed your name before the selection committee but I regret to inform you that due to your past record, your application was at first refused. However, my personal plea on your behalf, plus the £5 beer money, which you so kindly sent along, finally won the day. The voting went as follows; one in favour, one 'don't know', and four abstentions.

However, I must warn you that we will not tolerate the sort of 'yob' behaviour which is sinominous ~~synonminos~~ usually connected with your name. Since you are now one of us and not one of 'them', we expect you to behave in a dignified and upright manner. (Exept when you are doing 'that') Just watch it that's all.

Cookey rules O.K.

In late 1982 Bert Wijnands, Julie and I were Richard Charter's guests in South Africa with the primary aim of our visiting Sun City and to learn of his plans for the organisation of the 1983 RW World Championships. The four-star accommodation was to be in the complex itself with the support of two Pilatus PC6 Turbo Porters operating from the ninth fairway of the famous golf course providing the lifts to altitude. The drop zone was to be any open space close to the swimming pool chosen by the competitors themselves, thus enabling them, having landed, to quickly throw off their kit and dive straight into the water to cool off! All this was approved at the 1983 CIP Meeting as was my appointment as chief judge. In early December Julie and I, together with John Laing as video camera operator, Eveline, his wife and Brit RW judge, Martin Rennie, all arrived in Sun City as the only BPA representatives. The Championships benefited from perfect facilities, well-flown aircraft and excellent weather. The result was a hassle-free competition with no protests – the dream of every organiser, judge and competitor alike and not often achieved, but it certainly was at Sun City. Political interference had reduced the entry to nine nations, but those teams whose governments and/or aero clubs had been enlightened enough to allow them to enter, competed in a Championships that would become an example for the future with Switzerland and the USA deservedly winning the four-way and eight-way events respectively – and both with impressive scores.

For me personally it was the perfect judging swan song, but then I'd been so very fortunate to have had such great teams of judges working with me at three World Cham-

A Pilatus Porter lands on the ninth fairway of the golf course... while John Laing operates the video camera

pionships, and for that I'll always be extremely grateful. Richard Charter subsequently wrote me an interesting letter, from which the following is an extract:

> *I must be honest and say that I have a substantial twinge of guilt when I think of how much of the political responsibility you took in respect of the Bureau's decision to grant us the World Championships. Obviously we both did (and I hope still do) believe that the Bureau's decision was correct and at the end of the day it was all worthwhile. The standard of the judging at the World Championships was quite obviously excellent and I think that your dedication to detail was largely responsible for this. Your choice of John-Charles Portier as event judge in the tricky four-way event, I feel was a very wise one and contributed largely to the success of the event. In conversation with you, Bert, Uwe and many of the other CIP delegates at Sun City, it became obvious that there is a genuine desire by all of us to work towards a less politically orientated CIP meeting this year. I will be playing low-key at the coming meeting as there are no immediate issues that affect South Africa. I hope the 'South Africa issue' will not again raise its ugly head and, by so doing, create political barriers amongst the delegates.*

Amen to that, Richard!*

During the five years about which I have written in this chapter I was also enjoying some very interesting flying. I must therefore fast-rewind back to 1978 to start the next chapter.

---

* Tragically, Richard lost his life during a canoeing trip on the Orange River in 2004.

CHAPTER 17

THE TIGER CLUB AND THE DAWN TO DUSK

During the second half of 1978 and most of 1979 the majority of my flying had been for parachuting – indeed in the eighteen months I flew a total of 165 hours, of which 125 was in either the Red Devils' BN2A or in the APA's, and the balance in the APA's Cessna 206. I fell in love with the BN2A, so much so that during one weekend at Netheravon I flew fourteen hours for parachuting in Islander G-BBRP in the two days. But my Islander flying was about to be curtailed somewhat by the arrival of some new challenges appearing over the horizon. At a Royal Aero Club Council meeting in November 1979 we'd been discussing the subject of co-operation between aviation sports and this continued in a pub over the road afterwards. Here David Faulkner-Bryant, the then-chairman of the Popular Flying Association (now the Light Aircraft Association), quickly came to the point. 'How about my making a parachute jump?' he asked. 'No problem,' says I. Then, with tongue well in cheek, I suggested: 'Swap you for a flight in your Currie Wot?' 'Done!' he replied – and that's how it came about. A couple of weeks later we met at the Tiger Club's base at Redhill where the hangar full of beautiful aeroplanes set my mouth watering. Having extracted Currie Wot G-ARZW out on to the apron and having received a short but concise briefing from David, I found myself airborne in this captivating little aeroplane. She was an absolute delight to fly but I had no wish to take advantage of David's trusting generosity. After about half an hour

The John Urmston-built Currie Wot G-ARZW

I turned back towards Redhill to join the circuit. It was time to persuade Zulu Whisky to abandon her enjoyment of the sky. Downwind checks – turn base leg – ease back on the throttle and trim to 60kts. With the Walter Mikron engine popping gently away in front, we slid towards the green turf. I let her sink on. It wasn't a tidy arrival – a gentle bounce first to show me that she's the boss: 'Steady old girl, you've simply got to stay on the ground.' And the second time it's three points permanently on. I taxied back to the apron, shut down, and just sat there with a stupid grin on my face, savouring the memory. Later I wrote in my logbook: 'DF-B's fantastic Wot! Wot an aeroplane!' Wot I didn't know at the time was who had built this beautiful little aeroplane originally. I soon discovered that it had been one Dr John Urmston who, coincidentally, was the CAA approved medical examiner (AME) to whose scrutiny I subjected myself on a regular basis for the renewal of my flying medical. *Birds and Fools Fly* is his enchantingly written book about his learning to fly and his painstaking construction of his Currie Wot in 1966. John quickly became a good friend and for more than thirty years I was able to admire his engineering skills and delight in his wonderfully impish sense of humour. My experience of flying the Wot led directly to my being introduced to the Tiger Club which I joined there and then. The Tiger Club had been formed at Croydon in 1956 by Norman Jones, a colourful and, at times, cantankerous and mildly eccentric character, who had learnt to fly in the early 1920s. There is no shortage of Norman Jones stories. My favourite was told to me by Dr John Urmston. Late in his life, Norman, who was no lover of needless bureaucratic authority, had incurred the wrath of the CAA, the result of which required the immediate renewal of his flying medical. He phoned John, who was quickly ready to help with his professional expertise and, as they lived a good distance apart, John suggested they meet at the club's premises at Redhill which was about midway between the two of them.

'No,' replied Norman, 'that's not necessary – just put the medical certificate in the post to me!'

'I'm very sorry, Norman,' said John, 'but I really do have to see you.'

'Well, that's definitely not in the spirit of the Tiger Club!' was Norman's reply, then he hung up!

When Croydon closed in 1959 the club moved to Redhill at the same time as Norman's son, Michael, took over as manager. The club undertook no ab initio pilot training, restricting initial membership to only accepting pilots who had more than 100 hours' pilot-in-command time as the basic qualification. All new members were required to sign the Club Charter, which read:

> *As a member of the TIGER CLUB I undertake:*
> 1. *Always to go out of my way to assist other members in aeronautical matters.*
> 2. *Always to fly with courtesy and with especial attention to the safety and comfort of others.*
> 3. *Never to use an aeroplane for any disreputable or unworthy purpose.*

Michael Jones was very much more laid-back than his father and he quietly encouraged members' participation in all the club's activities whether it was display flying, aerobatics, air racing or touring, and in a wonderful variety of aircraft types – Tiger Moth, Stampe, Turbulent, Piper Cub and Jodel. Michael was a great enthusiast with the result that good-humoured, infectious enthusiasm was a quality that pervaded the entire membership – whatever their flying experience. On December 1, I drove to Redhill for my Tiger Moth check ride, the first hour and ten minutes of which I flew in G-AIVW with an experienced and helpful member by name of Freddie Stringer who gave me an unforgettable 'heads-up' about flying the DH82A. 'Remember,' he said, 'the most difficult decision you have to make when you're about to go Tiger flying, is whether you push it out of the shed or leave it hangared where it is.' A week later my final Tiger check ride – this time in G-ACDC, the oldest DH82A on the register – was thirty minutes with club check pilot Pete Kynsey. This modest, softly spoken man is now probably the most experienced and respected war bird display pilot in the country, and, as expected, my check ride was both comprehensive and enjoyable. Later the same day my check in Piper Super Cub G-AVPT was only fifteen minutes because, luckily, I was already current on the type. All my flying at the Tiger Club in January of the new year, less one trip in 'CDC, was in G-AWEF, one of the club's two Stampe SV4Bs. The Belgian Stampe et Vertongen SV is a two-seat biplane trainer of similar configuration to the DH82A Tiger Moth. Some 1,050 were manufactured mainly under licence in France just post-war. The designation 4B indicates that this version has a DH Gipsy Major X rated at 145HP, whereas the standard Gipsy Major in the DH82A Tiger Moth is rated at 130HP. Both types are 1930s designs with the 8,868 Tigers being built here in the UK, Canada, Australia and New Zealand. For my money the Stampe is a better aircraft than the Tiger from the flying perspective as it has ailerons on both top and bottom wings (making it more positive in roll), brakes, a tailwheel and, with its fifteen more horses pulling up front, it's a little quicker. During the next five months most of my flying was in G-AWEF as I attempted to thoroughly familiarise myself with this delightful aeroplane. Having been given a useful grounding in basic aerobatics by the modestly unassuming John Harper, one of the most accomplished aerobatic pilots in the club and a fine instructor, I threw in ten or so minutes at the end of every trip, which polished up my Stampe handling skills considerably. Michael Jones was a very relaxed club manager and he was always very accommodating in allowing me to take any of the club's aircraft away from Redhill's immediate airspace with Netheravon becoming a regular destination.

It was at this time that I learnt of the International Dawn to Dusk, one of the Tiger Club's annual competitions that took place every June. The idea of this unusual test of aviation skill is stated as being: 'To provide a means of encouraging the most fruitful and interesting employment of a light aircraft within the bounds of competent airmanship and to demonstrate the practical possibilities of a day's flying in terms of furthering some original and praiseworthy objective.' Having dreamed up a 'praiseworthy objective', which involves a day's flying of not less than eight hours between 4.30am and 8.15pm on any day in June, it is then necessary to present the project in flight plan form to the judges. The challenge is the map-reading necessary to fly the plan and, during the flight, have it certified as correct and subsequently recorded in a logbook. From the competitors' log books of their day's flying the judges determined the results. The initial problem, therefore, was to dream up a project that would produce an interesting day's flying. Because of my earlier connections with 'God's County' I came up with the idea of a flying celebration of Yorkshire's amazing contribution to the history of aviation – from Sir George Cayley, the 'Father of Aeronautics'; the UK's first aviation meeting held on Doncaster Racecourse in 1909; Sir Robert Blackburn, founder of the Blackburn Aeroplane Company; the R100 Airship first flown from Howden in 1929; to the incredible statistic of more than ninety military airfields being constructed in Yorkshire during the two world wars. The planning stage involved sending out more than a hundred letters to airfield owners, operators, air traffic controllers, farmers and aviation historians to seek their support. I had originally intended to fly the trip solo, but, while helping with some typing, long-standing family friend Amanda Mitchell, whose grandfather and my father had served in the same Fleet Air Arm Shark Squadron (755) together during the war, became so enthusiastic about the whole project that I invited her along as my co-pilot to share the workload – definitely one of my better decisions. The choice of aircraft was not difficult. I'd originally considered a Tiger Moth but because of all the landings planned for tarmac runways I chose a Stampe with its tail-wheel and brakes. From then on it became Tiger Club Stampe SV4b G-AWEF's Dawn to Dusk. She exalted in every flying moment, never gave a second's anxiety, patiently tolerated my clumsy handling at the low-speed end of her performance, and shared positively with Mandy and I our exhilaration of open cockpit-flying, especially when over the timeless beauty of the sunlit Yorkshire Wolds and Dales.

During March, April and May, WEF, Mandy and I made a number of flights together. We checked engine rpm and airspeed against fuel consumption, and discovered that with 1,900rpm we could achieve 80kts, burning about seven gallons of avgas and a quart of oil an hour. I also gave Mandy a few flying lessons during which we practised forced landings and short field landings. The replies to our letters came in thick and fast and finally we were able to work out a route that included two airports (Teesside and Leeds-Bradford), nine RAF airfields, eleven smaller airfields, eight disused military airfields and five farmer's airstrips. The en-route timings had to be accurate, not only for the competition itself, but also because of one minor operational detail – we'd planned to do it non-radio. And we were concerned as to how the RAF would react to that idea. We need not have worried – their reaction was: 'Interesting – now let's see how we can make it work!' And

WEF's crew, C S-S and Mandy... and the sparsely equipped rear cockpit

make it work they did. On Monday, June 16, we flew from Redhill to Leeds-Bradford airport with a refuelling stop at Sibson on the way. With the help of dear friend and my one-time boss at the Yorkshire Aeroplane Club, John Fenton, we topped up WEF with fuel and oil before checking Met Office reports for the next day. We then flew to Doncaster Racecourse which was our planned historic start point and chosen because the 'FIRST AVIATION MEETING IN ENGLAND' was held here from October 15-23, 1909.

The three of us just about to touch down on Doncaster Racecourse on Monday, June 16, 1980

Having landed between the railings on the racecourse we were delighted to find that Sara Hild, our energetic ground support team, had arrived with the caravan that was to be our overnight base. Having double-checked everything for the following morning's planned 4.30am start, we crashed out. The three alarm clocks went off almost simultaneously, spurring us awake to get the show on the road, seventy-one years since the first aviation meeting was held there in 1909 with the famous US aviator, Colonel Samuel Franklin Cody, being paid £2,000 to attend. While the girls produced toast, honey and coffee, I gave our precious Stampe a thorough check before Mandy climbed aboard and strapped herself in. Then it was time for WEF's Gipsy Major engine starting ritual and it obligingly burst into life on my second swing of the prop. I was in no hurry to climb aboard myself as this allowed the engine time to warm up. Checks completed, I waved 'chocks away' to Sara and we taxied WEF halfway up the 'Leger Mile' before swinging her around into wind for take-off. At precisely 4.30am, I eased the throttle wide open and pushed the stick gently forward; the tail rose immediately as the ASI recorded the airspeed quickly building up towards 40kts. I applied a touch of back pressure and we were airborne for our first take-off of the day – WEF just wanted to fly! However, our first leg was the shortest planned – only a mile to Doncaster airfield, the first of the thirty-two at which we landed during the course of the day – thirty of them in Yorkshire. In recounting our day, a catalogue of all our landings – and same number of take-offs – would be tedious, but in summary it's worth mentioning that we flew a total of 689 nautical miles in an elapsed time of nine hours and forty-three minutes at an average speed of 71kts, before landing back at Redhill at 8.17pm, fifteen hours and forty-seven minutes since starting at 4.30am. But there were plenty of lasting memories: the fickleness of the weather (we flew through more than enough rain); the kindness and enthusiasm of everyone we met en-route; the amazing support we received from the RAF (mention must be made of Sqn Ldr Simon Bostock, who persuaded the RAF to waive landing fees and who escorted us in his Hornet Moth into three of the RAF airfields); a great logbook comment from Mandy when I had a brain lock trying to find the disused military airfield of Marston Moor in the rain – she wrote 'Charlie lost his temper!' – too true; the total trust we had in the Stampe and, most importantly, the amazing support I received from Mandy throughout – she never stopped smiling!

Two pages from the log book we submitted to the judges

But it wasn't until November that we learned that we had won the 1980 Dawn to Dusk competition, and with a bonus of being informed that we had raised close to £5,000 in aid of SSAFA (the Soldiers' Sailors' and Airmen's' Families Association). And, of course, it was a special thrill for Mandy and I to have been presented with the Duke of Edinburgh Trophy in London by His Royal Highness himself.

Mandy receives the trophy from HRH the Duke of Edinburgh

Most of my immediate post-Dawn to Dusk flying seemed something of an anti-climax by comparison, so I started giving some thought as to what I might take on as a project for the 1981 competition. Like 1980 it had to be both enjoyable and challenging. Then in early March, Jackie Smith asked me if I could fix her up with a biplane jump for her to appear in an advertisement for Guinness.

I immediately asked Michael Jones if I could use one of the Tiger Club Stampes and he agreed without further ado. The result was that I flew G-ATKC down to Netheravon and mounted a camera on the starboard inter-plane strut. I then flew Jackie for four jumps over two days while the official Guinness photographer shot air-to-air photos from the APA Islander. One of the photos I took with the strut-mounted camera of Jackie's exit is reproduced here. It was all great fun and, of course, we also managed to down a few pints of Guinness – but after we'd stopped flying for the day!

Meanwhile, a possible Dawn to Dusk project germinated in two different ways. As in 1980 we had received such enthusiasm from the farmers into whose airstrips we had flown, I reckoned it would be a challenging idea just to use farmers' strips for 1981. Secondly I had met Judy Kay, the very capable and glamorous director of appeals of ASBAH, the Association of Spina Bifida and Hydrocephalus. She was aware of our 1980 success in the competition and suggested that ASBAH might benefit from any fundraising that might be included in the project this time, especially as 1981 had been designated as the International Year of Disabled People. My dear friend and 1980 co-pilot Mandy had landed herself a full-time job that sadly didn't allow her the necessary time off to join me on this occasion, so it seemed reasonable to offer Judy Kay the right-hand seat so that she could concentrate on all the fundraising, leaving me to apply myself to the flying side of the project. She agreed enthusiastically.

Now we needed an aeroplane and, although Stampe SV4b G-AWEF had been the perfect choice for our 1980 project, this year needed something with a greater range and a good short field capability. The choice seemed obvious – having been fortunate enough to have flown a Maule Lunar Rocket during my 1976 trip to South Africa and subsequently written it up for *Pilot* magazine the following year – the Maule had to be the answer. Designed in the USA by Belford Maule in 1971, the Maule Aircraft Company produced 855 of these exciting little four-seat flying machines during the nine years it was in production from 1974. With a cruising speed of 135kts, a range of nearly 550 nautical miles and a startling short field performance, it ticked all the boxes as a flying farmer's aeroplane. I therefore contacted Michael Collins of Capital Aviation Sales at Staverton, the UK agents, who was immediately enthusiastic about our project, promising to lend us a Mighty Maule M5-235 for the competition. We soon arranged a weekend in early March to familiarise ourselves with their pristine demonstrator, G-MAUL, which was to be our mount for the competition. The performance was everything we had been led to expect and more, and after four hours we had got to know her fairly well – with 235hp pulling an empty weight of 1,400lb (only 200lb more than a Tiger Moth) we soon learnt that she had to be treated with respect – especially on take-off. Meanwhile David Corbett, an old friend and ebullient secretary of the Flying Farmers Association, had provided us with the current FFA list so we were able to write to about fifty letters in our quest to find a flying farmer in each county, while Judy had decided that the Young Farmers could best handle the fundraising. The replies took longer to come in than expected, either proving that farmers are as genuinely overworked as they would have us believe, or that they simply don't like writing letters!

In early May I flew the APA Islander G-BBRP down to Goodwood to go back to school again to extend my flying instructor's rating to include instructing on multi-engined aircraft. I was fortunate in completing the course with Peter Philips whom I had known for years as he was married to special friend Sue Burges, who was the first British lady sport parachutist to compete in an international parachuting competition, in her case the Fourth World Parachuting Championships held in Czechoslovakia in 1958. Peter was a gifted pilot who had honed his aerobatic skills as a young fighter pilot in the RAF and, having left the service, he had become a Britten-Norman test pilot – therefore I couldn't have had anyone more qualified to take me on the course in the BN2A Islander. I flew a stimulating seven hours of the course with Peter in four days before successfully passing the test with Goodwood CFI, John Gratton, on the last day.

By the end of the second week in May the flight plan was complete – 42 strips in 42 different counties, three being in Wales. It immediately became apparent that we had two major problems: 1) locating all the strips accurately on the aeronautical chart and then being able to find them on the day and 2) the weather. The answer to the first problem was careful flight planning followed by accurate navigation during the flight itself – this time we had two radios, a VOR and an ADF to help us. But the answer to the second problem was largely in the lap of the gods!

While I was flying at Goodwood, disaster had struck – G-MAUL was written off in a flying accident. But Michael Collins immediately put his shock and dismay behind him before he generously made G-BICX available – she was an identical aeroplane. The rest of May was spent with Judy beavering away at the fundraising while I wrestled with the problems of refuelling and Met Office forecasting. With the plan of nearly 1,500 miles in eleven hours and forty-two landings on farmers' strips only, maybe we were being somewhat over-ambitious. One thing was certain, however – it was going to be interesting!

Four days before the 'off', scheduled for the first Monday in June, everything appeared to be progressing according to plan. Judy was on a cruise with her boyfriend and was due back on the Saturday. Then another setback – I received a message from Judy that, because of a strike at Southampton, the Canberra would be unable to dock until the following week – so I was now faced with the problem of finding another co-pilot. As I had been teaching Julie to fly, and because of her enthusiasm for the project, she was obviously my first choice to fill the right-hand seat. Fortunately for me she was then 'temping' and was thus able to agree to my short-notice request to join me as co-pilot. As she had originally told me that she had only agreed to go out with me because she'd fallen for Boomerang, I wasn't in the least bit surprised when she proposed that we should take

Maule M5-235 G-BICX with her crew   **….and the Maule's office**

my aviating canine with us as supernumerary crew and team mascot. As he'd notched up close to 500 hours' flying time I could think of no good reason why not! On the Sunday we flew BICX to Redhill from whence we had planned to start at 4.30am the following morning, although the forecast was far from optimistic. The weather was as forecast, with ominous-looking low cloud hanging over Redhill, but we decided to have a go with the very clear proviso that we would return immediately if the weather was as grim as it looked. It was! Having found ourselves in solid cloud at about 450ft, we descended back to Redhill having only been airborne for twenty minutes.

We decided to postpone a second attempt until the Wednesday and we contacted all the farmers accordingly. The alarms sounded off in the Tiger Club room at 3.15am and, in a repeat of Monday, the team mascot showed a marked reluctance to get up, but by the time he had, we had obtained a Met forecast which was this time much more encouraging. 'Let's go!' And present were two members of the local Young Farmers who had very kindly turned up to wish us well. At 4.30am, we took off, heading 281º for Tony Poulson's strip at Seale twenty-two nautical miles away. By 7.45am we had touched down near Truro for our tenth landing and a refuel having flown 263nm. Our twenty-second landing was made at 1.40pm, by which time we'd flown 792nm in seven hours and forty-seven minutes, before we finally landed back at Redhill at 8.51pm for our forty-first landing, having flown a total of 1,405nm in an elapsed time of thirteen hours and forty-six minutes at an average speed of 102.06kts – phew! The log we submitted to the judges still provides plenty of unforgettable memories: those who made generous donations to ASBAH during the day, especially the Hull Young Farmers who gave us a cheque for £500; the varying standard of the strips into which we flew, some were particularly 'hairy', like the one that had a 40º bend in it; and one farmer warned his field was a little wet, but he neglected to tell us it was a cow pasture – Julie recorded in the log: 'He didn't warn us about the cow muck which decorated the aeroplane as we

We receive the trophy for 1981 from HRH the Duke of Edinburgh

landed, and, after he got out, the dog!' The most striking aspects of the day were the Young Farmers and the not-so-young farmers who supported us so enthusiastically from start to finish, especially as more than £10,000 was raised for ASBAH – their cheerful encouragement was very much part of enabling us to win the 1981 Dawn to Dusk competition and to experience the thrill of being presented with the trophy by HRH the Duke of Edinburgh for the second time. Our only regret was that Boomerang couldn't be with us on that delightful occasion. Subsequently it prompted the question: 'Could we manage a hat-trick?' A definite 'NO!' was the answer as you will soon discover. In the middle of July I was asked by John Davis, a friend and organiser of the Badminton Air Day, if, with Julie, I could bring the Tiger Club's Super Tiger G-AOAA in its SOW (Standing on the Wing) configuration to the show. Once again Michael Jones generously acceded to my request and the day after we'd carried out a twenty-minute practice at Redhill we flew OAA down to Badminton for the Air Day itself. The hour-and-a-half early morning flight, with Julie and the SOW rig crammed together in the front cockpit, was in very murky weather which luckily improved as the day went on.

Julie, SOW Star of the Show at the Badminton Air Day 1981

Flying OAA for SOW was potentially more hazardous than I had expected. There was so much additional drag inherently caused by the luckless passenger mounted above the upper wing that most of the flight had to be conducted at full throttle – this was fine providing the engine behaved itself. If it didn't and a forced landing on to a hostile piece of real estate was necessary, the star of the show strapped into the SOW rig would be in big trouble if the Tiger nosed over on touchdown. As we had no desire to push our luck, Badminton Air Day 1981 was our only SOW display.

In his published history of the Tiger Club's latter days at Redhill, Michael Jones describes 1982 as the club's annus horribilis – the year in which the three Tigers, G-ACDC, G-AOAA and G-AIVW, all had serious prangs. In his account Michael did not name the three pilots but, and I'm not proud to admit it, I was the pilot of the club's flagship, G-ACDC, on Tuesday, June 8, 1982, when things didn't go exactly according to plan. While attempting to come up with a project for the 1982 Dawn to Dusk we received a letter from the editor of a well-known flying magazine. In rejecting my article on our 1981 entry he wrote: 'The Dawn to Dusk, like so much of what the Tiger Club does, is outdated and is more in keeping with the 1930s…' Maybe he had a point, but maybe that's the appeal of the Tiger Club – maybe the 1930s weren't too bad a time to be involved in light aviation. Maybe having to exercise greater airmanship because of no radios, maybe having to read a map accurately instead of relying on sophisticated aids to navigation – no GPS in the 1980s – maybe having to exercise greater skill in actually flying a pre-war biplane, than simply 'driving' a modern tricycled, plastic trimmed tin can from Wichita, weren't such unreasonable concepts. So, as we didn't agree with his comment about the Dawn to Dusk itself being outdated, we

DH82A Tiger Moth G-ACDC over Cranwell by aviation artist Gordon Wright

decided with our 1982 entry to find out what flying was all about in the 1930s. With Michael Jones agreeing to our using DH82A Tiger Moth G-ACDC – the oldest Tiger on the register, and who was approaching her fiftieth birthday – the stage was set.

This time the project was simply to fly around the country to visit as many places associated with Tiger Moths as we could. We started our day's flying at 4.30am from Hatfield where CDC had been based at the De Havilland School of Flying in the 1930s. The forecast was for anti-cyclonic conditions with any early morning mist clearing quickly and that once we were west of Odiham we'd be in the clear. The first leg was to Thruxton where twenty-six Tiger Moths had been converted into Jackaroos. Initially all went well until we passed Booker, but then as we approached Newbury any patchy early morning mist became more dense. This was the time, now blessed with 20/20 hindsight, that we should have turned back. A few minutes later, having passed Newbury, the visibility deteriorated rapidly around us so, when I saw a welcoming-looking grass field ahead of us, I decided a precautionary landing would be a sensible option. But it wasn't until the wheels touched that I realised the grass was in fact about 2ft 6in of wet standing corn. It seemed like we might get away with it, but the corn pulled CDC's nose firmly downwards, turning her over on to her back. Mercifully both Julie and I were unhurt, but the same couldn't be said of CDC – and my poor judgment was responsible. The rest of the day was spent with the help of local Mothing chums Tim Williams and Ben Cooper removing the wings before loading a very sad-looking CDC on to a borrowed a trailer. The

A sad looking G-ACDC after her cornfield landing on June 8, 1982

" I'VE GOT A GUT FEELING THAT THIS GUY IS NOT YOUR AVERAGE LOONEY CROP SPRAYER

" THIS SHOULD CREATE A STIR BACK AT THE STATION. YOU'RE SAYING IT'S ALRIGHT TO DRIVE THE SAID VEHICLE FROM THE BACK SEAT !

And as talented cartoonist chum Phil Wells saw it!

next day we towed the trailer and its cargo back to Redhill. Here Michael Jones put on an exceptionally brave face and, hiding his disappointment, he said: 'Well, I've seen her looking a lot worse!' And, as if to prove it, the club's engineering team had CDC back in the sky over Redhill less than two months later. Julie and I remember her with affection.

In 1983 I was appointed chief pilot of the Joint Services Parachute Centre and the Army Parachute Association by the then Commandant of JSPC, Major Gerry O'Hara MBE, ex-22 SAS and Parachute Regiment. This was a commitment I enjoyed for the next thirty years, and one that I could not have fulfilled without the fantastic support of so many splendid pilots too numerous to mention – although some inevitably will be during the telling of my story. One such pilot was Werner Kroeger. Werner had unstintingly and cheerfully devoted every weekend, and more, to jump flying at Netheravon for many years until he was suddenly stricken with cancer from which he tragically died in August 1984. Julie and I had already toyed with the idea of a round-Britain parachute marathon as a Dawn to Dusk project, but now it had some purpose. Thus a flight to visit (and jump into) all the parachute clubs in the country, in memory of Werner, to raise money for Cancer Research, was to became a Dawn to Dusk reality for the two of us. I had known Gerry

Golf Romeo Uniform on a winter's day at Netheravon

The team. Standing: Gerry O'Hara, Patrick Long, C S-S and Tony Rose.
Front: Simon Ward and Julie Hanks

O'Hara since he had taken over command of the Red Devils in 1975 and I held him in the highest regard. I felt sure that he would support the idea, which indeed he did enthusiastically; he also offered the JSPC BN2A Islander G-AYRU for the flight – she proved to be the perfect aircraft for the job. So Gerry had to be on the team as did his chief parachute instructor, WO Tony Rose, a commando gunner. As I envisaged making a few jumps myself during the day, it would mean recruiting another pilot who was also a jumper to share the flying with me, so Patrick Long virtually selected himself. He was an ex-Army Air Corps Beaver pilot and an experienced parachutist, and I also knew him well as a genial personality. The final member of our six-person team was Simon Ward, a good friend and hugely talented skydiver and photographer who was then working for GWR, a local radio station. We all knew each other well, as we did Werner, so the Werner Kroeger Memorial Flight proved to be both a challenging yet thoroughly enjoyable experience that benefited Cancer Research enormously. We decided to allow between fifteen and twenty minutes on the ground at each of the twenty drop zones to repack which, as it turned

Finally back at Netheravon: Gerry, Simon, C S-S, Tony, Julie and Patrick – cheers!

out, was barely enough time for the two or three of the team who jumped at each. Once again the weather was likely to be significant with the requirement for a minimum drop height of 2,000ft AGL and a maximum surface wind of 18kts. By the middle of May, Patrick and I had come up with the definitive flight plan, which produced 962 nautical miles and a total still air point-to-point time of eight hours and six minutes. Patrick and I would fly alternate legs and jump on each of the legs when we weren't flying, with the rest of the team helping out with co-pilot duties, log-keeping or photography. Meanwhile Simon swung into action with PR for both the plan and for the fundraising for Cancer Research. This year the rules allowed the competition to be flown in July as well as in June, so it was at 4.30am on Monday, July 8, and with a promising forecast, that we took off from Netheravon at the start of the Werner Kroeger Memorial Flight. Simply put, the day went roughly according to plan – the weather kindly allowed us to parachute into twenty parachute clubs covering 962 nautical miles in nine hours and fifty three minutes' flying time to arrive back at Netheravon at 8.36pm. I flew four hours and thirty-nine minutes, and Patrick flew five hours and fourteen minutes – and we both made eight jumps; Simon made fourteen jumps (twelve with a helmet-mounted camera), Gerry made thirteen jumps, Julie nine and Tony eight – a total of sixty. These statistics, however, don't reflect the magnificent support and the warm welcome we received throughout the day. There wasn't one airfield where we weren't greeted warmly and we couldn't help but believe that this demonstrated the sport parachuting fraternity's approval of what we were trying to achieve. The weather forecasters couldn't have done a more professional job, though we reckoned that Werner, bless him, had a hand in fixing the two fortuitous weather breaks that permitted us to jump at both Cark and Topcliffe. By July 1985 G-AYRU had already been flying for parachuting at Netheravon for twelve years, but her engines never missed a beat all day and her radios worked perfectly – much credit to the two Geoffs, Thirkell and Vincent, who maintained her. Much later we learned that the flight had not only raised more than £12,000 for Cancer Research, but it had also won us the Duke of Edinburgh Trophy for the 1985 Dawn to Dusk. And inevitably it was a lively party after we'd collected it from HRH the Duke of York in London that December. We counted ourselves fortunate indeed that we were able to participate in such a thoroughly enjoyable and worthwhile day of sporting aviation and, most importantly, we felt that Werner would definitely have approved. As flying competitions go, the Dawn to Dusk, now in its fifty-fifth year, is unique and, from where I'm sitting, it takes some beating.

CHAPTER 18
DH82A TIGER MOTH G-AGZZ

A year after I had joined the Tiger Club I was introduced to Ralph Hart, one of the members, who had built his own Lycoming-engined Currie Wot and which he now had up for sale. When he saw me admiring his beautiful little aeroplane, he rightly suspected that I was seriously tempted to make him an offer so he kindly suggested I took G-AYNA for a flight. It was every bit as memorable as flying Currie Wot G-ARZW the previous year, but, as I taxied back in after the flight, the fact that she was a single-seater was suddenly significant – if I did become her owner how could I share the enjoyment of flying her with anyone? Ralph was generous in his understanding of my decision not to buy his Wot and thereafter the acquisition of a two-seater open-cockpit biplane became my goal. Inevitably it was the choice between a Tiger Moth and a Stampe that became the focus of my attention and it quickly became apparent that the purchase of either in flying condition was well beyond my means at the time – especially as Julie and I were also considering setting up home together! So we started looking for a rebuild project, opting for a Tiger as I was advised that there were still plenty of spares available and that it was likely to be less problematical than restoring a Stampe. Apart from that Julie and I were aware of our developing a growing affection for Tigers.

The June 26, 1982, issue of *Flight International* contained the following classified advertisement: 'DH Tiger Moth 1940, complete, under restoration, for sale or completed to customer's specification, Tel…' It turned out later to be neither 1940 nor anywhere near complete, but a telephone call and a visit to Southampton in company of retired aircraft engineer Bill Cairns (an old friend who used to maintain the DH89A Rapides at Netheravon), revealed a sad pile of bits barely recognizable as a Tiger. I handed over a deposit to secure the purchase of what proved to be the remains of a DH82A Tiger Moth which had recently been registered as G-AGZZ. Both Julie and my father immediately declared their support for the project, with Bill Cairns agreeing to provide the necessary expertise. On Thursday, July 1, we collected the four wings, fin, rudder and tail plane – all uncovered – the engine and propeller, the fuel tank, the two side frames and rear fuselage, and any number of cardboard boxes containing a huge variety of uncatalogued bits and pieces. Luckily we had a spare corner of the family business premises where all the immediate restoration work could begin, with the first priority being to identify and catalogue everything in an attempt to discover what was missing. Meanwhile G-AGZZ's colourful history was being revealed from correspondence with various organizations in Australia – she was actually DH82A (Aust) Tiger Moth because she had been one of 1,125 built by de Havilland Australia Pty Ltd, of which 'ZZ was produced at Mascot NSW on April 15, 1942, with DHA construction No. 926 and given Royal Australian Air Force registration A17-503. She entered service with the RAAF in May 1942 principally at No. 5 Elementary Flying Training School at Narromine, NSW, until late 1944 when she was stored. In February 1944 she was purchased by Associated Aero Clubs for £90; they in turn sold her to the Newcastle Aero Club when she was re-registered as VH-BMY. She was again stored from 1951 and the Newcastle Aero Club brought her back to airworthy condition in 1956 when she became VH-RNM. Three years later she was sold to become a crop sprayer in Perth in Western Australia where she obtained yet another registration, VH-BTU. She had last flown in Australia on June 10, 1963, before being once again stored and, sadly, being allowed to deteriorate. In 1969 she was purchased by Robert Rust of Fayetteville, USA, who shipped her to North Carolina and obtained a US registration for her – N3862. Her planned restoration in the USA never happened and it was a pitiful pile of bits that found their way to the UK in 1981 via Cliff Lovell; it was here that she obtained her sixth registration, a period, out-of-sequence number that had never been issued – G-AGZZ. We christened her the Bunyip which, as any Australian will tell you, is an enchanting, mythical Australian animal.

The mutilated control box...   **... and the 'new' full length replacement**

The whole thirteen-month restoration was a period of excitement, frustration and achievement in varying degrees and one to which we devoted a huge amount of time and effort. Our flying and skydiving during the thirteen months was put very much on a back-burner – my logbooks reveal that I flew just over a hundred hours and only made eighteen skydives during the period of 'ZZ's re-birth. We kept an illustrated log of the whole project on an almost day to day basis, with the result that this unique volume has become a much treasured record. During the first month our enthusiasm was seriously dented when we realized just how much of 'ZZ was missing or damaged – for example half the vital control box, which is usually the length of the cockpit, was missing because when she had been operated as a crop sprayer everything in the front cockpit had been replaced by the huge hopper that contained the spray. The result was that we'd have to make a completely new control box, and find a front windscreen, seat, instrument panel and set of instruments. While we received little help in this respect from the gentleman who had sold us the 'complete' 'ZZ, Stuart McKay, the guru of the de Havilland Moth Club, put us in touch with any number of organisations and individuals from whom we were able to source so much of what was needed, as indeed did Ben and Jan Cooper of the Newbury Aeroplane Company. This delightful couple were in the aircraft restoration business and they gave us an amazing amount of help and advice – Ben was able to make the two new full-length sides for the control box, which was one irritating problem solved. We also found that one of the four inter-plane struts had at some stage been damaged and was 7/16 of an inch too short – it wasn't easy finding a replacement. I was relieved when my father appointed himself responsible for the engine refurbishment as it looked in a terrible condition – we even discovered the body of a large antipodean termite lodged between two of the cylinder barrels – he'd done well to make it to the UK from Oz via the USA! But when the engine was stripped down, however, it looked in reasonable condition with only a crack found in one of the exhaust valves and this was easily replaced. Meanwhile we'd been fortunate enough to meet with two local craftsmen whose expertise became essential to the project. Lionel Sheppard proved to be an amazing metal worker who tidied up the engine cowlings and fabricated the two new pieces of the firewall, while John Graves, a local Auster enthusiast and owner who was an ace with aircraft instruments, helped by restoring those we had and finding replacements for those which were still missing. Based in Salisbury, Ted Moslin had an unequalled reputation as the ultimate expert on magnetos and the result of his meticulous refurbishment of 'ZZ's was that we never had a magneto problem.

By the end of August, the fuselage was coming together and Julie and I flew a borrowed Tiger, G-AXAN, to the annual DH Moth Club Rally at Woburn Abbey. This was a most useful exercise in that a number of our ongoing queries were answered enthusiastically by the many Moth Club members who were keen to help. The star of the show was undoubtedly Henry Labouchere. Whoever bestowed the nickname 'Dr Moth' on Henry hit the nail on the head – his knowledge of de Havilland Moths is encyclopaedic and his skill as an engineer of 'Mothery' has no equal. He's also a pretty useful pilot as his flight to Australia in 1984 with Tim Williams in the latter's DH 80A Puss Moth and that in 1995 to the famous Air Rally at Oshkosh, Wisconsin, USA with Torquil Norman in the latter's DH 90 Dragonfly proved so conclusively. Apart from all that he has a wicked sense of humour which is always on standby to prick pomposity or ridicule unnecessary bureaucracy. Whilst Mothery in its many forms is Henry's livelihood, he's always been very generous in passing on the fruits of his knowledge when requested as he did with us on numerous occasions, especially when he learned that 'ZZ was, like his Tiger, built in Australia – he's owned his, G-BEWN, for nearly fifty years since he purchased her in 1971 in Australia for £600. An important milestone was reached by the end of October when 'ZZ got to stand on her own two wheels and when she could now be clearly identified as a Tiger Moth. In December and January we prepared the fuselage and flying surfaces for covering and this was made easier than anticipated because we had discovered a company in the USA – Air Tex Products of Pennsylvania – which could not only supply Grade A cotton fabric at half the price it was then available in the UK, but which could also make up the bags to order for most fabric covered aircraft types. We ordered a set right away. It was a good decision – it saved a considerable amount of time stitching the bags together ourselves, and that would have assumed we had some basic sewing machine skills, which we hadn't. At the beginning of March, and after an almost inevitable delay in customs, the bags arrived and the covering operation started immediately.

October 1982 – she stands on her own two wheels

Initially in the covering process we were concerned that, once we had pulled the fabric bags over the wings and fuselage, maybe Air Tex had made them too baggy. We needn't have worried – once we had sprayed them with water they tautened themselves up perfectly, as tight as a drum, ready for the required two coats of dope. For the next step we had to learn the simple sewing skills necessary to enable us to string the fabric on to the ribs of the flying surfaces – a laborious but essential process.

November 1982 – My father and I pose for the local press

In February 1982 the APA Islander G-BBRP was badly damaged when both engines failed soon after take-off with a full load of jumpers on board. Mercifully all on board survived the resultant very firm landing and were all uninjured. Unfortunately just before take-off the pilot had inadvertently switched to use the near-empty wingtip tanks instead of switching the fuel pumps on and using the main tanks, in which there was plenty of fuel. The pilot's decision to retract the flaps when the first engine failed hadn't helped the situation and the Islander was written off. Later in the year the APA purchased a new Pilatus PC-6 Turbo Porter to replace the Islander. It proved to be an exciting aeroplane to fly because of its startling short take-off and landing (STOL) performance and its ability

APA Pilatus PC-6 Turbo Porter G-OAPA at Netheravon, 1982

to easily beat the jumpers to the ground from 13,000ft. It served the APA well for the next five years.

Because of all the flying I was doing for parachuting at Netheravon at the time, I was confident that Gerry O'Hara would look favourably on my request to house 'ZZ in the APA hangar. Indeed he did and this quid pro quo arrangement worked well until the military 'powers that be' decided in the fullness of time that it was unacceptable. So in April we put 'ZZ on a trailer to move her to her new home in the APA hangar on the airfield. Meanwhile the engine restoration had been completed and Mike Inskip of the airworthiness branch of the CAA paid us a visit and, following a thorough inspection of airframe and engine, was able to approve everything we had done so far. We eagerly anticipated having 'ZZ in the sky during May – how wrong we were! A set of stainless steel flying wires had been manufactured in the USA for 'ZZ when she had been N3862 and these had been included among the essentials we had collected from Southampton way back in July. The only problem was there were no fork ends – the vital pieces of metalwork that

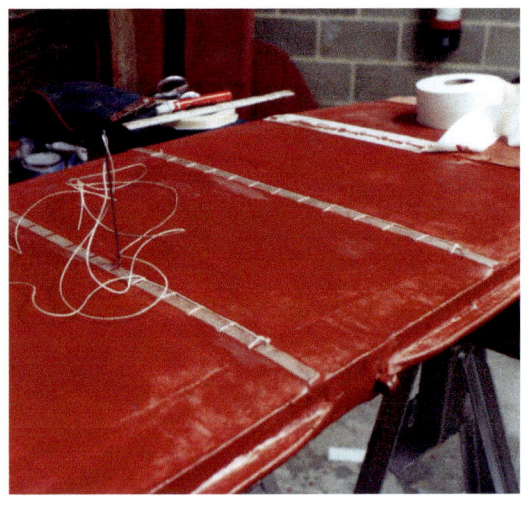

April 1983: the stringing process   'ZZ in the APA hangar at Netheravon

connect the wires to the attachment points on the flying surfaces and the fuselage. Not only that, we also discovered that the threads on the wires were American, not British, therefore the fork ends we had acquired didn't fit. I finally made contact with Robert Rust in the USA who had been sitting on the box containing the full set of American threaded fork ends waiting for them to be claimed – he sent them off to us right away.

The result of all this was that we didn't manage to have the wings and tailplane fitted or the engine installed until the end of June. Then we had to endure the almost inevitable frustration of dealing with CAA bureaucracy over the issue of the Certificate of Airworthiness. Firstly they were insistent that, as Australian Tigers had never been fitted with anti-spin strakes – ugly small flat surfaces fitted either side of the rear fuselage adjacent to the tailplane, aerobatics would not be permitted until the airworthiness branch of the CAA had conducted rigorous air testing of the aeroplane. My father and I agreed that we'd initially accept this restriction and maybe challenge it at a later date. The second restriction proposed was not to permit parachuting from 'ZZ and we went into battle on this one pointing out that, not only had Tigers had been used regularly for parachuting since the late 1950s, but that actually the DH82A Tiger Moth had been designed for parachuting. The Tiger's predecessor, the DH60T Moth Trainer, had straight wings placed one immediately above the other with the fuel tank positioned above the front cockpit. When offered as a trainer to the RAF it quickly became apparent that accessibility to the front cockpit by the instructor wearing a bulky seat parachute was far from easy. The result was that de Havillands moved the fuel tank forward by 22in which, while it improved accessibility, necessitated sweeping the wings back to maintain the position of the centre of gravity. This in turn meant that the lower wingtips would be positioned unacceptably closer to the ground, so that it was then necessary for a certain amount of dihedral had to be applied to the lower wings to solve the problem. Legend has it that Geoffrey de Havilland himself drew the required changes on the back of a fag packet – thus the DH82A Tiger Moth was born having been designed specifically for parachuting! G-AGZZ's C of A when issued reflected this piece of history.

On August 3 we gave 'ZZ her first engine run. On the 6th my Father carried out a taxi trial using the full length of the runway, though he denied getting airborne! On August 9 I took her on her first flight in the UK, twenty years since her last in Australia in 1963. The fifteen-minute flip was totally exhilarating, especially so because, just after I had touched down, I remembered the sad pile of bits she'd been thirteen months earlier. Importantly, however, it was to check there were no major snags that needed solving before I flew her on her C of A air test the following day – there were none and even the weather looked favourable. It was a perfect English summer's evening on August 10, which ensured ideal flying conditions. The fifty-minute flight went really well and all in accordance with the schedule, and for the last ten minutes I flew in formation with the APA Islander, G-AYRU, flown by Werner Kroeger, enabling Julie to take a memorable photo of G-AGZZ. Her Certificate of Airworthiness was issued by the CAA on August 18, three days before Julie and I flew her into the temporary airstrip at Woburn Abbey for the annual DH Moth Club Rally. It was an exciting climax to an extraordinarily memorable thirteen months of team effort that involved the skills of so many enthusiastic people – our sincerest thanks were extended to all of them. Following the restoration all we wanted to do was to fly this beautiful aeroplane and, now that she was once again perfectly serviceable, occasionally jump out of her – which reminds me:

> *Pilot: 'I can't understand why anyone should want to parachute out of a perfectly serviceable aeroplane.'*
>
> *Skydiver: 'Because if it wasn't perfectly serviceable, I wouldn't be jumping out of it!'*

A month later, and having already flown about six hours in her, Julie and I took off in her to fly to Goodwood. We were due to stay with Peter and Sue Phillips as I was to renew my flying instructor's rating with Peter the following day. It was a clear September evening and our route took us south of Andover and just to the north of Winchester. We'd been airborne for about twenty minutes and I had just informed Southampton ATC on the radio of our position when there was a loud bang followed by immediate severe vibration. Instinctively I closed the throttle, which restored some normality to the situation. The oil pressure gauge was indicating its normal 45psi (pounds per square inch) and the engine sounded OK – until I eased the power on again, whereupon mayhem returned once more. Having closed the throttle once more, I informed Southampton that we were about three miles north-west of Winchester and that, because we were experiencing engine trouble, it was my intention to land in a large stubble field which, conveniently, was almost immediately below us. I saw no need to make a 'mayday' call as there was nothing much that Southampton could do to help. In glancing at the rear mirror I detected some concern in Julie's eyes but I was unable to reassure her because at that time we had no intercom facility. The field was huge and there was little wind so I was confident of being able to pull off a reasonable landing. The moment I turned on to final approach at about 55kts I knew I was well placed, so I reached out with my left hand and turned off the ignition switches as we passed over the boundary hedge. The engine and propeller stopped simultaneously moments before we touched down safely

The Bunyip's damaged propeller. September 23, 1983

and without any further drama. Even the birds stopped singing! As soon as we had disembarked we were immediately aware of the cause of the vibration. About a foot of the metal leading edge of the propeller had broken away, causing massive imbalance between the two blades, thus the vibration. When we had stripped the propeller, cleaned it and repainted it, all had seemed OK, but it had not been possible to check the wood under the metal leading edge without removing it. The wood had clearly rotted, allowing a large piece of the leading edge to disappear.

Within fifteen minutes of our landing, the farmer/owner of the land had appeared and he couldn't have been more helpful. He kindly pointed to a box on a post at the edge of the field that contained a telephone which we used to contact Southampton ATC, the police, Peter and Sue Phillips, and chum Colonel David Mallam at Middle Wallop, who generously agreed to come and rescue us, but not before we'd secured 'ZZ and with the farmer agreeing to look after her. Later I phoned Tim Williams, my nearest Mothing chum, to see if he had a spare propeller. No such luck, but he generously suggested that if I could be at his house in Hungerford early the next day I could borrow the propeller from his Tiger Moth to enable us to get the Bunyip back to Netheravon. Having collected the propeller from Tim and armed with the necessary tools, Julie and I drove to

the field near Winchester where I removed the damaged propeller and fitted Tim's in its place. The return flight to Netheravon was uneventful and 'ZZ was back in the hangar by 11.30am, and thanks to Tim's brilliant support.

I made the first jump out of 'ZZ nine months later when I parachuted into Bob Pooley's annual garden party having been flown by John Taylor, and soon after that I flew Julie for her first jump from the Bunyip over Netheravon which we recorded photographically with a strut-mounted camera.

During the twenty-five years we operated 'ZZ there is an enduring memory that remains with us – the wonderfully infectious smiles of everyone who either flew her, flew in her or jumped out of her. This is best illustrated for me by Joce, wife of Jim Steele, the Commandant of JSPC in 1986. Joce hated flying, or the thought of flying, in any type of flying machine; for example, she always needed two or three stiff G&Ts before embarking on a civil airliner – mind you, I sympathise with her on that one! It was a beautiful summer's day at Netheravon and Jim had just enjoyed a jump out of the Bunyip, so of course I offered Joce a ride in her. The answer was a vehement, resounding 'NO!' So I made her an offer she couldn't, I hope, refuse. I explained that, as I just wanted her to enjoy the experience, we would simply take off, make a gentle circuit around the airfield, and land. I told her that we'd only be in the air for two or three minutes and if she didn't enjoy it she could signal a 'thumbs down' to me in the rearview mirror and we'd taxi back and shut down. Of course she loved it, as evidenced by the vigorous 'thumbs up' she signalled to me with both hands as we touched down. So I took off again, flew her around Stonehenge and pointed out their house to her. The radiance of her smile when we finally landed made it all so wonderfully worthwhile. Two more examples spring to

Simon's Dangle Dive   **'Pie in the Sky'**

mind. First was Simon Ward's extraordinary 'dangle dive' from the undercarriage of 'ZZ – to get there he had to climb out of the front cockpit, over the leading edge of the wing and pass within 18in of the spinning propeller – rather him than me. I was happy simply firing the camera's shutter from the rear cockpit! Simon's crazy imagination resulted in a unique photograph. On another occasion my airborne attempt to bite into a massive pork pie won second prize for Julie's 'Pie in the Sky' photo in a competition organized by the Royal Aero Club and sponsored by the Meat Marketing Board.

For the fifteen years between 1986 and 2000, involvement with the Diamond Nine Team of Tiger Moths provided numerous priceless opportunities for its special breed of pilots and parachutists to experience the very best of DH82A flying and skydiving. From the very start Julie and I, with G-AGZZ, were privileged to have been part of it and the amazing comradeship it generated. All is revealed in the next chapter.

G-AGZZ about to touch down at Netheravon

CHAPTER 19

THE TIGER MOTH DIAMOND NINE TEAM

The Diamond Nine Team had its origins in the both the Tiger Club and the DH Moth Club because at the time I was a member of both. A couple of weeks before the 1985 Moth Club Rally, Julie and I came up with the idea of a Tiger Moth display team as we felt there should be more to the rally than simply turning up and wandering around admiring each others' aeroplanes. 'How many aircraft?' she queried. 'Nine,' I said carelessly, with little thought to potential problems, 'just like the Red Arrows.' Later it occurred to us that having a team of Tiger Moths displaying at airshows would provide a splendid opportunity to pay tribute publicly to an iconic aeroplane that had proved to have been such a successful basic trainer for all three services in times of both peace and war. And so it came to pass at Woburn that we sounded out kindred spirits as to the feasibility of a Tiger Moth Diamond Nine Team. The result was that nine of us, complete with Tigers, met the following spring at Badminton, and, having taken to the air in two groups, we formed our first Diamond Nine overhead the field on April 26, 1986. The participants were Colin Dodds, David Baker, Joe Frankel, Robin Livett, Jonathan Elwes, Nick Parkhouse, Keith Palmer, Pete Harrison and, because nobody else wanted the job, myself at the front. Later that year at the Woburn weekend, we flew a Diamond Nine on each of the two days with Henry Labouchere, David Cyster, Pete Jackson and Martin Gambrell also participating. With our skydiving backgrounds, Julie and I had formed an informal parachute team to jump from Tigers and Stampes and five of us performed successfully that year at Woburn.

During the fifteen years the Diamond Team were operational the birds were only very occasionally obliged to stop singing – yet on June 24, 1985, Julie, her friend Jakki, the Ruiz twins Julian and Martin and I took off from Denham in three Tigers and two Stampes to parachute into the Guild of Air Pilots and Air Navigators' Garden Party being held on the airfield. I was being flown in G-ACDC by Pete Jarvis and was communicating with him using hand signals via the rear view mirror. He gave me a 'thumbs up' as we ran in for the drop-in at 3,000ft and, when we were over the exit point, I drew my open-hand palm downwards across my throat to signal Pete to cut the engine so I could climb out on to the wing – this was also the signal for the other four to follow suit. I was positioning myself for exit when Pete started signalling frantically that I should climb back in so that we could make another circuit over the field before we could jump. As

I did so, Pete opened the throttle to initiate our going around again. Jakki and I managed to climb back into the Tigers' front cockpits, Julie finished up half-in and half-out, while the twins found that they couldn't move in the slipstream so they were left hanging grimly on to the Stampes' struts for the whole additional circuit above Denham. We were able to jump on that second run-in, the need for which was the result of London ATC holding us at altitude and their not appreciating how dangerous it was for the twins. If either of their parachutes had deployed while they were immobile on the Stampes' wings the canopies could easily have wrapped around the tailplane or fin and rudder. The birds were definitely on stand-by to stop singing on that one!

But stop singing they certainly did on a subsequent jump on June 21 the following year. The DH Moth Club had raised the splendid sum of £10,000 in aid of the Harefield Heart Transplant Hospital and it had been arranged that our parachute team would jump on to a playing field in Harefield where, having landed safely, Julie would hand over the cheque to the Mayor. By this time the team's regular jumpers had each paired up with one of the pilots. I always enjoyed being flown in G-AGZZ by dear long-standing friend Sue Thompson. She was a reassuringly experienced Tiger pilot who always looked after the Bunyip as meticulously as if she had owned her herself. Julie more often than not was flown by Pete LeCoyte, whereas irrepressible London copper Steve Plank was destined to be teamed up with Joe Frankel. With me, Joe was one of the team's ex-regular Army officers, having served in the Royal Tank Regiment, and the third was Nigel Yonge, one of the regular parachutists, who had served with the 60th Rifles in Palestine where he'd had the misfortune to lose an eye when his armoured car hit a land mine. We mounted the display from Denham and, without any disruption this time from ATC, we successfully jumped to be met by the Mayor and his entourage. Julie handed over the cheque and we repaired to the hospital for a cup of tea. What we, the parachute team, didn't know was there had been something of a drama after we had jumped. Joe Frankel's Tiger was unserviceable so he had borrowed the Tiger Club's Super Tiger G-AOAA which, as part of its streamlining modifications, had the ignition switches repositioned inside the cockpits. At the appropriate moment over Harefield Joe closed the throttle and Steve climbed out of the cockpit on to the wing, whence he and 'AA parted company. Joe re-opened the throttle – nothing! He called Denham ATC on the radio to inform them of his engine failure. He was cleared for an immediate landing on to Denham's 24 runway about a mile-and-a-half away. It was touch and go if he could glide that far. The other pilots transmitted their encouragement. 'Good luck, Joe!… Go for it, Joe!… Hang in there, Joe!'

Joe coolly flew a faultless approach and safe landing after which all was revealed. The switches in the front cockpit were found to be in the 'off' position – while climbing out, Steve, who is a big man, had inadvertently knocked them off! In spite of that adrenalin-pumping few minutes for Joe, we decided that the parachute team would be a unique addition to the Diamond Niners. As there was no way I could lead both teams and, as the BPA required any parachute display team to be led by a parachute instructor, Steve Plank agreed to assume this responsibility. His was an inspired appointment that resulted in a wonderfully entertaining bunch of jumpers with whom Julie and I enjoyed every jump we made with them.

The following month, and by a strange twist of fate, I was elected chairman of the Royal Aero Club. I had been a vice-chairman for a couple of years following a stint as treasurer, while another vice-chairman was James Black, a successful lawyer, who was an accomplished competitive aerobatic pilot. It seemed to me that James was destined to be elected chairman and he certainly deserved the job, but his company unexpectedly posted him to Hong Kong. The result was that I found myself sitting in the hot seat of an historic organisation that dates back to 1901 and whose principle object then was 'To encourage the study of aeronautics and develop the sciences connected therewith.' Now, with its patron, Her Majesty the Queen, and its president, HRH the Duke of York, the Royal Aero Club's modern-day role is to be the coordinator of sporting aviation

The 1986 Royal Aero Club Council with Royal supporters. Ann Welch sitting second left, C S-S sitting next to the RAeC president, HRH the Duke of York, and Eric Brown standing extreme right

governing bodies and their link with the FAI – the International Aviation Federation. Serving with me on the RAeC Council throughout my two-year stint as chairman were a loyal and enthusiastic group of aviators whose flying achievements in the majority of cases far exceeded my own. For example Captain Eric 'Winkle' Brown CBE, DSC, AFC, had been a distinguished naval test pilot who, in an utterly amazing career, had flown 487 different types of aircraft, had 2,407 carrier landings to his credit during which he'd made the first carrier landing in a jet-engined aircraft and the first carrier landing in a twin-engined aircraft. And Ann Welch OBE was another extraordinary aviator who was also one of our vice-chairmen. Pre-war, Ann had flown both gliders and powered aircraft and during the war she became one of the exclusive band of 166 women ATA (Air Transport Auxiliary) ferry pilots. She flew everything from Tiger Moths, Swordfish and Gladiators to Spitfires, Blenheims and Wellingtons. After the war she worked tirelessly for the British Gliding Association. I was fortunate and privileged indeed to have known and worked with so many experienced aviators on the council of the Royal Aero Club. I owe them all a massive vote of thanks.

A 1987 Diamond Nine Team, from left: Steve Bohill-Smith, Pete LeCoyte, John Webb, C S-S, Colin Dodds, Pete Harrison, Len Mitton, David Baker and Jonathan Elwes

1987 was the Diamond Nine Team's first proper display season with our appearances at Denham, Old Warden (always one of our favourite venues), Hatfield, Cranfield, Middle Wallop, Badminton, Woburn, Silverstone and Duxford, prompting British Aerospace to sponsor us with a welcome cheque for £400 – recognition indeed. The parachute team also joined us for three of our nine displays. Initially our routine was simple and unsophisticated with our taking off in three groups of three to form up and fly by in diamond nine after which we broke into line astern for a fly-by, the crowd waving cheerfully as we sped by before landing.

That July I made what was nearly my last parachute jump. Julie, 'ZZ and I had been invited to a posh aviation garden party near Hungerford into which we'd agreed to parachute. On the day chum Tim Williams flew me in 'ZZ while Julie was flown by another chum, consultant plastic surgeon, Nick Parkhouse, in his Tiger. It was a perfect summer's day with a warm breeze. We climbed to altitude and ran in at 3,000ft over the field where the spectating ranks of the 'quality' waited expectantly. Julie sensibly decided to land well out into the field while I was aiming for an open space in the line of parked aircraft. At about 200ft I flew into some vicious turbulence, which caused one side of my canopy to collapse completely. I instantaneously became a swaying human pendulum. I'd never seen the ground coming up so dramatically. 'This looks like the big one!' I thought. Hanging on grimly, I hit the ground hard with my right shoulder being my first point of contact. My acromion was smashed, and it hurt! Even the birds stopped singing! The local hospital suggested that physiotherapy would be the solution but that evening Nick Parkhouse phoned to say he'd made an appointment the next day for me to see Ian Bailey, the country's number one shoulder consultant. Some 24 hours later Ian operated, and to him I can be grateful for the 100% restoration of the use of my right arm. But I'd been well shaken with the result that I didn't parachute again until June of the following year when Julie, the Twins, Nigel, Steve and I jumped into Old Warden. Thereafter I only

The Diamond Nine Parachute Team at Old Warden, June 26, 1988:
Martin and Julian Ruiz, C S-S, Julie, Steve Plank and Nigel Yonge

parachuted twice more before my last and 2,107th jump, which was on July 8, 1989, into Bob Pooley's garden party at Felden Grange. The Guest of Honour was Queen Noor of Jordan and I agreed with Steve that on landing I would, as usual, jump with a bunch of a dozen red roses for Lyn Pooley, while Steve would do likewise but with a bunch for Queen Noor. Once more dear Sue Thompson was flying me in 'ZZ as the lead of the first three Tigers for the drop, while Steve would lead the second trio. When we got airborne it was drizzling with rain and almost immediately we were flying in and out of the cloud. We started a somewhat forlorn run in at about 1,500ft and I had just signalled Sue to descend and land when, glancing ahead, it appeared to be a little brighter. I swiftly changed my mind and frantically signalled Sue to climb and continue running in. She managed to give me about 1,800ft. 'Good enough!' I reckoned and, signalling 'CUT!' to Sue, I stepped off the wing. On deploying my canopy I saw the twins had both managed to follow me, but Steve's trio of Tigers were well into their descent to land. I landed safely, shrugged off my parachute and approached Lyn and Queen Noor, fully aware that Steve still had possession of the roses intended for the Queen. She was highly amused when she learned what had occurred before graciously suggesting that I split the roses I was carrying between herself and Lyn. It was the perfect solution and an appropriate moment on which to hang up my boots. Every jump I'd made since my bone-crunching landing two years earlier shook me up for days afterwards. It was obviously time to call it a day after twenty-seven memorable years of jumping out of perfectly serviceable aeroplanes and making numerous lifelong friends along the way.

In April 1988 I received a telephone call from Lt Col Colin Sibun, the Commanding Officer of 7 Regiment, Army Air Corps, at Netheravon. The regiment was to receive a visit from ninety-year-old Cecil Lewis who, as a young pilot in the Royal Flying Corps, had won an MC over the Somme in 1916 aged eighteen. *Sagittarius Rising*, his inspirational book about flying in that appalling conflict, was first published in 1936 and has never been out of print since then. Colin asked me if I would fly Cecil from Netheravon to Middle Wallop in 'ZZ at the end of his visit and, having devoured *Sagittarius Rising* years before, my response was a no-brainer. Cecil turned out to be a tall, erect, utterly charming man, who possessed all the demeanour of a sprightly seventy-year-old – not what I might have expected of a First World War veteran of ninety. Once airborne I asked him if he'd like to do the flying and he took over immediately and with complete confidence before, some twenty minutes later, he executed a tidy landing on to the grass at Middle Wallop. Having taxied in and shut down, the infectious laughter between us was evidence of how much we'd both enjoyed the experience, so I was delighted when he signed my copy of *Sagittarius Rising*: 'For Charlie from Cecil Lewis with warmest

2nd Lt Cecil Lewis, Royal Flying Corps 1916

C S-S, Cecil and DH82A Tiger Moth G-AGZZ, 1988

thanks and memories!' We agreed to keep in touch with the result that we flew together again during our 1992 Diamond Nine Team training weekend at Badminton where he kindly accepted an invitation to become the Team's president. Then aged ninety-four, he excelled himself when he pulled off an immaculate landing in the Bunyip in a 90°, 15kt crosswind – not easily done in a Tiger and one I'd have been delighted to have done myself. In 1996 I was able to visit him and his lovely wife, Fanny, at their home in Corfu when we cooked up a plan to fly together again in two years' time when he would be 100. Sadly it wasn't to be – he passed away peacefully the following year aged ninety-nine. He was an amazing man who certainly lived 'Gloriously, generously, dangerously. Safety last!'

At the end of the month the annual Jersey Rally was to be our objective for the third time. 'ZZ's first overseas flight had been for the rally in 1986 when we flew the long sea crossing direct from Bournemouth to Jersey – two hours' Tiger flying over the water was more than enough! This time we crossed the Channel by way of a much shorter crossing from Lydd to Le Touquet and from there, having cleared customs, we continued to Caen. Here we met up with good friends Pete and Mary LeCoyte and their Tiger. The next day the weather for our planned final leg across the water to Jersey looked decidedly unfriendly, though a clearance was predicted for later that afternoon. From a phone call to Jersey we learned that a number of rally aircraft had flown into Granville, a small airfield on the west coast of the Cherbourg peninsula handily situated for a sea crossing to Jersey when the weather cleared. We soon took off to join them though the forty-minute flight through drizzle and limited visibility was none too pleasant. With about ten miles to run I called Granville on the radio only to be informed that the airfield was now closed. This presented us with something of a problem as we had planned to don our lifejackets for our flight across the water once we had landed there – but the all important lifejackets were stowed behind us in the baggage locker and thus unavailable – bugger! I called Pete and suggested to him that we fly up the coast to the estuary at Lessay, and there turn sharp left for the now shortest sea crossing to Jersey. Pete LeCoyte's laid-back response was typically Pete trying to be helpful: 'I'll just follow you,' he said. At Lessay I banked 'ZZ left and out across the water towards Jersey praying that her Gipsy Major would keep going for at least another fifteen minutes. Julie's head disappeared down into the front cockpit so she didn't have to be aware of the sea all around and below us and confirming our mutual unease at flying a forty-six-year-old single-engined open cockpit biplane over the sea – something we'd never get used to. I'd just made the initial radio call to Jersey when, having just passed over a bank of cloud, the island, now bathed in welcoming bright sunshine, was suddenly there straight ahead of us. Our arrival, which was marked by a successful crosswind landing from the Bunyip on Jersey's hard asphalt runway, was a welcome climax to our flight. It has to be recorded that my beloved required a couple of large G&Ts before she unwound enough to talk to me. When she did, she extracted a promise from me that we would never fly over the sea in 'ZZ together again without wearing lifejackets – and nor we ever did!

Added for the Diamond Nine Team's 1988 season were displays at Biggin Hill, Dunsfold, Henlow, Booker and Leavesden to make a total of fourteen between June and October. The first of these was to be at Biggin Hill for the two days of Jock Maitland's prestigious International Air Fair. The plan was for us to display at Biggin before flying on to the display at Dunsfold for the British Aerospace families day. It was one of those occasions when we had ten pilots and Tigers raring to go. John Webb agreed to be the reserve for our first display and to take off with us. He would then hold off and wait to join us en-route for Dunsfold, where he'd fly in the nine for our second show. We lined up and I called: 'Tigers, rolling, rolling, GO!' We took off in three groups of three with John bringing up the rear as No 10.

Climbing through 200ft the radio crackled into life in my helmet – it was David Baker's calm Cathay Pacific captain's voice: 'Tiger Lead, this is 9 – engine failure – I'm landing back on!'

Tiger Diamond Nine

I fear that my response was probably a little more anxious. 'Roger 9 – out to you. 10 this is Lead, fill 9's slot, over!'

John's voice came back swiftly. 'Roger Lead, understood – wilco!'

Mercifully, David's engine failure had occurred moments after he'd got airborne so he was easily able to land back on to the airfield. Meanwhile, John flew into the number 9 slot before completing the display in that position demonstrating considerable panache! Both the display at Dunsfold, and our second back at Biggin on the Sunday, went well. David and John had both flown with skill and flair and we, the rest of the team, were proud of them.

Having originally learnt to fly in the RAF, Victor Gauntlett was a petroleum entrepreneur who had also become the chairman of Aston Martin. He had collected some classic cars and some classic aircraft and among the latter was ex-APA DH89A Rapide G-AJHO. Before 'HO had been acquired by Victor the previous owner had her resprayed so that she represented the King's Flight's first aircraft, the 1936 DH89A Rapide complete in Brigade of Guards colours of dark red and navy blue, and the registration G-ADDD. However the 'powers that be' had taken umbrage at this unauthorised cloning of the original G-ADDD so Victor had her resprayed yet again so that she became G-AJHO once more. But before that happened, however, it had been agreed that 'HO, posing as G-ADDD, could be 'on parade' in July for the 1988 Queen's Flight Families'

Day at RAF Benson and I was lucky enough to have been the pilot asked to fly her on that occasion. It was at Benson that I met Air Vice-Marshal Sir John Severne. John had enjoyed a wonderfully colourful career in the RAF, culminating in his final appointment as Captain of the Queen's flight. It was in 1960 that he won the prestigious King's Cup Air Race in the Tiger Club's Turbulent G-APNZ, a year after he had fixed it for HRH the Duke of Edinburgh to fly the self-same aircraft, making him the only member of

G-AJHO posing as G-ADDD – airborne and at RAF Benson with one of the Queen's Flight's BAe 146

the Royal Family to fly a single-seat aircraft. John later became a good friend and, to fulfil a secret wish to fly a Tiger Moth on his 80th birthday, he flew G-AGZZ with me in 2005 – he recalls the occasion in his delightful 2007 memoir, *Silvered Wings*. 'Charlie Shea-Simonds made this possible for me by letting me fly with him from Netheravon in the beautiful aircraft he had restored himself. After I touched down on my first landing Charlie said, "Now go round again and prove to me that it wasn't a fluke!"' Indeed, it wasn't a fluke – both John's landings were textbook!

The year 1989 didn't start well! At 11.07am on February 5 I found myself piloting Rapide G-AJHO when it caught fire over the Oxfordshire countryside – an incident recounted in the first chapter of this book. In April we were joined in time for team training sessions at White Waltham and Badminton by Ken Whitehead, Pete Thorn, Mike Gibbs and Mike Blee. I was delighted when Ken agreed to take on the job as team manager – it made my job as leader much easier – and Pete Thorn became our head of training. Pete had not only been an instructor in the RAF, he'd also been a member of the Battle of Britain Memorial Flight, so his experience became a priceless asset.

In May the team met at Sibson prior to a splendidly memorable visit to the Red Arrows the following day. We always held the 'Reds' in the highest regard, especially as they had been our initial inspiration, so we felt especially privileged that they had agreed to our spending a day with them. The next morning, May 26, we took off from Sibson and formed ourselves into diamond nine for the 48-mile transit flight north to RAF Scampton. Our route took us smack overhead both RAF Cranwell and RAF Waddington so we tightened up the formation, which resulted in our receiving much-appreciated complimentary comments from the air traffic controllers at both. We had agreed to appear overhead Scampton at 10am and fly straight into our display routine. Having arrived excitedly within a few seconds of our planned start time, we certainly didn't disgrace ourselves and on landing we were warmly welcomed by our opposite numbers in the Reds – in my case Red One, Tim Miller; he and his fellow team members were the perfect hosts. It transpired that they had videoed our performance – the first time this had been done. The evidence of our shortcomings was revealed for all to see, so it proved to be an excellent training aid! Apart from that it was also interesting to spend the day at this historic RAF airfield from where the 'Dam Busters' raid – 'Operation Chastise' – was launched by the Lancasters of 617 Squadron on May 16, 1943. After lunch we attended the Reds' briefing for a full practice display and I was particularly fortunate to have been nominated to fly with Red One Tim in the back seat of Hawk XX264 during this sortie. It was an exhilarating flight of breathtaking precision. Then it was time for the Reds to fly with us in the Tigers for one of our display practices and, of course, Tim flew with me. He had to experience being in the back seat to be in command in the Tiger. I briefed him to do everything I would do as leader except the radio calls, which I did. It came as no surprise that he did a fantastic job and loved every second of it. Our visit heightened our respect for the Red Arrows and in thanking them for an unforgettable day I said that we didn't envy their flying the Hawk or the support they received from the RAF, but we were, however, hugely envious of the amount of time they were able to spend together in the air – no wonder that they had attained such team flying brilliance! In 1995 we enjoyed a second visit to the Reds when John Rands was Red One – it was every bit as memorable as the first in 1989.

C S-S with Tim Miller (Red One) having flown together at Scampton, May 26, 1989

The 1989 season turned out to be our busiest so far with eighteen successfully flown displays and with our parachute team, now joined by Dennis Jones and Pete Carey, flying with us for five of them. As usual the Moth Club Rally at Woburn in August was a memorable weekend, principally because we discovered we had enough pilots with reasonable formation flying skills for us to attempt to fly a diamond sixteen of Tigers in the sky before seven would break away to allow the remaining nine of us to fly our usual diamond nine display. It was definitely something of an organisational challenge with the sixteen of us walking through the routine several times before we then managed to achieve sixteen Tigers with Gipsy Major engines running and lined up on Woburn's grass and ready to go. Simon Bostock, now a Group Captain, had been appointed to co-ordinate the afternoon's flying activities and it was his voice that came through on the radio: 'Tiger Lead, this is Woburn radio – you are to return to dispersal and shut down!'

After all we'd been through, I was not about to comply without there being a very good reason. 'Lead, what's the problem?'

'You no longer have any fire cover so you are return to dispersal immediately!'

As Woburn Radio was a temporary advisory facility for the weekend and, as many of us operated out of unlicensed strips with no fire cover available anyway, I was distinctly unhappy to receive Simon's unwelcome, terse command. I glanced around the Tigers closest to me only to receive hand signals urging me to go. I needed little encouragement. 'Tigers, rolling, rolling – GO!' Sixteen Tigers roared into life and accelerated along the grass. Once airborne we climbed skywards and it wasn't too long before I was able to call: 'Tigers running in, in diamond sixteen!' It wasn't an especially tidy sixteen, but it wasn't bad for a first effort. However, our subsequent nine display was a very much more polished affair. Having landed, taxied in and shut down I saw Simon striding purposefully in my direction as I climbed out of the cockpit. 'Charlie, I think we'd better go for a little walk!'

With the adrenalin still flowing I couldn't stop myself. 'I don't think so,' I said, before explicitly telling him in good old Anglo-Saxon exactly what he could do instead!

In May 1990 we were completely devastated to learn of Joe Frankel's tragic, untimely death as the result of a freak mid-air collision near Redhill. The loss of one of our most enthusiastic founder members was an awful blow, particularly as Joe's unique brand of humour, his delightful personality and his dedication to Tiger flying exemplified what the team was all about. At the request of Joe's wife, Alex, we paid our own special tribute to Joe with a formation flypast of twelve Tigers at his funeral. He will certainly never be forgotten by any of us who were privileged to know him.

At Colerne for our first training weekend that year we were joined by Pete Colman, who brought our British Airways pilots' strength to four, and by Mike Vaisey whose considerable Gipsy Major engineering expertise proved fortuitous on a number of occasions thereafter. At a second training session at White Waltham we totally revamped our display routine for the start of our display season at the Biggin Hill Air Fair weekend later in the month. After our display on the Saturday we were delighted to learn that we had been voted runners-up for the team display trophy – an accolade definitely worth celebrating. As always at the end of the first day, Jock Maitland generously hosted a drinks party in the RAF Biggin Hill Officers' Mess for all the air fair participants. It was a perfect early summer's evening, allowing us to relax and unwind outside on the lawn and the first pint of Shepherd Neame's best slid down without touching the sides. I was halfway through my third pint when my attention was drawn to a pilot in an RAF flying suit who had just started to climb the impressively high but naked flagpole that stood proudly on the roof of the mess building. At roughly the halfway point he produced one of his squadron stickers and stuck it on the pole. Having descended safely back on to the roof he received a well-deserved round of applause from all of us below. The Royal Navy couldn't ignore the challenge, whereupon a Fleet Air Arm pilot managed to climb higher up the pole to place his nautical aviation sticker about a foot above that of the RAF. After the applause for the Navy's effort had died away, I remember thinking that perhaps one of the Army Air Corps display pilots might be up to challenging the Senior Service, but it was not to be and I was suddenly aware that all my Diamond Nine colleagues were now looking at me. 'Come off it, Chaps, I can't stand heights!' (Like a good many aviators I know, I genuinely can't!) But moments later Mary LeCoyte had firmly grabbed my upper arm and was steering me towards the building. She must have realised that, if I'd been left to my own devices, I would have probably (no, definitely!) found a place to hide and remained quietly hidden there sipping my beer until the dust had finally settled. My only hope was that by now one of the Mess staff had secured any further access to the roof so that any possible attempt by the Army would be stillborn – but no such luck! Having negotiated half a dozen flights of stairs, Mary guided me on to the roof where I found myself facing the challenge of the heavenward-pointing flagpole, which must have been at least 20ft high and secured to the roof by a trio of taut steel wires. With my escort providing verbal encouragement and standing by to catch me in the event of my parting company with the pole, I wrapped my arms and legs around the wretched thing and, pulling with sweaty hands, inched myself precariously skywards, and at the same time constantly reminding myself not to look downwards. Keeping my face a couple of inches from the pole, I was suddenly aware that I'd passed both RAF and RN stickers. I've no idea how I kept going as I was finding it more and more difficult to concentrate and NOT LOOK DOWN! Unexpectedly the 'button' was suddenly there at my eye level and I was able to stick a Diamond Nine team sticker right on the top of it. The descent was considerably easier, but I was still concentrating grimly and hoping desperately to make it back on to the roof in one piece. At one stage, and still not daring to look down, I managed to place my legs on either side of one of the steel wire stays – ouch! Very carefully inching my way back up and over it, I found myself moments later standing on the mess roof with both hands shaking like leaves as I reached out and carefully retrieved the pint pot that Mary had been kindly nursing for me throughout the entire harebrained contest. The remaining contents disappeared in seconds and it immediately made me realise that there was no way I could ever have tackled the flagpole while stone-cold sober, and I had been concentrating so resolutely that I was unaware whether the birds were singing or not. Still, it had all seemed like a good idea at the time!

I have to admit to feeling not too sparky at the following morning's briefing where Walter Eichhorn and I acknowledged each other's presence. Walter had been the team leader of Walter's Vogel, our skydiving rivals in a number of ten-man competitions in the 1970s. Walter was now one of the most well-respected display pilots anywhere and he regularly flew Germany's only surviving ME 109 at European airshows. Every year at Biggin Hill, at the conclusion of the Battle of Britain re-enactment display, Walter inevitably got 'shot down' – a requirement that he always accepted with patient good humour. The briefing itself was finally wound up with the usual: 'Are there any questions?'

'Ja,' said Walter, rising to his feet, 'after our display please may I fly off without landing first?'

'No problem, Walter,' was the helpful reply, 'what is your destination?'

'Germany,' replied a grinning Walter, as the response from the back of the room was almost predictable as some wag spontaneously suggested: 'Just like old times then!'

Later our Sunday display at Biggin had been a good one and, still on something of a high, I had just climbed out of 'ZZ when I was approached by a Squadron Leader in RAF uniform. 'Are you de team leader?' he inquired in a broad Irish accent. I admitted somewhat sheepishly that I was but, at the same time, pondering what I might have done to upset him. 'Roight,' he announced firmly, 'you'll be doing de Cottesmore Air Show!' He enlightened me further. 'Me name's Michael Kennedy and I'm de show organiser.' I replied that I didn't think it was one of our displays in our 1990 calendar. 'Well, it is now!' he informed me with a broad grin.

And that's how it came about and a couple of months later we performed at RAF Cottesmore, whereupon Michael Kennedy was quick to tell me we were booked to display there for the following year. For that 1991 display the weather forecast was depressingly 'iffy'. As usual team members who were based at a variety of different airfields, would soon be phoning in to see if it was it was a 'GO', so I called Michael at Cottesmore to find out what the weather was like there. 'It's not a problem, Charlie, de weather's foine here.' I passed on Michael's reassuring news to the team and an hour later Julie and I were airborne in 'ZZ, initially to meet up in the air with Nigel Wookey, a local farmer, who had only recently joined the team. Having done so, we set course for Cottesmore 120 miles away. The further north-east we flew, the lower the cloud became with Nigel's Tiger sticking to 'ZZ like glue in the deteriorating visibility. It wasn't very pleasant flying and somewhere near Kettering I started looking for an open space that might be suitable for a precautionary landing should it prove necessary. Looking ahead it looked like the cloud might have lifted a little. From my time at Uppingham I was able to recognise some helpful local landmarks. We pressed on and, having passed over the considerable expanse of Rutland Water, I was still unable to identify RAF Cottesmore until we had about three or four miles to run. Having landed safely we were comparing notes when a grinning Michael Kennedy appeared. 'Good to see you, Charlie,' he said, 'welcome to Cottesmore!' I let him have it, as I was very much aware that the birds had been on standby to stop singing! 'Michael, you told me that the weather wasn't a problem – it was crap!'

'I know,' he said, 'but if I'd told you de truth yer never would have come!'

'Too bloody true, Michael, too bloody true!'

Back to 1990 where there were other memorable displays. In July, Airborne Forces celebrated their fiftieth anniversary with a show in Aldershot's Rushmoor Arena over which we had been asked to display to mark the role that the Tiger Moth had played in providing ab-initio flying training for pilots of the Glider Pilot Regiment. The organisers had obtained permission for us to mount our display from Queen's Parade and the team arrived from different directions and landed in plenty of time to prepare our Tigers and walk through the routine. But we hadn't reckoned on the appearance of two overly zealous military policemen who were convinced that nine Tigers neatly lined up on Queen's Parade were clearly up to no good and should be arrested. Mercifully we survived the threat of being incarcerated in an Aldershot military 'nick' and our display went ahead on time without any further hiccups. In early September we made our first appearance at what was to become one of our favourite venues – the Shepway Show. Having taken off from Headcorn, we displayed off Folkestone sea front over the water to huge crowds stretched along about a mile and a half of clifftop and, yes, we all wore lifejackets! Jeanne Fraser, a dear friend from Tiger Club days at Redhill, was the Shepway Show organiser and she quickly gained our respect as she was one of the few airshow organisers who fully understood our Tigers' limitations. Our final 1990 display was our second

The team at West Malling, 1990. Standing: John Webb, Colin Dodds, C S-S, John Watkins (reserve), Pete LeCoyte, Ken Whitehead; Kneeling: Steve Bohill-Smith, Martin Gambrell, Len Mitton, Pete Jackson

appearance at the Great Warbirds Air Show at West Malling. It had become another favourite where three years later we collected the trophy for the best team display. In 1991, and having been joined by Roger Fiennes and Dave Chalmers, we displayed on sixteen occasions and among them was our first overseas display at Abbeville in France where the organisers were suitably impressed when Pete LeCoyte's wife and our team commentator, Mary, delivered her entire commentary in faultless French. 1992 was notable for its unkind weather but, now joined by Paul Chapman, we still managed to perform fifteen displays with the parachute team jumping from the Tigers on five occasions. The Woodcote Steam Rally was one of our new display venues and, having dropped the parachute team, we, the pilots, joined them for a wander around the showground. Intrepid sixty-six-year-old Nigel Yonge, complete with one glass eye, spotted a bungee-jumping crane with the other. 'I rather fancy having a go at that,' says he. Moments later he was seen climbing up the ladder to the launch platform, to the accompaniment of much ribald encouragement from his parachute team members, especially Steve, whose warning: 'Keep your eyes shut, Nigel, you don't want to lose your glass one!' was appropriately delivered just as our hero was having the bungee straps secured tightly around his ankles and while another of our number quietly muttered: 'Silly old sod!' The gentleman concerned then launched himself vigorously off the platform into a spread-eagled skydiving exit. 'YEEE-HAARRRR!' he cried, while we all cheered. After the bungee boings had died down and his ankles had been released, he was asked what it was like. 'Bloody marvellous!' he replied proudly and, still sporting his glass eye, 'but for gawd's sake don't tell the Mem Sahib!'

We gained two notable sponsors in 1993. The first was Castrol, which generously quenched our Gipsy Majors' raging thirsts for oil for the next eight years, while the

G-AGZZ poses in Olympus livery **The Olympus Diamond Nine team poster**

second was Olympus Cameras, which, through Ian Dickens, its enthusiastic communications and marketing director, helped us in more ways than we could have dreamed possible with everything from corporate clothing, including our iconic straw boaters, to posters publicising our appearances at shows. G-AGZZ now appeared in Olympus livery. In turn all this benefited the two charities we supported, initially Cancer Research and later the Anthony Nolan Trust. It's worth mentioning that we never charged for our displays. We simply asked the airshow organisers to fill up our fuel tanks before our departure and to make donations to our team funds, from which we gave a percentage to our chosen charity. For the two-day shows such as Biggin Hill and Duxford, overnight

With the 'Reds' at Scampton, July 1995. Kneeling: Pete Colman, Pete LeCoyte, Mike Vaisey, Pete Jackson, C S-S, Roger Hanauer, Nigel Wookey, Len Mitton and Ken Whitehead

accommodation was provided and, as can be imagined, this led to some memorable parties on the Saturday night! That year we flew seventeen displays and were joined by the parachute team for five; in 1994 the numbers were twenty and nine and in 1995 they were twenty and seven. During those years we were joined by Pete Henley, Roger Hanauer, Doug Collyer and Dave Kirkham. Inevitably some of our pilots discovered that the flying of so many displays – 149 in our first ten years – was a huge commitment that forced them to fall by the wayside, but luckily others replaced them. Earlier that year we enjoyed our second visit to the 'Reds' at Scampton. Now led by John Rands, they once again proved to be enthusiastic hosts, even if our joint attempt at a photograph of the two teams in the sky together wasn't wholly successful – with our 250kts speed differential and indifferent visibility it wasn't altogether surprising.

An early team outing the following year was to Old Warden in early July. For our practice day on the Saturday I had suggested to Kim Ross, dear family friend and now Adjutant of the Royal Hospital, that he bring some of the Chelsea Pensioners to the

Shuttleworth Trust to fly with us. Six of these stalwart veterans flew with us during a full display routine – my co-pilot for the occasion was Sid Tweedale, a splendid character who'd won a Military Medal on D-Day. After landing the Pensioners donned their iconic scarlet jackets and we all repaired to the Crown for a memorably entertaining lunch generously organised by Ian Dickens on behalf of our sponsors. The rest of the season saw us displaying on sixteen occasions with the jumpers joining us on nine of them.

Diamond geezers fly Chelsea pensioners

The six Chelsea Pensioners and Diamond 9 team get ready for take-off by a Tiger Moth plane

AS A part of the 10th anniversary celebrations of the Olympus-sponsored Diamond 9 Tiger Moth display, the pilots offered to take six grand old soldiers from the Royal Hospital in Chelsea up in the skies.

The idea came from Diamond 9 team leader Charlie Shea-Simonds, and the eldest Chelsea pensioner to fly from the Old Warden Airfield in Bedfordshire was 79.

Tiger Moth planes were originally introduced in the late 1920s and at that time their open cockpits, wooden spars and fabric covered wings were regarded as innovative.

After a 20 minute flight the party retired to a local pub to compare flights over a pint.

Six Chelsea Pensioners with the team at Old Warden, July 1996. Standing: Pete Thorn, Noel Wright RH, Sid Tweedale MM RH, Sid Hazell RH, ????, Alf Amphlett BEM, RH, Tom Parnell RH, Pete Jackson. Kneeling: Doug Collyer, Pete LeCoyte, Mike Vaisey, C S-S, Ken Whitehead, Nigel Wookey, Len Mitton and Roger Hanauer

In 1997 our first training weekend was at Rendcomb, an historic disused First World War grass airfield in the Cotswolds, and home of Vic Norman's Aerosuperbatics Flying Circus and the world's only Formation Wing Walking Team flying immaculately maintained Boeing Stearman biplanes. The Stearman is the US equivalent of the Tiger, but with a 450hp engine up front instead of the Tiger's more modest 130hp. Since 1987 Vic, a wonderfully enthusiastic and hugely respected display pilot, has led his splendid team of pilots and glamorous lady wing-walkers for the past thirty-plus years with charismatic commitment and good-humoured professionalism, and with much welcomed sponsorship over the years from, in turn, Yugo Cars, Cadbury's Crunchie, St Ivel's Utterly Butterly, Guinot and, more recently, Breitling. Vic always enjoyed our presence at Rencombe whether it was for one of our training sessions, for a Diamond Nine display at one of the Rendcomb Air Shows or whether it was our using his facilities to mount one of our displays for one of the massive Royal International Air Tattoos at Fairford. He even flew with us in the Nine on a couple of occasions when we only had eight Tigers and pilots on parade – his support of the team was always generous and always much appreciated. He became a staunch friend.

Another regular team supporter was Al Mathie, a wonderfully charismatic aviator who just lived to fly. Not only was he an exceptional pilot but he was also a very useful engineer – while he was an officer cadet at the RAF College Cranwell he managed to rebuild a Gipsy Major engine in his room in the Mess! He flew both Hunters and Jaguars while serving in the RAF, and during these years he became an Auster devotee and an acknowledged expert on the type, both as a pilot and as an engineer. Later his lovely wife, Dot, also became an accomplished Auster pilot; she was extraordinary as she always seemed impervious to Al's use of their house as a hangar overspill – on arriving to stay with them on one memorable occasion Julie and I discovered the fuselage of an Andreasson BA4, which Al was restoring, resting across the arms of two large comfy chairs and which filled their sitting room! Al was one of the most genial and lovable characters imaginable and he would always generously agree to provide support for anything to do with flying, especially if it included him – he even allowed me to fly the Andreasson BA4 once he'd restored it. This little single-seat aerobatic biplane was so exhilarating to fly and I think Al really appreciated my adrenalin-fired enthusiasm in recounting the flight to him after I'd landed – especially my first roll off the top of a loop from level flight. We always enjoyed Al's association with the team and usually this was when he joined us at training weekends flying his Auster G-AKSZ around us while acting as a camera platform.

Thus he was with us at Middle Wallop for our second training session of the season and at the end of the day we were all packing up before flying back home. I thanked him for his enthusiastic support and watched him taxi out across Wallop's grass to line up into wind for take-off. He opened the throttle and the Auster quickly gathered speed to lift off the ground after a couple of hundred yards before climbing away. He can't have been more than 200ft up when the engine suddenly quit. Every pilot practises the action to be taken in the event of an EFAT (engine failure after take-off) – quickly select an open space somewhere ahead of the aircraft into which to attempt a landing – and never turn back towards the field is the golden rule, as there is a very real danger of spinning into the ground off the turn as the speed decays. On this occasion, however, and in front of him, Al was faced with the busy A343 road beyond which were the multiple buildings of a firework factory. But Al clearly believed that rules were for fools and for the guidance of wise men. He immediately flew straight into a stall turn, simultaneously selecting full flap and, at the same time, rotating the Auster around its vertical axis and allowing its speed to decay to 28kts – the aircraft's full-flap stalling speed. Seconds later he pulled off an impeccable downwind landing back on to Wallop's grass acres. It was a brilliant piece of flying and it happened so quickly that the birds had no time at all to even consider stopping singing! We all lent a hand to push the Auster off the runway, whereupon Al produced his ubiquitous bag of tools and, within a few minutes, he'd removed the engine cowlings and diagnosed the cause of the problem. 'Just a bit of shit in the carburettor,' he announced cheerfully, after which he swiftly rectified the problem and, having completed a successful ground run of the engine and now covered in oil, he took off a second time to return happily to Upavon where the Auster was hangared.

Al, Dot and 'SZ often joined Julie, 'ZZ and I for aerial outings together as they were such delightful company. On one such occasion we flew in formation down to Sandown on the Isle of Wight just to get ice creams – a simple piece of ridiculous fun! In 2012 we were totally devastated to learn of Al's death in a tragic accident. So many of us in aviation lost an especially dear friend about whom Julie and I never heard an unkind word said, while dearest Dot lost an amazing husband. He enriched the lives of all of us who were fortunate to have known him – he was a 'one-off' who will always be remembered with great affection.

Other characters have to be mentioned because of the encouragement they always gave us whenever we met during the air display season. The first is Brendan O'Brien, who, for me at any rate, was the ultimate air display showman. Not only was he an accomplished and talented pilot, but his displays were, and probably still are, highly original, always wonderfully entertaining and every time flown with a flair that reflected the innate charm of his charismatic personality. As experienced by so many of us, Brendan's enthusiasm for air display flying was initially nurtured at the Tiger Club where his flying showmanship was effectively demonstrated during his dazzling Tiger Moth Crazy Flying performances. With John Taylor as his partner, he then went on to create the RF4 Duo, flying two Fournier motor gliders for a graceful formation aerobatic ballet with smoke trailing from their wingtips and beautifully choreographed to the music of Pink Floyd. His next display routine was a US import – the Truck Top Landing using a Piper Cub, one of a much loved, ubiquitous aircraft type with a useful STOL (short take off and landing) performance. While landing the Cub on top of a large truck being driven down the runway requires a little more than usual flying skill, Brendan added his own special brand of showmanship to produce a wonderfully entertaining air display routine. He was always full of surprises. One festive season Julie answered the phone – it was Brendan calling to wish us 'Happy Christmas' while airborne in the Antarctic Survey Twin Otter. He informed us he was some fifty nautical miles from the South Pole – it made our day!

Then there is Paul Bonhomme, an amazingly accomplished pilot who took to the skies early in life, becoming British Airways' youngest captain before he was thirty at much the same age as he started flying historic 'war birds' on the air display scene. He is a thoroughly genial, always smiling, modest character who became well-respected by the team. I well remember one of our appearances at Duxford when we were parked in isolation at the far south-western end of the crowd line and a long walk from all the essential facilities. A gaggle of war birds were taxiing past us towards the downwind end of the runway for take-off. Paul's mount was a pristine example of the massive Vought F4V Corsair fighter powered by the equally massive 2,000hp Pratt & Whitney radial engine. He was the first of the pilots taxiing past who acknowledged our presence with a cheerful grin and encouraging salute – after which our remote parking didn't seem so bad after all. Later at one of the two-day White Waltham air shows, Paul was the display director. On the Saturday he gave a comprehensive pilot's briefing, which ensured a successful afternoon's flying. On the Sunday we were all seated, awaiting Paul's briefing which, on this occasion, was attended by a gentleman from the CAA who was monitoring the proceedings. Paul stood up and cheerfully announced: 'Good afternoon everyone – same as yesterday – any questions?' Of course there were none. The authority's representative, not having been present at Saturday's briefing, was not amused, but the rest of us most certainly were. Having been given a copy of the afternoon's flying programme, officialdom had the good sense to leave it at that and, unsurprisingly, the show went like clockwork! Well done Paul! This talented pilot went on to the become the undisputed star of Red Bull Air Racing – indeed, from 2005 until he stood down in 2015, he was the unrivalled Red Bull World Air Racing Champion on three occasions, which can only have been the result of his meticulously precise, disciplined flying. And he's still flying both historic war birds and formation aerobatic displays with his Matador team partner, Steve Jones, utilising the exciting little 315hp German built XtremeAir XA41 aircraft. Long may he continue to do so.

Air Chief Marshal Sir John Allison had enjoyed a glitteringly distinguished military career in the Royal Air Force before retiring in 1999 as Air Officer Commanding (AOC) Strike Command. Both during and after his service career, John was one of the few senior RAF officers who made their mark on the civilian air display scene, and, as an outstanding pilot and one who had benefited from the Tiger Club membership, he eventually went on to became the respected chairman of the Historic Aircraft Association. HAA was founded in 1979 to support those of us who owned or operated historic aircraft, especially when they were being flown in air displays. Under John's resolute and charismatic leadership a much-needed system for qualifying display pilots was established with the most experienced being appointed display authorisation evaluators (DAEs) who, in turn, checked out newcomers to the scene to enable them to be issued with display authorisations (DAs). Initially the CAA accepted HAA's self-regulatory DA system as being a sensible means of promoting air display safety. In 1991 John was appointed AOC No. 11 Group RAF so, and unfortunately for HAA, he decided to step down as chairman. I suddenly found myself being elected in his place. He proved to be a ridiculously hard act to follow. Initially all went well with HAA members who quickly accepted that their DAs or DAE appointments would be important benefits of HAA membership – until the CAA decided to muscle in with its own system of qualifying display pilots. It quickly realised, however, that the HAA system was a good one, with the result that we were

Nine of the team during our penultimate season: John Watkins, Pete LeCoyte, Pete Jackson, C S-S, Mike Vaisey, Ken Whitehead, Pete Thorn, Len Mitton and Nigel Wookey. Interestingly there are only three of us in this team photo who are also in all the other team photos in this book: Pete LeC, C S-S and Len

informed that it would be adopting it lock, stock and barrel. Of course we protested vigorously, but to no avail. The authority finally adopted the HAA system with our reluctant agreement, but, even then only subject to its assurance that it would make no charge for its implementation. How naive I must have been to rely on its assurance! Within a very short space of time the CAA had not only adopted our system, but it was also making a substantial annual charge for issuing a DA – currently £298 against today's HAA annual membership fee of £25. Whether the authority's DA system has proved itself any more relevant to the promotion of display pilot ability, and thus air display safety, is debatable.

By the end of the 1998 season it became obvious that we were finding it more and more difficult to enjoy having nine team members flying with us for each of the air shows to which we were committed – and none of us was getting any younger! That year we only flew six displays and eleven the year after, with the parachute team only jumping with us five times during the 1998-99 seasons combined. Not only that but it was becoming increasingly more expensive to keep our beautiful Tigers airworthy and Olympus was due to terminate its splendid sponsorship. We sadly decided to announce that the 2000 display season would be our last, while appreciating that it would be far better to call it a day while we were still capable of pleasing the air display crowds rather than trying to continue, thereby risking a slow decline in our performances. But at the end of the season we'd completed another fourteen Diamond Nine displays with, of the original parachutists, only Steve Plank and Julian Ruiz still jumping out of our Tigers. We agreed that our final public Diamond Nine team display would be at the Shuttleworth Collection Autumn Air Day at Old Warden on Sunday, October 1. I told the team that we'd

The programme for our Diamond Nine farewell display

work it so that whoever turned up would definitely be included in the display providing they arrived the day before for a practice. With thirteen – lucky for some – Tigers and pilots on parade we improvised a formation to fly a vic of nine with a diamond four in the middle. It looked good and Saturday's two rehearsals went well, as did the team party in the Crown later. Sunday dawned bright and sunny and, having successfully dropped the jumpers for the last time, we took off and flew our final display. I didn't land afterwards but flew straight back to Netheravon – I just knew that it would all get too emotional. It was my 224th Diamond Nine display.

Our final thirteen fly-by – good enough for government work!

A couple of weeks later and accompanied in 'ZZ by Holly, a dear family friend whom I was teaching to fly, eight of us flew down to Lee-on-Solent to display a Diamond Eight 'thank you' over the start of the Clipper Ventures Round the World Yacht Race for Ian Dickens, who was one of the crew members. He kindly wrote in his delightful book, *Sea Change*: 'And then Charlie and the team centred their Tiger Moth display right overhead and gave a beautiful send-off with the tightest and sharpest formation, waving from their cockpits on the downwind flyby.' We landed back at Lee and it was only then that it hit me. It was now definitely all over – that was it! I parked, flicked off the ignition switches and the prop coughed to a standstill. I just sat there unsuccessfully trying to hold back the tears. Now remain just logbooks and photo albums full of memories. And they are precious.

Perhaps 224 Diamond Nine displays in fifteen years is not an awe-inspiring total, but consider, if you will, that they were flown with iconic aircraft that were then more than fifty years old with a modest cruising speed of 75kts and by pilots of a similar age, and you may then more readily understand why we loved flying our DH82A Tiger Moths in the way that we did. And during all the displays we flew we only had two accidents – the first was a minor taxiing accident and the second a gentle touch between two team members flying in formation which, fortunately, left their paintwork undamaged. And what of the Diamond Niners themselves? They were, without exception, members of a very special team of enthusiastic aviators of which I was not only massively privileged to have been a member, but also Tiger Lead. Sadly there isn't room here to record all the splendid stories from our fifteen years together, but in my case two treasured snapshots remain. Whenever Len Mitton flew into any of our display venues he would immediately seek me out to inquire where and when lunch was. To my shame I seldom ever did know, but he continued to ask me anyway! And then there was the occasion we had overnighted the Tigers between shows at Pete Jackson's strip near Huntingdon. We got airborne the following morning and Pete slipped into formation on my left. Then I spotted it. He'd obviously mislaid his pitot head cover because, still held in its place by an elastic band, was an empty crisp packet. 'Useful pre-flight inspection, PJ!' was our cruel taunt, and, of course he was never allowed to forget it! They were an extraordinarily special bunch of guys who will remain unforgettable. Sir John Allison was a great Diamond Nine team supporter so we were thrilled to receive his generous tribute to the team, which is reproduced below.

A TRIBUTE BY AIR CHIEF MARSHAL SIR JOHN ALLISON KCB CBE

I would like to say to all the Diamond Nine team, on the day that you conclude your long and very successful air display career, how much I have appreciated and enjoyed your presence on the scene over the years. I have admired firstly the professionalism you have brought to the flying – and in this matter I suspect many people do not fully appreciate just how difficult it is to achieve a high standard of formation flying, as you have done, with Tiger Moths. As someone who was fortunate enough to have learnt to fly on the Tiger, and who has kept in touch with the type subsequently, I think I know. I have also observed with admiration (and even perhaps a little wistful envy) the team's sense of style, your goodfellowship and ability to enjoy life. You have enriched the air display community with your presence and we are the poorer for your departure which, typically, you have done with wisdom, grace and style.

CHAPTER 20
TURBINE TIME – THANK YOU, DR PEARSON!

As recounted earlier, I was bitterly disappointed when my application to go flying with the Army Air Corps was derailed by Dr Pearson, CME's ENT specialist, who had decided that my high-tone deafness was such that it would prevent my ever flying turbine-engine aircraft. It didn't, however, and I now have to admit that, had I been able to fly with the Army Air Corps, life might well have been very different, but probably nowhere near as fulfilling as it has been. Perhaps therefore, Dr Pearson, I should be thanking you rather than allowing your decision to continue to fester.

By the early 1980s, BN2A piston-engined Islanders had given reliable service to skydiving but the sport was now looking for a replacement that could provide a swifter climb to altitude. Turbine-engined aircraft now became de rigueur for the larger parachute centres as they were appreciably quicker in the climb to altitude and, unlike piston-engine aircraft that required descending with care to prevent over-cooling, they could be returned to the ground very swiftly. As mentioned earlier, the Army Parachute Association purchased a Pilatus PC-6 Turbo Porter in 1982, which did the job admirably for the next five years. In 1983 I was appointed APA's chief pilot and a CAA PPL examiner – two roles that I was to enjoy for the next thirty years. Flying for the Joint Services Parachute Centre, co-located with APA at Netheravon to provide adventurous training courses for the three services, was undertaken by a small pool of RAF Hercules pilots on secondment from Lyneham. They were never entirely comfortable flying single-engined aircraft for parachuting and thus their influence played a substantial part in the decision to replace the Porter with a BN2T Turbine Islander. Engines provide the major cost of aircraft maintenance so lifting ten jumpers to altitude in the twin-engined BN2T Islander was, per capita, considerably more expensive than lifting ten in the single-engined Pilatus PC-6 Turbo Porter. In May 1986 I was fortunate enough to fly the European demonstrator Cessna 208B Grand Caravan when it visited Netheravon. I was immediately impressed with its ability to lift sixteen jumpers swiftly to altitude when powered by one 675HP Pratt & Whitney PT6A turbo-prop engine. Why should the expense of twin-engined safety be a necessity for parachuting operations when the jump aircraft is seldom far away from gliding distance of the departure airfield? Surely the Cessna Grand Caravan was the obvious way forward, but it took a further fourteen years before enlightenment became reality, which I will recall later. In the meantime there were more than enough aviation experiences to enjoy, a number of which I hadn't anticipated.

During the summer of 1987 I received a call from Herbie Knott, a talented photographer, who had been asked by *The Independent* to take some photographs to mark the restoration of a steam rail locomotive, SR N Class 2-6-0 No. 31874, for the Watercress Line, a heritage railway that runs from New Alresford to Alton in Hampshire. To add a pre-war period atmosphere to the photo, he thought it would be interesting to have a Tiger Moth flying close to and in the same direction as the locomotive. When he asked me if I would be interested in being involved, I quickly agreed. The immediate problem was 'ZZ's speed of 75kts (86mph) compared with the locomotive's chuffing-contentedly-along-speed of 25mph would make it difficult for Herbie to photograph both locomotive and Tiger in the same frame. Herbie found a suitable spot for the photo, however, where the locomotive would be passing along an embankment, and I contacted the CAA to obtain an exemption from Rule 5 of the ANO which stated in part that: 'Except with the permission in writing of the CAA, an aircraft shall not be flown closer than 500ft to any person, vessel, vehicle or structure.' The authority was very helpful and provided me with the necessary exemption; included eight conditions, two of which were that I was not permitted to fly: '(iv) at a height of less than 200ft above the ground level'; and '(v) above any point on the ground closer than 110 metres to any area occupied by spectators or their vehicles.' As all the spectators would be in the train, the second condition quoted seemed somewhat superfluous. On August 13, the weather was perfect as I circled over the line waiting for the locomotive's approach to the embankment. When it finally did and, aware that I only had one attempt at getting it right, I descended on to a heading parallel with the line, hoping that my timing worked and that I remained above 200ft AGL. Herbie's photo was a winner and it subsequently appeared in both *The Independent* and in *One Day for Life*, a fundraising book in aid of four cancer charities. It's certainly one of our favourite photos of G-AGZZ.

G-AGZZ over the Watercress Line, August 13, 1987 – photo by Herbie Knott

As a flying instructor I only twice had the opportunity to train a student pilot through a complete private pilot's licence course and in the early 1980s I was regularly instructing for the Army Flying Association at Middle Wallop, home of the Army Air Corps Centre in Hampshire. The then Commandant was Colonel David Mallam who, during his tenure, saw the establishment of the Museum of Army Flying, the ultimate success of which was in no small way due to his energy and enthusiasm. He was to become a staunch friend. As Lloyds Bank was involved in sponsoring the Wallop Air Show, which raised money for the Museum, Colonel David met Fred Crawley, its deputy chief executive, who had, during one of their meetings, expressed an interest in learning to fly. David suggested that I might consider teaching him with the Army Flying Association, so the three of us met to discuss it further. As he was the highly respected second-in-command of the bank, I initially found myself somewhat in awe of him – it was almost as if I was being interviewed by him about an increase to my overdraft facility! Nonetheless, having agreed to instruct him and having started flying with him, I gradually warmed to him as I discovered he possessed a delightful, self-deprecating sense of humour. He certainly didn't find flying a skill for which he had any natural aptitude – but, as he must have then been in his late fifties, this was not altogether surprising. The other problem was that Fred was often out of the country for weeks at a time on Lloyds business, with the result that his flying lessons suffered from a lack of continuity – but he battled on with great determination anyway.

Coincidentally, I had got to know Peter Richie, a regular skydiver at Netheravon, who was at the time the manager of the Petersfield branch of Lloyds Bank. Because of his financial expertise Peter had been persuaded to become treasurer of the Royal Aero Club – a job for which he was well qualified. In a local pub after a RAeC council meeting, I suggested to Peter that we might have a bit of fun with Fred, who was one of his bosses and whom he'd never met. The idea was that Peter would come to Wallop to make a skydive from the Army Flying Association's Cessna 172 at the same time that Fred was due to have his next lesson. Having assured Peter that the prank was unlikely to be detrimental to his Lloyds Bank career, he agreed and the date was set. By the time Fred arrived at Wallop I'd removed the 172's starboard door and briefed Peter and another chum, Andy Grice, an ex-Royal Marine skydiver whose sister, Ruth, was my secretary in the family business. While the two jumpers climbed into the back of the 172 I explained to Fred that he was about to fly his first parachute sortie for which I'd instruct him as we climbed to altitude. Over the airfield at 3,000ft Fred eased off the power – Andy exited first closely followed by Peter. 'By the way, Fred,' I announced, 'that second jumper is the manager of your Petersfield branch!' Fred was delighted and, after introductions on the ground, we adjourned to the nearest pub to celebrate. I was able to instruct Fred for the rest of his course and, having been the first student whom I'd instructed throughout, he finally gained his PPL in September 1985. A couple of months later Fred gave me a large parcel with instructions that I was not to open it until I got home. When I did open it I discovered a beautiful 16in wingspan model of G-AGZZ, which was perfect in every detail and with a note from Fred which read: 'Charles, with grateful thanks for all your efforts spread over two years in teaching a slowcoach to fly. Fred.' It's a much-treasured memento.

By May 1986, David Mallam was working for the Lady Hoare Trust, a charity devoted to the support of physically disabled children. David had organised a fundraising fête in aid of the charity to be held on the playing fields of Blundell's school in Devon and he'd persuaded Lewis Collins, the actor, to officially 'open' the event. Lewis had by this time made a name for himself playing the part of Bodie in *The Professionals*, a highly successful television series. David asked me if I would fly Lewis down to Devon in 'ZZ for the occasion which I did and my VIP passenger obviously enjoyed the flight.

Lewis Collins and C S-S in G-AGZZ, May 1990

Having duly opened the fête he was introduced to a number of the children for whom the charity was providing much-needed support. One of these was a chronically disabled and disfigured young lady in a wheelchair who had no power of speech – it was impossible not be moved by the utter helplessness of her situation. Lewis Collins spontaneously knelt down alongside her, put his arms compassionately around her and gave her a massive cuddle – her whole face lit up. I remember thinking, 'Lewis Collins, you're OK!' Subsequently I got to know Lew well – he was such a genuine Mr Nice Guy that he became a good friend and, because he was a competent skydiver, he often jumped with the Diamond Nine parachute team. Finally, after a five-year fight against cancer, he tragically died aged only sixty-seven in 2013. Not only is he sorely missed by his dear wife, Michelle, and their three splendid boys, but also by all of us who were fortunate enough to have known him.

During the twenty-four years since her restoration in 1983, our much-loved DH82A Tiger Moth, G-AGZZ, flew just over 1,100 hours and had provided some special memories, not only for Julie and me, but also for so many others – pilots, passengers and parachutists alike. Apart from the details being recorded in my logbook, the two-week trip Julie and I made to France in 'ZZ in the autumn of 1990 was especially memorable. The third of our eight outbound legs finished at Alençon, which was also our first night stop. A few minutes after we landed we were approached by an enthusiastic French aviator whose delight at seeing 'un Teeger Moth' prompted him to arrange free overnight hangarage for 'ZZ before kindly giving us a lift into town to the B&B accommodation he'd recommended. The next morning he picked us up and drove us back to the airfield. All this was typical of the warmth of the welcomes we received everywhere. From Alençon we continued on to Dax in south-west France. Here we picked up a hire car that Julie drove to the little coastal airfield of Mimizan and to which I flew 'ZZ. We chilled out there for five days of sun, sea and sand – bliss! When it was time to depart homeward-bound I felt distinctly uneasy about flying my solo leg from Mimizan back to Dax. Forty minutes later my sixth-sense apprehension was explained. My landing on the single hard runway at Dax was fine and, as I wasn't too happy about taxiing all the way along the hard with no brakes, ATC gave me clearance to taxi across the grass to the flying club. Unfortunately the longish grass concealed an uncovered drainage sump about 18in in diameter. I simply didn't see it and the Tiger's port wheel rolled into it. 'ZZ tipped forward, smashing the propeller. The French ATC were very helpful, but then so perhaps they should have been – the sump should surely have had a cover. By the time Julie arrived with the hire car I'd removed the prop and telephoned the Henry Labouchere Hotline. Swinging into immediate action, Henry excelled himself. He removed the prop from his Tiger, G-BEWN, packaged it up and gave it to one of his chums who was about to fly to Booker and who was happy to deliver it thence. John Laing then kindly collected it from Booker and took it to Air France cargo at Heathrow for its onward journey to Bordeaux. The next day Julie and I drove to Bordeaux-Merignac airport to collect Henry's generously loaned propeller. As soon as we had found our way into the Customs office we spotted the long box on which was written in bold print: G-AGZZ WITH LOVE FROM G-BEWN! 'Qu'est-ce que c'est?' inquired the Customs Officer. 'C'est une hélice pour un avion ancien,' was the best I could come up with, but he seemed happy enough, so we hurried back to Dax to fit G-BEWN's prop to G-AGZZ. The next day, after a quick test flight to check all was well, we set off on the first of seven legs homeward, arriving back at Netheravon three days later. In spite of the prop drama it had been a thoroughly enjoyable trip and made especially memorable by Dr Moth's timely support. Thank you Henry!

PPL examiners are authorised by the CAA to check the logbooks of PPL holders as required to certify that a minimum number of flying hours have been achieved during the previous one or, later, two years. In early 1992 Tim Williams, one of my regular PPL 'customers', contacted me as his logbook needed certificating. Now Penny, Tim's lovely, elegant wife, could not be described as an aviation enthusiast – I think it would be fair to say that she tolerates flying graciously – so I was amused to read of four flights they made together in his DH80A Puss Moth recorded for the same day in his logbook: 1. Folly Farm – Lydd. 2. Lydd – Le Touquet. 3. Le Touquet – Southend. 4. Southend – Folly Farm; and in the remarks column it simply said: 'Penny's Holiday'! Tim also owned a 1939 DH82A Tiger Moth G-APAM, which had been converted to become a Thruxton

Jackaroo in the 1960s, during which time she had been owned by the aviatrix Sheila Scott. When Tim acquired her (the Jackaroo, not Sheila Scott!) he converted her back to being a Tiger Moth and so it came to pass that Tim asked me if I'd like to teach his delightful daughter, Harriet, to fly in the family Tiger. The idea of instructing Harriet throughout a complete PPL course on a Tiger was hugely appealing as it was something I had yet to do, and Harriet was a bright young lady who I was sure would have inherited some of her father's flying genes. And so it proved.

We made our first instructional trip together in 'PAM on May 18, and, three days later, I sent her solo after fourteen instructional sorties totalling eleven hours and thirty-five minutes! With this extraordinary achievement Harriet set the unusually high standard she went on to achieve throughout the rest of the course. Not only did she have huge enthusiasm for learning to fly, she was, and probably still is, an accomplished equestrienne. Anyone who can successfully ride horses usually discovers that flying presents few difficulties and this is why so many pilots in the early days of the Royal Flying Corps were cavalry officers. If you can tame a horse, you can usually tame an aeroplane! I found that every sortie with Harriet was enjoyable and fulfilling, and there were some memorable moments. We were well into the navigation flight test (NFT) part of the course when I was expected to give her a diversion because of notional bad weather – but this time the bad weather unexpectedly became the real thing as it started to rain. Over the intercom I asked her what she was going to do given the circumstances. 'If I was my dad, I'd probably continue on a bit further,' she mischievously replied, 'but as I'm not, I'm going to divert to the nearest airfield.' Which was what she did very proficiently, though later, when I submitted all her paperwork to the CAA to support her PPL application, I attached a covering letter to her rain-soaked NFT flight log to explain how it came to be in such a sorry state. Maintaining a flight log in an open cockpit biplane in the pouring rain is not an easy exercise. A couple of weeks later we were in the air together revising all aspects of the course in preparation for her general flying test (GFT) that she was due to fly with fellow examiner Pete Thorn. I was more than happy with her performance so I decided to present her with a final challenge. I'd always stressed to her the need, especially when flying old aeroplanes, to keep a good lookout for fields in which it might be possible to land in the event of engine failure or poor weather. We were overhead the expanse of Savernake Forest when I spotted the only such suitable field, so I waited until we had flown past it and, hoping to catch her out, I closed the throttle and told her: 'You have a total engine failure – carry on!' She coolly trimmed 'PAM to glide and at the same time turned the Tiger gently towards the only field in the forest as she replied: 'I think I can make the field, now in our left ten o'clock!' Had it been a genuine engine failure I have no doubt she would have made it to the field and landed safely. As a result I was confident that Harriet was now fully prepared to fly her GFT with Pete Thorn. The weather on the morrow was perfect as Tim and I waited patiently at Folly Farm for the arrival of 'PAM. Harriet joined overhead and as she did so, the familiar note of the Gipsy Major died away to comparative silence. In the dying minutes of her GFT, Pete Thorn had given her an engine failure right over the field from where a relatively safe approach and landing could only be made through a gap in the line of trees bordering the north side of the strip. She handled it immaculately, gliding 'PAM gently through the gap before pulling off a perfect landing. Tim's massive grin of paternal pride said it all. Even the birds sang fortissimo! We strolled over as Harriet shut down the Tiger's engine – Tim for a quiet word with his talented daughter who was sitting in the rear cockpit removing her helmet and goggles, while I approached a smiling Pete who was doing likewise in the front.

Before I could ask him how she'd got on, Pete's question gave me a clue. 'Where did you find her?!'

'May I assume she passed, Pete?' I replied, knowing full well from the manner of his question that she must have done OK – as indeed she had. It had been an amazing privilege to have had the opportunity to teach this talented young lady to fly – we'd flown thirty-four Tiger hours together and the entire experience had been happily unforgettable. Dear Harriet, thanks for the memories!

Julie records C S-S at the helm of DH85 Leopard Moth G-ACMN over Salisbury Plain, 1993

The DH85 Leopard Moth is a classic de Havilland-designed monoplane powered by a Gipsy Major engine. Capable of carrying the pilot and two in an enclosed cabin, it had innovative folding wings that allowed it to be stored in a large garage. The type first flew in May 1933 and two months later Geoffrey de Havilland won the Kings Cup Air Race in G-ACHD with an average speed of 139mph. One hundred and thirty three were originally built, but when Henry owned G-ACMN there were only six left in the UK. Thus it is a priceless vintage aeroplane and, in early March 1993, having flown 'ZZ to Langham for its annual check, Henry offered to lend me 'MN to fly home – and I'd never flown a Leopard! He reassured me this wouldn't be a problem as he briefed me on another of the Leopard's interesting design features. As the aircraft had no flaps, the aerodynamically shaped fairings over the telescopic undercarriage legs could be turned through 90° in flight to act as effective airbrakes. After lunch, and with my passenger, a BA Concorde pilot, strapped into the seat behind me, I took off and climbed away from Langham heading for Booker just over 100 nautical miles away to the south-west. The Leopard was a delight to fly and I was savouring every second while soaking up the nostalgic smell of its original leather upholstery, when suddenly there was a loud 'BANG!'

'WHAT THE BLOODY HELL WAS THAT?' exclaimed Mr Concorde Man in the back as I immediately sought a clue from the oil pressure gauge; 45psi was the reassuring reading. The Gipsy Major purred away purposefully in front of me. 'I've absolutely no idea!' I replied, 'I've never flown a Leopard before!' Mr Concorde Man was obviously shocked into silence as he said not another word throughout the rest of the flight to Booker where, barely had we come to stop, he scuttled away from 'MN in double-quick time. From Booker the flight back to Netheravon was incident-free, enabling me to report by phone to Henry of my safe return. At the same time, and seeking enlightenment, I told him of the sudden bang. 'Oh, I should have warned you about that,' I remember him saying, 'just occasionally the port oleo leg is reluctant to extend after take-off and when it does it does make quite a bang!' As I had discovered for myself, Henry – thanks a lot! But subsequently, and thanks to his amazingly trusting generosity, I flew Henry's beautiful Leopard on numerous occasions and it became a firm favourite.

Thanks to the Royal Air Force I was fortunate indeed to get my hands on two exciting types of fast jet aircraft – the BAE Hawk and the joint British/French SEPECAT Jaguar. My first Hawk ride had, as already described in these pages, been with the Red Arrows when I was very much just a passenger – my second and third Hawk trips were very different. In early 1990 I had met Fl Lt Jim Gosling who was at the time a Hawk pilot with 151 Squadron at RAF Chivenor in north Devon. He asked me if I would like to display 'ZZ at the Chivenor Air Day that July, with a very strong hint that there might be a Hawk flight for me in exchange – which indeed there was! All went well at the air day including the Tiger ride I donated as a prize in the associated raffle – the latter was won and enjoyed by one of the Officers' Mess barmen who ensured that I was well looked-after at the post-display party that same evening!

I had to wait, probably too impatiently, until the following January for the promised Hawk flight. This was with Jim when we took off just before first light in Hawk T1A XX320 for an exhilarating one hour, ten minute sortie to check out the weather over south-west Wales during which Jim kindly allowed me to do much of the flying. Three months later I was able to show my appreciation to Jim by checking him out and sending him solo in 'ZZ. It was at about this time that I learned that my cousin, Group Captain Andy Griffin, who was enjoying a splendidly fulfilling career in the RAF during which he had notably flown the supersonic English Electric Lightning, was the Station Commander at RAF Valley in Anglesey. RAF Valley was then, and still is, the home of No. 4 Flying Training School operating Hawks for advanced fast jet training. I made contact with Andy and cheekily suggested that I swap a ride for him in the Tiger for a ride for me in the Hawk, to which he readily agreed. My flight up to Valley that May provided two hours and fifty minutes of bitter cold, head winds and turbulence through the Welsh hills. Andy welcomed me on arrival at Valley when he cheerfully told me that he'd been monitoring my progress on radar and the Bunyip's blip on the screen had been almost stationary for its final thirty miles. The following morning he introduced me to Chris Taylor, his deputy chief flying instructor, who had accumulated thousands of hours on Hawks. 'This is my cousin, Charlie – let him do whatever he wants!' Wow – what an introduction! My log book entries sum up the day's flying:

> *With Chris, Hawk T1 XX234, 55mins, a great trip – low level through mountains, aerobatics and circuits. With Chris, Tiger G-AGZZ, 45 minutes, Chris having a go in return plus aerobatics. With Station Boss, Andy, Tiger G-AGZZ, 60 minutes, Andy effectively demonstrating his Tiger competence.*

I haven't had too many days' flying as memorable as that one, and my two Hawk trips had revealed just how delightful this little trainer was to fly. Fast-forward to early 1994 when I received a call from Jim Gosling who was by this time a Squadron Leader flying Jaguars with 54 Squadron at Coltishall in Norfolk. He asked me if Nigel Wookey and I could fly our Tigers up to Coltishall in July for a 54 Squadron reunion to give some of the veterans flights in the Tigers. In return he offered us both a Jaguar trip. We took no time at all to agree to his request. On the first Saturday of the month we flew up to Coltishall to enjoy two days of RAF hospitality during which time Nigel and I had the privilege of flying twenty-four of 54 Squadron's 'Old & Bold' in our two Tigers – they were a great bunch, the majority of whom had lost little of their old flying skills. And on Monday we were ready to fly the Jaguar. This amazingly successful front-line strike aircraft completed thirty-three years in RAF service and now Jim conducted the briefing, which was for us to fly a pair of Jaguars to notionally 'take out' Peter Phillips' strip in South Wales, followed by a similar 'attack' on Henry Labouchere's on the north Norfolk coast. I was

C S-S, Jim Gosling and SEPECAT Jaguar T2 XX 839

to fly with Jim as the lead while Nigel was number two with Chris Carder. We blasted off towards our first 'target' to discover that it was wreathed in low cloud, making it too dangerous to continue – we therefore broke away before heading off towards our secondary 'target'. With about ten miles to run we picked up Henry's strip visually. Jim announced 'I have control', and, timing it to perfection, he pulled the Jaguar into the vertical right over Henry's hangar. Then it was a descent back to Coltishall for what proved to be my only brake 'chute assisted landing – an awesome conclusion to an exhilarating, never-to-be-forgotten sortie. And, of course, I couldn't resist phoning Henry to ask him if he had enjoyed our 'attack'. 'I might have known it was you, you hooligan – you had me off me bike!' I wish I'd seen that!

I have been fortunate enough to have known Nick O'Brien since 1973, when we first met at LBA as recounted earlier in Chapter 14. Nick's military career started in the Parachute Regiment and, while serving in 2 PARA, he became interested in changing direction to go flying with the Army Air Corps. The initial problem was that applicants were required to be at least full corporals before they could even be considered. So Nick hit upon the jolly wheeze of initially transferring to the Royal Army Pay Corps where, because Corps personnel would be trusted to handle large amounts of cash, he was immediately promoted to the Corps' minimum rank of corporal. Having received an interview of welcome from the Major General who was the Paymaster in Chief, he wasted no time in applying to go to flying with the Army Air Corps – this could not be refused because at that time the Army was short of pilots. Thus his spell in the RAPC must have been the shortest on record! Nick's Army flying career must have been unique. He eventually found himself flying both rotary and fixed-wing aircraft on active service, and having been commissioned, he successfully completed his flying instructor's course with the RAF on BAC Jet Provosts. He then followed this with a spell instructing for the RAF on JPs. Back with the Army he brought the BN2T Islander into military service and, as an experienced skydiver, he also enjoyed a spell as Commandant of the Rhine Army Parachute Centre at Bad Lippspringe. The last job Major Nick O'Brien enjoyed with the Army Air Corps was as 'guru' of all fixed-wing flying in the Army and this included his giving spirited air displays in the replica Fokker Triplane owned by the Army Air Corps and based at Middle Wallop. He finally retired from the Army in early 2000.

By this time, Major John Horne, another very experienced skydiver who, like Nick, had also been Commandant of the Rhine Army Parachute Centre, had now become Commandant of the Joint Services Parachute Centre at Netheravon. John had appreciated the wisdom of acquiring a Cessna 208B Grand Caravan and one had been ordered by the APA. The RAF had by now stopped providing service pilots to fly the services Adventurous Training parachute courses and finances were in place to pay for a full-time civilian pilot. With John Horne's support I set about persuading Nick that he was the best man for this job, which he undoubtedly was as there was no other pilot around who had more relevant qualifications or experience. I couldn't have been more delighted when Nick agreed to take on the job. Of course he knew everyone at Netheravon well as he'd already been flying part time for the APA for a good many years. I was privileged to work with Nick for the next fourteen, all the while doing our best to ensure that the Netheravon aircraft were being safely flown for parachuting by a dedicated bunch of enthusiastic pilots.

In late February 2000 our first task together was to fly out to Wichita, the home of the Cessna Aircraft Company in Kansas, to undergo a course on the aeroplane provided by Flight Safety International before taking delivery of the APA's brand spanking new Cessna 208B Grand Caravan. We then had to fly it across the States to Portland, Maine, before handing it over to a ferry pilot who would then fly it back to the UK. The course, which was part of the purchase package, principally consisted of eight hours in a Caravan simulator with an associated ground school. Simulator flying was a new experience for both of us. Lowell, my instructor, was like all the best teachers – enthusiastic and patient and I still remember the important things he taught me about flying the Caravan. On the other hand Nick's young instructor was too keen by half, taking pleasure in throwing emergencies at Nick at every conceivable opportunity – not the most constructive introduction to Caravan flying. One afternoon I suggested to Nick that we should visit the local flying club to acquire some charts to enable us to navigate the Caravan across the States. He reckoned he had a better idea – as he was still technically in the Army and enjoying his terminal leave, he believed that we ought to be able to bluff our way into McConnell Air Force Base, the colossal USAF airfield on the other side of Wichita, and scrounge the charts from Uncle Sam – it was certainly worth a try.

The following day we arrived in our hire car at the main gate of the airbase. We were greeted by a gorgeous young lady dressed in camouflage kit and toting a massive firearm. 'Good afternoon, gentlemen, what can I do for you?' she inquired.

Nick replied in an outrageously posh English accent, offering his ID card to her at the same time. 'Major O'Brien, British Army, we've come to visit Base Operations.'

'Very well, Major, have you got your orders?'

The American military love their orders, so it looked like we were to be unhorsed at the first fence. But I hadn't reckoned on my chum's skill in the art of bluffmanship. 'I'm terribly sorry,' he said, maintaining his wonderfully over the top accent, 'I'm afraid we left them back at the hotel!'

'Very well, Major,' she replied cheerfully, 'I shouldn't really let you in, but you've got such a cute accent, you go right ahead!'

Later, having collected a huge bundle of charts from Base Operations, Nick suggested we visit the PX, the US equivalent of the NAAFI. Mercifully I was able to persuade him that we should quit while we were still ahead, so we waved a grateful farewell to the lovely lady sentry on the gate before returning to our hotel to study the charts and produce our flight plans. Three days later on February 29, we finally got our hands on the real thing, APA's new Grand Caravan, adorned with its temporary US registration N51960. We each enjoyed a forty-minute flight with Scott Bengtson, one of the Cessna salesmen,

C S-S and Nick O'Brien with Cessna 208B Grand Caravan G-BZAH at Witchita, March 1, 2000

from Wichita to Hutchinson, fifty miles away – and back. The next morning, March 1, 2000, Cessna Grand Caravan, now proudly displaying its UK registration, G-BZAH, waited patiently for its crew. Nick, having won the toss to have the honour of flying the first leg, climbed up into the left-hand seat – I into the right, and we were on our way. The first leg to Quincy, Illinois, took us over both the Missouri and the Mississippi before I flew the second leg to Findlay, Ohio. The next day we weren't so lucky with the weather and Nick, flying the third leg of the trip to Binghampton, New York State, had to cope with appalling weather. During the descent through solid cloud until we got ground contact at about 200ft, we collected a considerable amount of airframe ice before we finally saw the runway lights at less than half a mile. I was mightily relieved that this was Nick's leg as his instrument flying was much more current than mine. 'AH and her crew overnighted in Binghampton before, the next day, March 3, I flew the relatively easy final leg into Portland, Maine. Here that evening we celebrated our safe arrival at J's Oyster Bar, where Nick's cute posh English accent once again did the business and got us the best seats, and where, as he had promised, the Maine lobsters were worth waiting for. Job done and with more than four hours of Caravan experience apiece, we felt confident enough to pass on what we had learned to our APA pilot team to enable all of them to qualify on type. Now, eighteen years down the line, Cessna 208B Grand Caravan G-BZAH is still dropping skydivers over Netheravon.

On December 17, 2003, Julie and I, together with dear chums John and Lizzie Ball, were among the crowd of thousands at Kitty Hawk, North Carolina, to celebrate the 100th anniversary of the Wright brothers' first powered flight and to pay tribute to them and to recognise their extraordinary aeronautical achievements. Having chosen the area for its prevailing onshore breezes, they taught themselves to fly over a four-year period of painstaking experiments in gliders of their own design. They not only designed and built their own 12hp aero-engine that weighed in at 180lb, but also the propellers that they tested in a wind tunnel – also of their own design! The Wright 'Flyer' had two propellers that were chain-driven from the little engine, and the brothers were concerned that, with the propellers rotating in the same direction, they might produce unacceptable torque. Their solution was to 'figure of eight' the left-hand chain drive to produce contra-rotating propellers – clearly visible in the iconic photo of the first powered twelve-second and 120ft flight with Orville at the controls.

With Orville Wright at the controls and Wilbur watching, the Flyer gets airborne on December 17, 1903

The brothers made four flights that day, the final one of which was Wilbur's of 852ft and fifty-nine seconds. Now, exactly 100 years later, we all waited patiently in depressing light drizzle for the meticulously constructed replica of the Flyer to re-enact the first powered flight. But there was simply not enough wind for the replica to get airborne and, while everyone was disappointed, it demonstrated the enormity of the Wright brothers' accomplishments. It was humbling to have been there in 2003.

By 2007 we had found that the operation and maintenance of G-AGZZ was becoming more and more expensive, with the result that Julie and I made the difficult decision that we had to sell her. Interestingly we had never considered ourselves to have been 'ZZ's owners – we were simply privileged to have been able to have restored her and to have been her custodians for twenty-four years. Luckily, Malcolm Jordan, a retired airline pilot, took over as her custodian and she now lives in Devon. My last flight in 'ZZ was for an hour with Nick when, on October 30, 2007, he revalidated the Single Engine Piston (Land) rating on my licence.

In 2011 the British Parachute Association decided to prohibit pilots over the age of seventy from flying parachutists. There seemed to be no logical reason for this other than perhaps the association was intimidated by the fear of upsetting the Health and

Safety Executive. As I was then approaching seventy, I wrote to the BPA requesting an exemption to this rule. I pointed out that I held a UK CAA commercial pilot's licence and a current CAA Class One Medical, the latter which was renewable every six months. I also explained that I had been flying parachutists since 1971 and had held a full flying instructor's rating continuously since 1972. I also reckoned it was relevant to inform the BPA that I had held a CAA PPL examiner's rating continuously since 1983 – the latter also being the year I was appointed chief pilot of the Army Parachute Association. Perhaps a trifle flippantly, I also suggested that if a jump pilot was incapacitated in any way, the jumpers were equipped and trained to abandon the aircraft and parachute to safety! My request was put on hold and, as there were other experienced jump pilots who were also approaching seventy, the association set up a pilots' age working group, PAWG, to resolve the matter. Those of us affected sought expert advice, both to ascertain whether the BPA was in breach of any age discrimination legislation, and whether pilots over seventy could continue to be medically fit to fly for parachuting. The BPA unwisely chose to ignore the advice of stalwart friend Jim Crocker, who was not only one of the association's vice-presidents, he was also a hugely experienced pilot, parachutist and lawyer, and one-time chairman of the BPA Safety and Training Committee. The association's medical adviser, who held no aviation medicine qualifications, continued to insist that seventy should be the maximum age; indeed, he had previously assured Jim that this was not an arbitrary figure. All of those of us affected held CAA medical certificates as the result of having been examined by CAA-approved aeromedical examiners, the latter who are all required to be qualified specialists in aviation medicine.

Eventually the whole sorry saga went to arbitration where Professor Mike Bagshaw, the UK's most respected specialist in aviation medicine, went into bat very professionally on behalf of those of us who wished to continue to fly for parachuting providing we held CAA medical certificates. The turning point at the tribunal was when the BPA medical advisor was obliged to admit that seventy was an arbitrarily chosen age, which might just as well have been sixty-nine or seventy-one! The judge ruled in our favour, so we were able to continue flying for parachuting. And while I continued to do so until well past my seventy-second birthday, I have to admit that, because of the BPA's extraordinary intransigence, I lost much of my enthusiasm for jump flying. I flew my last Caravan load of jumpers at the conclusion of the Army Parachute Championships at Netheravon on August 23, 2014. And appropriately, my dear chum, Ed Gardener, was sitting in the right-hand seat; exactly fifty years earlier we had been competing against each other in the 1964 Army Parachute Championships at Netheravon – he beat me!